The Fourth Education Revolution

Will Artificial Intelligence liberate or infantilise humanity

Anthony Seldon

with
Oladimeji Abidoye

The University of Buckingham Press

ISBN 978-1-908684-95-0

Dedication

To Tim and Sarah Bunting, inspirers and supporters of many remarkable education projects over the last ten years.

All royalties from the sale of the book go to the
Jo Cox Foundation

Jo Cox personified human intelligence at its best

Metal & coach workers pose in front of the Benz & Co factory in Mannheim.

"AI is coming. To understand the stage we are with its arrival, we can draw an analogy from the car industry in 1886. Karl Benz had just invented the internal combustion engine. People had no idea how the invention would take off, or that it would transform human life across the planet. The comparison is wrong though in one respect. AI is far more wide-ranging than the car, and will carry humans much further."

From Chapter Five

Anthony Seldon: Publication List

Churchill's Indian Summer: The Conservative Government, 1951-55 (Hodder & Stoughton, 1981)

By Word of Mouth: Elite Oral History (with Joanna Pappworth, Methuen, 1983)

Ruling Performance: Governments since 1945 (ed., with Peter Hennessy, Blackwell, 1987)

Political Parties Since 1945 (ed., Philip Allan, 1988)

The Thatcher Effect (ed., with Dennis Kavanagh, Oxford Paperbacks, 1989)

Politics UK (Joint author, Philip Allan, 1991)

Conservative Century (ed., with Stuart Ball, Oxford University Press, 1994)

The Major Effect (ed., with Dennis Kavanagh, Macmillan, 1994)

The Heath Government 1970-1974 (ed., with Stuart Ball, Routledge, 1996)

The Contemporary History Handbook (ed., with Brian Brivati etc, Manchester University Press, 1996)

The Ideas that Shaped Post-war Britain (ed., with David Marquand, Fontana Press, 1996)

How Tory Governments Fall (ed., Fontana, 1997)

Major: A Political Life (Weidenfeld and Nicolson, 1997)

10 Downing Street: An Illustrated History (HarperCollins Illustrated, 1999)

The Powers Behind the Prime Minister (with Dennis Kavanagh, HarperCollins, 1999)

Britain under Thatcher (with Daniel Collings, Routledge, 2000)

The Foreign Office: An Illustrated History (HarperCollins Illustrated, 2000)

A New Conservative Century (with Peter Snowdon, Centre for Policy Studies, 2001)

The Blair Effect 1997-2001 (ed., Little, Brown, 2001)

Public and Private Education: The Divide Must End (Social Market Foundation, 2001)

Partnership not Paternalism (Institute for Public Policy Research, 2002)

Brave New City: Brighton & Hove, Past, Present, Future (Pomegranate Press, 2002)

The Conservative Party: An Illustrated History (with Peter Snowdon, Sutton Press, 2004)

New Labour, Old Labour: The Labour Government, 1974-79 (ed., with Kevin Hickson, Routledge, 2004)

Blair: The Biography, Vol I (Free Press, 2004)

The Blair Effect 2001-05 (ed., with Dennis Kavanagh, Cambridge University Press, 2005)

Recovering Power: The Conservatives in Opposition since 1867 (ed., with Stuart Ball, Palgrave Macmillan, 2005)

Blair Unbound: The Biography, Vol II (with Peter Snowdon and Daniel Collings, Simon & Schuster, 2007)

Blair's Britain 1997-2007 (ed., Cambridge University Press, 2007)

Trust: How We Lost it and How to Get It Back (Biteback Publishing, 2009)

An End to Factory Schools (Centre for Policy Studies, 2009)

Why Schools, Why Universities? (Cass, 2010)

Brown at 10 (with Guy Lodge, Biteback Publishing, 2011)

Public Schools and the Great War (with David Walsh, Pen & Sword Military, 2013)

Schools United (Social Market Foundation, 2014)

The Architecture of Diplomacy: The British Ambassador's Residence in Washington (with Daniel Collings, Flammarion, 2014)

Beyond Happiness: The Trap of Happiness and How to Find Deeper Meaning and Joy (Yellow Kite, 2015)

The Coalition Effect, 2010-2015 (ed., with Mike Finn, Cambridge University Press, 2015)

Contents

Education has been the Cinderella of the AI story – largely ignored in the literature and by governments, companies and educational institutions worldwide. This needs to change rapidly: AI could be the Princess Charming or the Ugly Sisters in education.

Introduction:

Education, the Cinderella of the AI Story

There is no more important issue facing education, or humanity at large, than the fast approaching revolution of Artificial Intelligence, or AI. This book is a call to educators everywhere, in primary, secondary, further and higher education (HE), and in all countries, to open our eyes to what is coming towards us. If we do so, then the future will be shaped by us in the interests of all. If not, others, the large tech companies, governments and even the bad guys will decide, and we will have only ourselves to blame.

Education is truly the Cinderella subject of AI. We hear much about its application in transport, in medicine, on the factory production line, and even in warfare. But education has been comparatively overlooked. In Jim Al-Khalili's popular science book *What Is Next?* where an array of writers imagine the future, almost all topics are covered for example, bar schools and universities.[1] A succession of booklets on the impact of AI published in the last three years have all but

---

[1] Al-Khalili, J., (2017) *What is Next? Even Scientists Can't Predict the Future – or Can They?* London: Profile Books.

ignored education.[2] Margaret Boden a distinguished professor of cognitive science and author of many books on AI from her *Artificial Intelligence and Natural Man* (1977) agrees "the applications of AI in schools and universities has been relatively ignored but needs our urgent attention".[3] A host of other distinguished figures in the AI field interviewed for the book, including Sir Timothy O'Shea and Sir Nigel Shadbolt, think similarly.

This book develops its argument for radical and urgent change over ten chapters. In Chapter One, we look at the three previous education revolutions in history that preceded the AI or fourth, which allows us to see its impact with a sense of perspective. The last revolution began 500 years ago and, for all the impact of new technology and digitalisation during the last fifty years, the task of teaching and the classroom/lecture hall remains fundamentally the same as it was in 1600.

In Chapter Two, we break down education into our five stages of teaching and five stages of learning, which is the necessary precursor to considering how AI might make its revolutionary impact. We examine who, or what, an educated person might be, and how we have allowed far too narrow a vision of the purpose of education in schools and universities to continue across the world.

Chapter Three looks at how the third education revolution, which introduced mass schooling and universities on an industrial scale, failed to conquer five enduring problems. Elites have continued to dominate top educational

---

[2] See for example Microsoft, (2018) 'The Future Computed: Artificial Intelligence and its role in society'.

[3] Interview with Margaret Boden, 27.02.18

institutions, and social mobility has been disappointing. Students have to make progress at a set rate, which demotivates some and bores others. For all the new technologies, teachers remain weighed down by routine administration, which prevents them from concentrating their best efforts on actually teaching students. Only a narrow range of our intelligences or aptitudes is prioritised and educated in the current model. Finally, education is too often passive, and does little to encourage the development of individuality, because the system teaches students to give the 'right' answers. It homogenises rather than individuates students.

Chapter Four looks at the question of human intelligence. It explores whether there is one form of intelligence or many, and explores the impact of dominant cultures being allowed to define intelligence in their own image. It explores different varieties of intelligence, including military and state intelligence, 'collective intelligence', and emotional, spiritual, inquiring and natural intelligences. It concludes that the third education revolution era did a poor job in defining what we mean by, and what we need to mean by, 'intelligence'.

Chapter Five examines the evolution of AI, and explores whether machines will ever be able to think, and whether they will always be subordinate to the will of humans, and, if so, which humans. It further explains why AI, together with Virtual Reality (VR) and Augmented Reality (AR) are of a totally different level of sophistication and potentiality compared to current digital technologies. It introduces us finally to a range of concepts we will need to reckon with, including robotics, face recognition, transhumanism and the singularity.

The next three chapters examine how the AI revolution might evolve in the next 12 to 25 years. It began just a few years ago but is still in its infancy compared to the impact that it will shortly have on schools and universities. The chapters return to the ten-part model for teaching and learning, and reveal that many of the tasks that we have allowed ourselves to believe can be done uniquely by the teacher, can in fact be as well, or better carried out by AI machines. They look at the impact on the developing world, where there are over one billion children who need to be educated. These young people will never receive sufficient teachers of quality for them all to be educated. AI is an altogether new way of spreading quality education across the world, above all in Africa, South America and the Indian subcontinent, as well as to disadvantaged students elsewhere in the developed world.

The final two chapters look at the wider impact of AI. Chapter Nine discusses the risks and benefits for education from the imminent advent of the fourth education revolution. Chapter Ten looks more broadly at the threats and the unprecedented opportunities for AI to provide a much better educational and human experience for all.

The book finishes with a series of recommendations. Above all, it stresses that we have to place education and its responsibility for developing human skills at the heart of our strategy of AI. Nothing matters more. We must embrace AI and ensure that we shape it to the best advantage of humanity. There can be no excuses for hiding. If we get this wrong, there may be no second opportunity.

Anthony Seldon, March 2018

5

The third educational revolution introduced the factory model where massed ranks of students sat in front of a teacher/lecturer at the front of the room, all moving at the same pace and all trying to learn the right answers in the right way.

Chapter One:

The First Three Education Revolutions

The history of education is the history of humanity. Only three education revolutions can be said to have occurred during the last three to five million years.[1] The next, involving Artificial Intelligence (AI), alongside Augmented Reality (AR) and Virtual Reality (VR), will be the fourth education revolution. AI, *et al.* are that important. We have heard much since the World Economic Forum in January 2016 about the so-called 'Fourth Industrial Revolution'. We need to wake up still more to the Fourth Education Revolution. Now.

Schools and universities today would be recognised by our forebears in the year 1600. Why do we say this? The teacher or lecturer today remains the dominant presence: they

---

[1] The term 'Third Revolution' in education was coined as early as 1941: see [Anon.], 'Education. The Third Revolution?', *Time*, 10 March 1941; and among the books and articles addressing this theme is Lee Benson and Ira Harkavy, 'Higher Education's Third Revolution: the emergence of the democratic cosmopolitan civic university', *Cityscape*, 5 (2000), 47-57; Ronaldo Mota and David Scott, *Education for Innovation and Independent Learning* (Oxford and Waltham, MA: Elsevier, 2014), Ch. 4 'The Third Educational Revolution'. For a recent case, see Jeffrey Selingo's 'The Third Education Revolution' in *The Atlantic*:
https://www.theatlantic.com/education/archive/2018/03/the-third-education-revolution/556091/
Thanks to John Adamson, email 16.04.18.

are *an* authority (i.e. a master of their subject) and *in* authority (i.e. they command the learning environment). They generally stand at the front of the learning space; students are organised into groups by age; class size typically varies between 20 and 50; the day is divided into the teaching of different 'subjects'; older school students may study in libraries stocked full of books and audio-visual resources; teachers and lecturers prepare students for, oversee and mark regular tests and periodic exams; and these result in students passing with various grades or categories, or failing a subject/course/degree.

Most of this will be swept away by the fourth education revolution. Barely a single facet of this education model will remain unchanged.

The First Education Revolution: Organised Learning; Necessary Education

The beginnings of learning from others, in family units, groups and tribes, constitute the first education revolution. This can also be said to constitute the origins of mankind. This development did not take place in one precise place on earth, nor at a precise time; it took place over hundreds of thousands of years and in diverse places. We can however highlight key moments. Dating back some 2.5 million years, some of the earliest stone tools to have been used have been discovered in Ethiopia, which suggests that learning was being handed down from generation to generation, with knowledge about how to use the tools to cut open animal flesh and grind bones passed down from parent to child. *Hominids* (i.e. great apes, including human antecedents) began transferring knowledge systematically about how to hunt, how to build seasonal camps, how to use fire, and how to migrate over long distances.

Daily life during the period of the first education revolution revolved around mere survival and bringing up the next generation; it left little time for leisure, the arts or for conjecture. Pleasure came from bodily experience. Life was harsh and itinerant, and changed little for a very long time. *Homo erectus*, a species of human antecedent, began to colonise areas in sub-Saharan Africa some 1.8 million years ago, migrating approximately 1 million years ago into North Africa and the Near East, reaching northern Europe 500,000 years later.

Homo sapiens ('wise human being') did not emerge in Africa until approximately 200,000 years ago. Their cerebrum had evolved to approximately its present size and their vocal apparatus gradually modified to enhance the development of language. Some 100,000 years ago, *Homo sapiens* started a migration northwards out of Africa, reaching Australia 50,000 years ago, and the Americas some 35,000 years later. *Homo sapiens* co-existed for a time alongside *Homo erectus* in eastern Asia and with *Neanderthals* in West Asia and Europe. But the more sophisticated social understanding and adaptability of *Homo sapiens* allowed them to triumph and to spread more successfully than other early *hominids: Homo erectus* died out approximately 140,000 years ago, while *Neanderthals* remained until some 40,000 years before the present day. Both types left behind large numbers of stone tools, showing us that the knowledge of how to use them had been successfully transmitted down the generations.

9

By the end of this first phase of education, *Homo sapiens* might have triumphed. But life consisted of bands of hunter-gatherers eking out life, with daily existence differing little from their predecessors at the very beginning of the first education revolution.

The Second Education Revolution: The Coming of Schools and Universities: Institutionalised Education

This second phase, institutionalised education, was ushered in following the end of the last Ice Age in 10,000 BC. Now we see the origins of settled life, with developments in the stable production of food and urbanisation. Improvements to agriculture made possible a growth in human population between 8000 and 4000 BC, and encouraged human beings to work together cooperatively. This new lifestyle allowed humans, for the first time in history, to live in settled places. Remarkably quickly, villages, followed by towns and cities, began to appear. Here is the start of civilisation.

Urbanisation began to occur in four diverse areas, almost concurrently: in the valley of the Nile in Egypt; in the lower Tigris and Euphrates valley in Mesopotamia; along the Yellow River in China; and in the Indus valley in India. By 3500 BC, cities had grown up in Mesopotamia, in Egypt by 3200 BC, in India by 2500 BC and in China some 500 years later. The emergence of writing was common to all four civilisations, along with political, commercial and legal systems to assist the administrative task of running more complex societies. Ruling classes emerged in all four, along with distinctive religious systems.

These new societies demanded a new range of specialisms, including learning about agriculture, trade, law, civic society, technology and religion. The sophistication of the emerging civilisation called for an altogether more systematic form of education than had been possible with the *ad hoc* transference of applied knowledge in the first education revolution phase.

Writing was essential to keep track of commerce, to record details of taxes and wages, and to record legal proceedings. It was widely used too in religion and in the recording of sacred texts, traditions and myths. It seems to have emerged first in Egypt and Mesopotamia towards the end of the fourth millennium BC. The Sumerians wrote their language, cuneiform, on clay tablets that were then dried and baked, whereas the Egyptians wrote on papyrus, made from overlaid and interwoven pith of the papyrus reed, which grew along the banks of the Nile. Each society evolved a representational form of language, including 'phonetic' forms of language. Sumerian, for example, was additive: each syllable had a meaning, and these could be combined to create new meanings. The symbols for 'water' and 'head' could thus be placed next to one another to represent 'headwater' or 'origin'. The oldest known alphabet was developed in Egypt circa 2000 BC.[2]

Writing was a precise and sophisticated skill that needed to be learnt. The need to teach it in a systematic and disciplined manner almost inevitably led to the development of institutional places of learning. The word 'school' has its

---

[2] Good, H.G. & Teller, J.D., (1969). *A History of Western Education*. London: Macmillan, p.7.

11

origins in the Greek word *skholē,* meaning 'leisure, philosophy, or lecture place', and is the root of the word 'scholastic'. The Greek for education, *paideia,* was synonymous with culture and civilisation. It suggested something that modern education systems have tended to forget: the development of the 'whole' person, physical as well as spiritual, and not just the mind or brain.

The first schools to teach writing had emerged by circa 2500 BC, known in Babylon in Mesopotamia as 'tablet houses'. The strong association between state or religious organisations and school has been a common feature of education from the very earliest recorded schools in history. Many of the school tablets that have survived have been discovered in temples, and indicated important day-to-day business being transacted. Plato's Academy and Aristotle's Lyceum were both nominally places of worship, while religious schools were the only formal educational institutions in many areas.[3]

A tablet dating from circa 2000 BC provides an idea of life relating to Sumerian education. The student brought his lunch to school, where he would consume it under supervision. His teacher, known as the 'school father', would instruct the boy (no girls) by rote repetition and by overseeing the copying out of texts. Subjects taught included Sumerian, arithmetic and bookkeeping. Discipline in the classroom was maintained by a 'porter', the classroom pedagogue and a 'superintendent', who administered lashings for petty offences that we would still recognise today: for being late to school; speaking out of turn; and getting up to leave without

---

[3] Ibid. p.10.

asking.[4] School was divided into three separate grades. In the first, students learnt the fundamentals of writing by copying extracts from lexical lists. In the second, more complicated exercises were taught, including some complicated cultural concepts, and the values of Babylonian culture. In the third grade, scribes specialised in administration, accounting or religious writing.[5]

In Athens, schools flourished from the fifth and fourth centuries BC, although, aside from military training, the state played little formal part in schooling. Basic schooling included learning how to read and write, after which the young from less well-off families would learn a trade, while richer students would study drawing, painting and sculpture, as well as rhetoric, mathematics, geography, natural history, politics and logic. In Sparta, education differed, with the state very much interested in the physical development of young men. The skills of obedience, courage and maintaining bodily perfection were taught, and discipline was harsh.

Universities

Universities have been seen, rather Eurocentrically, as a particularly western European inspiration. David Willetts opens his seminal *A University Education* by saying: "The

---

[4] Kramer, S.N., (1949). 'Schooldays: A Sumerian Composition Relating to the Education of a Scribe'. *Journal of the American Oriental Society,* 69, pp.199–215.
[5] Gesche, P., (2000). *Schulunterricht in Babylonien im ersten Jahrtausend v. Chr. Alter Orient und Altes Testament.* Muenster: Ugarit-Velag, pp. 476–7. In Radner, K. & Robson. E. (eds.), *The Oxford Handbook of Cuneiform Culture*, pp.190–1.

university is one of Europe's great gifts to the world ... It is Europe's universities which gave birth to the humanism of the Renaissance, drove the Reformation, led the rise of empirical science, and promoted the emergence of critical history".[6]

It appears to have been only chance that the Latin word *universitas* came to be part of the nomenclature. A term with wide applications during the medieval period, the word denoted any kind of 'aggregate or body of persons with common interests and independent legal status'. *Studium generale* is the contemporary term that better fits our understanding of the role of the emerging medieval university. *Studium* was a school with defined courses of study, and *generale* indicated people coming in from beyond the locality. The most important specific right of the *studium generale* was, in Latin, that of *ius ubique docendi*, that is, "the right of the holder of a degree from a *studium generale* to teach in any other university without undergoing further examination."[7] This power gave the *studium generale*'s masters a teaching licence with universal validity.

The first university to be created in Europe was in Bologna in northern Italy in 1088, which was secular in origin, followed by the University of Paris, founded around 1150, which had a Christian origin, both receiving their charters in 1158 and 1200, respectively. The first English university, the University of Oxford, came into being when Henry II banned students from travelling to Paris in 1167. Cambridge and Montpellier in southern France were

---

[6] Willetts, D., (2017). *A University Education.* Oxford: Oxford University Press, p. 13.
[7] Cobban, A. B., (1975). *The Medieval Universities.* London: Methuen, p.27.

chartered shortly afterwards, followed by several others in France, Italy and Spain, while the first 'German' university, Prague, came into being in 1347, followed by Vienna in 1365. Bologna and Paris were the first universities under the *studium generale* system to acquire the right to elect their own officers, to have statute-making powers and a common seal.

The establishment of institutions of higher education worldwide, however, predated these European developments. In East India, Nalanda was set up as a centre of study during the fifth century CE, where students would come to translate texts for a few years and then return home.[8] Other centres of learning offered instruction in Mahayana Buddhism along with the study of philosophy, Sanskrit grammar, logic and medicine.[9] These early blossomings of learning, which were highly specific in purpose, were destroyed by Muslim invaders during the late twelfth century.

In China, Confucianism prompted the early development of other centres of learning: thinkers inspired by the philosophy regarded education as essential to the cultivation of human nature and good governance in society.[10] As early as 124 BC, a university was established by imperial order, and by the end of the first century BC it was teaching some 3,000 students the art of bureaucracy.[11] The development of printing in China from the seventh century CE encouraged the

---

[8] Kulke, H. and Rothermund, D., (1990). *A History of India.* London: Routledge, pp.167–9.
[9] Walton, L., (2015). 'Educational Institutions'. In *The Cambridge World History,* vol. 5, pp.116–44.
[10] Ibid.
[11] Theodore de Bary, W.M., et al., (1960). *Sources of Chinese Tradition.* New York, NY: Columbia University Press, pp.157–8.

development of libraries and learning in these early Chinese universities, which highlighted the concern of the Sung dynasty for cultural achievement as opposed to mere military aggrandisement.

In western Europe, the emergence of universities was powerfully boosted by the revival of learning and use of the Latin language during the twelfth-century renaissance (circa 1060–1160). It saw translations from Arabic and Greek into Latin, allowed European scholars to read lost works by Plato, Aristotle, Ptolemy and Euclid, among others, and prompted a rediscovery of interest in Roman law.[12] These texts provided a powerful boost to the study and dissemination of knowledge about humanity and its ability to master its environment through the intellect, cumulative knowledge and experience.

Universities taught the liberal arts, the *trivium* (grammar, rhetoric, dialectical reasoning) and, to a lesser extent, the *quadrivium* (music, astronomy, geometry and arithmetic), followed by one of three advanced subjects: medicine, law or theology. Taken together, the subjects of the *trivium* and *quadrivium* constituted the seven subjects of the liberal arts, and allowed students benefitting from the study to become a 'free' person, able to think independently and for themselves, thereby transcending the more limited mindset of the artisan or labourer, destined to spend a life in repetitive tasks, such as farming or stonemasonry.[13]

Oxford gained a particular reputation for mathematics and the natural sciences, along with Cambridge. Students engaged

[12] Walton, L., Op. cit., pp.116–44.
[13] Robinson, M., (2013). *Trivium 21C: Preparing Young People for the Future with Lessons from the Past.* London: Independent Thinking Press.

in disputations with masters and prepared 'summas' or 'compendiums', which were summaries of various fields of knowledge. University life across western Europe was restricted to the few: the educated elites who could read and who could benefit from the learning. All teaching still took place in Latin, which remained the *lingua franca* in western Europe throughout the Middle Ages.

The Third Education Revolution: Printing and Secularisation; Education for the Masses

Education remained throughout the second education revolution phase for the privileged few, both secular and religious, largely because texts had to be copied in Europe by hand and so were highly restricted in number. All this was to change with the advent of printing. Xylography, or wood printing, had come to be used in China from the late seventh century CE, with fine paper then being produced which facilitated printing using wooden blocks and a brush. While in some ways inferior to the movable type printing which emerged in Europe during the fifteenth century, it made possible a widespread dissemination of texts.

The development of the printing press in Europe was to transform learning and education. Attributed to Gutenberg in 1436, the moveable type printing method was to revolutionise the production of literature across Western Europe and beyond. By the end of the fifteenth century, some 75 towns in Europe had established a printing house. Between the invention of the press and the year 1500, an estimated 27,000 to 29,000 books had been produced. If we make the assumption that the average print run was approximately 500, it would suggest 13 million to 15 million printed books were in circulation by the year 1500, an increase of 6,000 per cent in the production of books compared to the world of manuscript writing alone in Europe in 1400.[14]

Textbooks began to be widely produced for the first time, covering a variety of different academic disciplines and for students at different levels to suit those of different ages and at varying stages in their development.[15] Books soon began to emerge in a recognisably modern form. Indexed alphabetically, their publication rapidly became subject to the criteria of unity, internal consistency, and harmony in the presentation of the material for the readers.[16] Printing catalysed change. Double-entry bookkeeping was codified by an Italian friar and professor of sacred theology, Luca Pacioli, in 1494, and is seen as the foundation of modern accounting. Books significantly came to be written in the vernacular, which made them more understandable to the non-fluent than Latin, which considerably boosted their readership. Learners could now read and learn unencumbered by the need to find teaching by academics at universities and schools.

Existing subjects began to change, often quite fundamentally. Legal codes and points of disagreement could now be debated far and wide across national frontiers. The

---

[14] Barbier, F., (2016) *Gutenberg's Europe*, New Jersey: John Wiley. p. 239.

[15] Strauss, G., (1965). 'A Sixteenth Century Encyclopaedia: Sebastian Muenster Cosmography and its Edition'. In Charter, C. H. (ed.), (1965). *From the Renaissance to the Counter Reformation.* New York, NY: Random House, p.152.

[16] Eisenstein, E. L., (1993). *The Printing Revolution in Early Modern Europe*, Cambridge: Cambridge University Press, pp.77–8.

study of medicine was one subject to be revolutionised. Latest research and thinking on medical method spread rapidly, facilitating the dissemination of knowledge based on the beginnings of rigorous scientific method. The Reformation from the early sixteenth century spread far more swiftly because of the printing press. Martin Luther, who famously initiated the Reformation with his 95 theses or disputations in 1517, was a supporter of widespread education and the use of the vernacular rather than Latin. Religious texts were translated into many different languages and spread far and wide. The use of small bibles, unsuitable for reading from fixed pulpits in Catholic churches, gives an indication of the spread of reading. Estimates suggest that a quarter or more of those living in German lands could read by 1600.[17] Universities in Germany were one of the agencies to channel the spread of the Reformation. In England too, Oxford and Cambridge grew in size, albeit still confined to a very small segment of society. By 1600, some 2.5 per cent of young men attended university.[18]

The growth during the late Middle Ages of the complexity of statecraft, law and commerce, and the later spread of Protestantism, played their part in the spread of schools and universities. But it was the coming of industrialisation in Britain from the early eighteenth century, and the spread of the franchise in the nineteenth, which gave the decisive push to the spread of mass schooling to educate the urbanised population. In Britain, a series of Parliamentary Acts in 1833,

---

[17] Maag, K., (2000). 'Education and Literacy'. In Pettegree, A. (ed.), *The Reformation World*. London: Routledge, pp.535–44.
[18] Willetts, D., (2017). *A University Education.* Oxford: Oxford University Press, p.17.

1870 and 1902 saw the state become increasingly involved in schools.

The new provision of schools in the United States was given a major push after independence in 1776, with states passing laws to make schooling compulsory between 1852 (Massachusetts) and 1917 (Mississippi). Its first university, Harvard was founded in 1636, with Yale (1701) and Princeton (1747) following. Universal and state schooling during early nineteenth-century France had been energised by the French Revolution after 1789, inspired by among others the ideals of Jean-Jacques Rousseau. Education in this third era was very much an instrument of state control and reach, which helps explain why the spread of education across Europe was piecemeal, and progress gradual and uneven.

A new style of university began to spread from the early nineteenth century. Napoleon tolerated the old medieval universities but established the University of France in 1808 at their head, and developed existing *écoles*, teaching subjects required for national supremacy. Partly in response, Wilhelm von Humboldt founded the Friedrich Wilhelm University in Berlin in 1810 (renamed in his honour in 1949), which became the model for the new breed of universities with an emphasis on research and an understanding of culture. The practice grew across German universities for lecturers to have completed a research doctorate or PhD. In the USA, the first PhD was awarded at Yale in 1861, from where it spread to the UK. The first to be instituted in the UK was in 1917 at Oxford (with the title DPhil).

In Britain more widely, once the government had overcome the opposition of Oxford and Cambridge to the creation of other universities, they were founded across the country initially in larger cities like Manchester (1824) and Liverpool (1881). Local industrialists encouraged this move in their bid to harness research and the education of future employees for their commercial advantage.[19] The rapidly evolving Industrial Revolution also saw a whole swathe of private schools, including, in Britain, Brighton College in 1845 and Wellington College in 1859, while the much older foundations, including Eton and Winchester Colleges, began to expand significantly under the pressure to educate the children of the new bourgeoisie. State education lagged behind these private schools in quality and quantity during the nineteenth century. The long overdue expansion of state schools was driven in part in response to the need to find meaningful occupation for children, who the Factory Acts dictated would no longer be allowed to be occupied at work.[20]

Despite schools spreading steadily across Britain, the curriculum remained very traditional, much as it had been since the start of the third education revolution era. Science and technology teaching, stimulated by the Industrial Revolution, took time to permeate into the classroom, and was then mainly limited to private schools, alongside their adherence to the teaching of Latin and Greek. Public examinations began at Cambridge from the late eighteenth century and at Oxford from early the following century and, by the 1830s, a system for university entrance had become firmly established, which played an important part in bolstering standards for leavers at schools to help ensure entry

---

[19] Willetts, D., (2017). Op. cit.
[20] Musgrove, F., (1964). *Youth and the Social Order*. London: Routledge and Kegan Paul, pp 33-57.

for them.[21] The focus remained on rote-learning from standardised textbooks. Mr Gradgrind's insistence, in Charles Dickens's *Hard Times,* that children were little pitchers "to be filled so full of facts" may always have been something of a caricature. But the reality of fact-based learning remained the norm up to the present day, bolstered during the last two decades by a new band of enthusiasts for exam success as the sole validator of school success.[22]

The advent of modern technologies, including reprographics during the 1960s, the photocopier during the 1970s, the word processor during the 1980s, computers during the 1990s and smartboards during the twenty-first century, all improved in some ways the quality of life for the learner, although they did little, if anything, to lighten the burden of work on the teacher. None changed the fundamental model of education; they merely led to a partially improved, more efficient and quicker, delivery of the third education revolution.

Very fundamental problems remained with the mass model, which rendered a high quality education across the world the preserve of the elites. Add to this, only a narrow segment of each child's capabilities was being developed at school. For most, these remained dormant all life.

This is why the promise of the fourth education revolution is so significant and profound.

---

[21] Gillard, D., (2011). 'Education in England: a Brief History'. [Online]. Available at:
http://www.educationengland.org.uk/history/chapter02.html
[22] Christodoulou, D., (2014). *Seven Myths about Education.* London: Routledge.

22

British Labour Parliamentarian, Jo Cox (1974-2016) was murdered by a far-right obsessive during the Referendum campaign in June 2016. She epitomises what it means to be a fully educated person, and to display multiple intelligences. She attended a state grammar school before going to university at Cambridge and the London School of Economics. She was widely involved in humanitarian work and became a Labour MP in 2015, while bringing up two children and living with her husband on a houseboat.

Chapter Two:

What is Education? What is an Educated Person?

What is Education?

The first chapter described how education emerged gradually over time in three successive revolutions in response to economic and technological change, shaped by societal, religious, and governmental needs. But what does 'education' entail? I am constantly surprised, when I ask colleagues in the profession the question, to be greeted by blank faces. If those most directly involved in education are not clear what the word means, including some leaders of higher education institutions (HEIs), it suggests some exploration of the concept is first needed, before assessing the potential impact on it of AI. Probing the meaning of education is the subject of this second chapter.

The word 'educate' has its roots in Latin in the act of leading a person from a place. *Educatus* is the past participle of *educare*, translated as 'bringing out or leading forth', from the words *ex*, meaning 'out', and *ducere*, to lead. So the idea of a journey is integral to education. Humans are born into the world, if not with a blank slate, then certainly "illiterate and innumerate, and ignorant of the norms and cultural achievements of the community or society into which they have been thrust."[1] We can conceive of education thus as a *journey* as in this diagram below:

Ignorance   —————————▶   *Fully educated*

But what does it mean to become 'fully' educated, and who decides what the measure is? It is our contention that the educational institutions of the third revolution era had a very partial notion: but let's first examine how and where education has occurred.

How Does Education take Place?

i) Formal education

A formalised education structure provided by an institution, sees teachers or lecturers organising the learning experience for students, who are sub-divided into classes, seminars or lecture groups. Across the world, school is traditionally divided into a *primary* level, which may finish between 11 and 13, a *secondary* phase, which further educates students and continues, in more economically advanced societies, until the ages of 16 to 18 or 19, and a *higher education* or university phase, the prerogative of a still more narrow elite, divided into undergraduate and postgraduate levels. An additional level which exists in many countries is *further education*, separate to secondary and higher education, which offers a series of

---

[1] Phillips, D.C. & Siegel, S., (2013). 'Philosophy of Education'. *Stanford Encyclopaedia of Philosophy*. [Online]. Available at: https://plato.stanford.edu/entries/education-philosophy/

diplomas and certificates to allow students to progress on to higher education (HE) or to give them a dedicated education to start on a career typically in areas like engineering or accountancy. Common to all these formal institutions, if only implicitly, is the notion that education finishes when the student leaves their last formal institution.

ii) Formal education not by educational bodies

Many professions, including medicine, the law, accountancy and finance, require employees to be continuously updated on recent knowledge all the way through their careers, and often involve professional qualifications or thresholds which allow progression to higher levels. With the growing complexity and sophistication of knowledge, and changes in the job market, indeed, most young graduates entering any career after university will need regular updates in knowledge. Education needs to do more to develop curiosity, enquiring minds and a commitment to self-improvement and to be constantly learning.

Professions, and many businesses, are increasingly attracting school leavers at age 18, believing that they can offer a more bespoke education than if the young people had gone off to university. We will see more professions and companies in future setting up their own higher and further education branches. Many voluntary organisations, including the Scouts and the Guides for the young, trade union-affiliated bodies (for example, workers' education bodies) and organisations like the National Trust are in the business of education through exposure to outdoor activities, to culture and to history.

iii) 'Informal' learning

From the moment of birth, a child will be learning from their parents and others in close proximity. Parents can indeed be considered the most important teachers in any young person's life. For many children across the world, home-schooling is a necessity, while in the UK up to 30,000 children were by choice home-schooled in 2016/17, and in the US, some 2 million are home-schooled.[2] In one sense, each individual is their own educator; we learn more from and by ourselves than from anyone else or from any institution. The rise of online learning and the internet imparts powerful new opportunities to us to become our own teacher. Almost anything we could want to know, if we can access it, is available on the internet. This ease of access has never been the case before in history.

We would therefore be wrong to equate what happens in education solely with what happens in schools and universities, or in workplace learning. Oddly, governments the world over make this very mistake.

What are the Purposes of Education?

If we are to understand how AI might assist in the education process, and compensate for the limitations of the third education revolution, we need to be clear about the *purposes* of education, so we can see how it might achieve them as well or better. We can view the purposes, historically,

---

[2] Yorke, H., (2017). 'Number of Children Home Taught doubles in six years amid increased Competition for School Places' *The Daily Telegraph* 7 July 2017. [Online]. Available at: http://www.telegraph.co.uk/education/2017/07/07/number-children-home-taught-doubles-six-years-amid-increased/

understanding why formal education institutions emerged at different points in history, or functionally, emphasising the roles education has fulfilled, or inspirationally, the objectives we might like it to have. Our approach below is a combination of all three.

i) Educating citizens to play a productive economic and military role

Governments rarely take decisions for benign, high-minded reasons; an ulterior motive usually lurks below the surface. There is nothing dishonourable about governments worldwide wanting schools and universities to train future workers in relevant skills, as well as preparing the young to maintain internal order, and to fight to defend the nation at home and abroad. After all, if schools are not preparing people for jobs, then they will have fallen short of their responsibility, and a country unable to defend itself against outside aggressors and internal purveyors of violence will not be serving its citizens.

Physical education (PE) or physical training (PT) was developed in Britain from 1860 (the first gymnasium opened at Oxford University), but took off seriously after the Boer War (1899–1902), in part to improve the physical health of the children in the hope that, should there be another war, most immediately in Europe, those called upon to fight would be in better physical condition than many of the young who went off to fight in that war in South Africa. It is no surprise that the Education Act of 1902, which set up local education authorities to improve primary schools and create secondary schools, should have followed that war. The need to have the young on permanent military preparedness might not be an imperative for many educators today, but health professionals believe that the young would benefit from daily exercise as a boost to their physical and mental health.

The utilitarian purpose of education remains a powerful strand. In February 2018, Robert Halfon, Chairman of the UK Parliament's Education Select Committee, stated that too many university students were receiving "paltry returns" for their effort and money rather than job preparation because, he said, "we have become obsessed with full academic degrees in this country". In the eyes of those who think similarly, education is above all designed to give people skills for employment. There is a danger we lose balance and perspective here: 'pure' university degrees can seem an indulgence, but the skills that employees need will change over time, and an education that develops human qualities and curiosity will prepare students well for future work and life, perhaps even better than a purely transactional training.

ii) Socialisation

From the earliest moments outside the womb, each child is socialised into the norms of society. Schools and universities arrive late in this prolonged socialisation process. Nations that are less democratic typically insist on tight control over education, for example in China and Russia. "In China today, as in many other nation-states, the inculcation of patriotism is an essential element in the construction of citizenship."[3] But

---

[3] Benei, V., (2005). 'Introduction: manufacturing citizenship: confronting public spheres and education in contemporary worlds'. In, Benei, V., (ed.), *Manufacturing Citizenship: Education and nationalism in Europe, South Asia and China*. New York: Routledge, p. 20.

then countries that are representative democracies, including the USA, equally emphasise nationhood and their own values of political and economic freedom.[4] In public schools in all states of the USA except Hawaii, Iowa, Vermont and Wyoming, teachers must schedule regular recitations of the 'Pledge of Allegiance' (although this practice is increasingly challenged). "National states have, until recently, penetrated down to the minutest details of everyday life in order to instil a sense of loyalty in their citizens", writes educationalist Veronique Benei.[5]

In Britain, concern over the last 30 years has focussed on the content of the history curriculum, with traditionalists wanting to emphasise *British* history, and progressives downplaying it in order to favour world history. Traditionalists prefer history to focus on the leaders of society, whereas progressives want it switched to the working class, the history of women, ethnic minorities and LGBTQ groups. Both sides recognise that, if they can captivate the minds of the young, they may win them over to their particular perspectives on life.

Not all of the role of socialisation is contentious within and between nations. Most from all quarters agree on the importance of teaching the young to be law abiding, to overcome antisocial impulses, to participate fully in civic life, to work hard at their chosen job, and to become valued and supportive members of society.

---

[4] Omar, L., (1991). 'Schools as agents of cultural transmission and social control'. *Revue Sciences Humaines* 12, pp. 41–51.
[5] Benei, V., (2005). Op. cit., p. 2.

Much of the debate in Britain today over the role of character formation in schools revolves around this very differing emphasis on the purpose of education. Traditionalists, including the last and current Chief Inspector of Schools, Michael Wilshaw and Amanda Spielman, believe that the focus of schools should be on the taught curriculum in class, and that morally uplifting messages should be delivered through it rather than through specific lessons or extra-curricular emphasis upon the development of virtues and good character. To them, character virtues and civic education can be a distraction and waste of time at best, and at worst a disincentive to emulate the very qualities that are being exhorted. The notion of the development of virtue as integral to education goes back to Aristotle and before.[6] Advocates like the Jubilee Centre for Character and Virtues at the University of Birmingham draw inspiration from a wide range of philosophers in asserting that the shaping of good character is a necessary and vital aspect of education.

Some European countries, with Christianity or Islam, see – or have seen – the teaching of religion in schools as integral to socialisation. Even religious sceptics can argue that the young brought up with a religious education might be less troublesome as mature citizens, and more likely to be responsive to the wishes of government.

iii) Cultural transfer

The scale of human achievement is unimaginably broader than any school or university can possibly cover. But the sheer

---

[6] 'Nicomachean Ethics', Book X, 1172a.17 / (1984). *The Complete Works of Aristotle: The Revised Oxford Translation*. Barnes. J., (ed.) 2 vols. Princeton, NJ: Princeton Univ. Press.

scale should not deter educational institutions from attempting to inspire and enrich students with cultural riches and heights of human achievement. Can children be properly educated if they have not been exposed to the paintings of Leonardo da Vinci, the plays of William Shakespeare, the music of Wolfgang Amadeus Mozart, the civilisations of ancient China, Greece and Rome, the literature of Jane Austen or Harper-Lee, the religious insights of Buddha and Jesus Christ, the leadership messages of Abraham Lincoln, Mahatma Gandhi, Winston Churchill and Nelson Mandela, or the scientific insights of Ada Lovelace and Charles Darwin?

Education is a meagre experience if it does not include at its core an appreciation of such giants across the field of human interest and endeavour. As Matthew Arnold, the nineteenth-century British poet, social commentator and inspector of schools wrote in *Culture and Anarchy* (1869), the importance of education is "learning about the best that has been thought and said". A rounded education needs to have such breadth, alongside grounding in science and maths, humanities and social sciences, languages and philosophy. Early specialisation can too easily lose sight of the context of the academic subject from which it springs, and the wider fields of human learning. Education worldwide has too often become a narrow transactional exercise, based upon the rote and superficial learning of a narrow curriculum, without insights into the depths of human experience and achievement. All students, regardless of nationality, social background or intellectual ability, have an entitlement and the potential to appreciate these profundities.

iv) The development of innate human potential

Institutions in the third education era concentrated on the development of measurable and practical skills of literacy, numeracy, scientific knowledge and technical skills. This approach also has left little space for the exploration of the inner talents of each child. Education is too often regarded as a process done *to* students, to make them better able to manage themselves in society and to succeed in the job market, rather than *for* them, giving them real opportunities for the development of their innate potentialities.

The Indian economist Amartya Sen during the 1980s developed his 'Capability Approach' for individual potential which drew on Aristotle's thinking about human flourishing and what makes life worthwhile. It envisages a wider vision for education than the maximisation of an individual's capacity to earn money and to develop purely cognitive skills to succeed in employment.

The work of Howard Gardner of Harvard University builds on the idea of the holistic development of human potential. He first wrote about his theory in *Frames of Mind: The Theory of Multiple Intelligences* (1983), in which he stated that humans have a variety of different intelligences rather than just one. The purpose of education, he argued, should be to develop these intelligences and help students reach "vocational and avocational goals that are appropriate to their particular spectrum of intelligences".[7] Gardner is

---

[7] Wikipedia. 'Theory of Multiple Intelligences'. [Online]. Available at:
https://en.wikipedia.org/wiki/Theory_of_multiple_intelligences (accessed on: 16 January 2018).

sceptical about the dominance across education of IQ tests in widespread use since before the First World War, which he believes narrow formal education down to just measurable intelligences: the logical and the linguistic. He argues that one of the dangers of the traditional model is that superior schooling gives a disproportionate advantage to elites who can excel at these specific IQ tests and the exam system which is based upon them. If students are given a broader education, however, embracing a much wider notion of intelligence, they will find it much more rewarding as well as enriching, allowing them to focus on what they *can do* rather than what they cannot. Gardner's approach can be summed up by the saying "Don't ask how intelligent a child is, ask how is a child intelligent". Throughout my own career in education there was no quotation that I would cite more regularly or with such strong recognition from teachers and parents.

Gardner's work has been criticised by many academics, but less so by those with prolonged experience of teaching in schools.[8] To many of these, Gardner's approach makes admirable sense. It ennobles, rather than belittles and constricts human potential. Detractors have to provide a convincing answer to the question: "If schools do not develop

---

[8] Cf. Waterhouse, L., (2006a). 'Inadequate Evidence for Multiple Intelligences, Mozart Effect, and Emotional Intelligence Theories'. *Educational Psychologist*, 41(4), pp. 247–255. doi: 10.1207/s15326985ep4104_5 / Waterhouse, L., (2006b). 'Multiple Intelligences, the Mozart Effect, and Emotional Intelligence: A Critical Review'. *Educational Psychologist*, 41(4), pp. 207-225. doi: 10.1207/s15326985ep4104_1 / Klein, P. D., (1997). 'Multiplying the Problems of Intelligence by Eight: A Critique of Gardner's Theory'. *Canadian Journal of Education,* 22(4), pp. 377–94. doi:10.2307/1585790.

these wider human potentialities, who will?" It is those young people across the world fortunate enough to go to well-endowed educational institutions who have their wider intelligences, including creative, sporting, moral and personal, nurtured and developed. It is the less well-off who attend schools that cannot afford co-curricular activities or who focus just on exam results who lose out. Lives are stunted because children have not had their wider aptitudes identified, nurtured and developed. It is no surprise that young people from disadvantaged backgrounds find it hard to be offered jobs at the most prestigious companies, who look beyond exam results to character traits that their schools did not develop.

v) Self-knowledge, the discernment of wisdom and the development of individuality

A final purpose of education is the most high minded, and the least likely to be focussed upon in purely utilitarian education requirements. The possession of financial, political or military power is no guarantee that one is an educated person. The analogy of Plato reminds us why: many people, he believed, are stuck in a cave of ignorance, taking the shadows playing on the wall lit by a fire as reality. But they are not reality. Only the intrepid person is capable of stepping outside the cave and seeing the real world as it is. But some wisdom is required to realise one is stuck in the cave. Humility is equally required. Socrates said "I am wiser than this man, for neither of us appears to know anything great and good; but he fancies he knows something, although he knows nothing; whereas I, as I do not know anything, so I do not fancy I do. In this trifling particular, then, I appear to be wiser than he, because I do not fancy I know what I do not know."[9]

Helping each student to acquire a genuine humility and curiosity for life, and become grounded in their own deepest identity, rather than learning to give the 'right' answers is a priceless quality of education and one which is often lacking in the factory education systems of today.

What are the Stages of Teaching and Learning?

Education is not a mystical, unknowable art, though many have treated it as if it is. It can be broken down into distinct stages which hold true for teaching and learning in all separate places on earth and at all points in history. By examining these separate stages, we can gain a clearer understanding of the role of human agency, and the extent to which AI might be able to assist or even replace human input for each particular function.

First, we will look at the five tasks in *teaching*.

1. *Preparation of material.* The teacher or lecturer has to plan out each lesson, decide what material is going to be required to be provided to students, and in what form, and, if worksheets or handouts need to be given out, these need to be prepared. This is often a laborious mechanical process, leaving little scope or time for the teacher to allow individuation of material for specific student capabilities and needs. The teacher in this role is the *curator* of knowledge, selecting appropriate facts from an

---

[9] Plato's Apology.

almost limitless bank, deciding what, how much and in what form to pass it on to students. The school teacher often has to spend further time preparing detailed 'lesson plans', especially if inspectors are calling, or senior leaders are 'on the prowl', some of the best classes I observed had a 'lesson plan': many of the most arid and worst had laborious ones.

2. *Organisation of the classroom.* The teacher or lecturer needs to ensure that he or she is in command of their classroom, that the space is optimally organised for learning, that any visual displays in the space are attractive and stimulating, that mechanical devices are working properly, that the lesson is orderly and well-disciplined, and that the time is effectively used. In this particular role, the teacher or lecturer is *in* authority and, without that overall control and structure, lesson time will not be optimised.

3. *Ensuring that all students are engaged in learning.* Teachers and lecturers need to keep the whole class under observation to ensure that good progress is being made by all students, and they notice and act when students lose focus. The larger the class, and the more distracted the students, the harder this is to do. The task becomes much simpler when students are well-motivated, well-socialised and are willing to follow the teacher's instructions. Teachers need to be skilled in conveying material to students in a way that engages all their differing needs and interests, and optimises their learning.

4. *Setting and marking assignments.* Teachers need to ensure and monitor that learning is taking place. They do this by observing behaviour, by asking questions orally in class, and by setting written assignments, which they must ensure are marked accurately and fairly, and that they make comments which help students to learn from their errors. Preparation of appropriate assignments can be time-consuming, but assessing and marking assignments, and offering constructive comments, is far more demanding still of the teacher's time.

5. *Preparation for terminal examinations and writing summative reports.* Teachers and lecturers are involved in preparing their students for terminal tests and examinations. If these are internal to the school or university, they themselves may be setting the examinations. They are responsible for the collection of data on the performance of every student in the class and for the writing of reports on the students for communication internally within the school and to home. Terminal exams at the end of courses of study spread rapidly last century as the standardised way of assessing and ranking students. Bodies or exam boards set and assess exams in schools in most countries. Transnational school curricula and examinations are unusual: the International Baccalaureate (IB), set up in 1968, is a rare exception, offering programmes of assessment at primary, middle and diploma (for ages 16–18) levels. Universities worldwide generally set and mark their own exams, but the quality of their assessment is closely monitored again by external bodies. Notionally at least, a

first class degree nationally (and indeed internationally) is of the same quality regardless of the institution that has made the award. Standardised testing and written entry exams in Britain were first introduced at Oxford and Cambridge in 1857 and 1858, respectively. Nationally standardised testing was introduced in English schools in 1917 with the 'School' and 'Higher School' Certificates, to be replaced by 'O' or Ordinary Levels in 1951 (succeeded by GCSE from 1988) and 'A' or Advanced Levels for the 16–18 year olds. In the United States, students leave with a final Grade Point Average (GPA) based on their high school performance. These can be supplemented by further tests, including American College Testing (ACT) and Scholastic Aptitude Test (SAT) for entry to university.

Learning by students also has five distinctive activities.

1. *Memorising knowledge.* Students at schools or universities are presented with knowledge, segmented into separate academic subjects, and into different levels of difficulty depending upon age. In the third revolution period of education, this material came in the form of monographs, textbooks and articles but, for the last 20 years, increasingly digitally. Students are able to read this material and to absorb it on their own, but the agency of a teacher, usually a specialist in the age group or the subject, or both, is responsible for 'parcelling up' the knowledge and explaining it to the students, especially younger ones. In schools, the method of teaching is normally highly directed, utilising question and answer,

whereas at university, the lecture is a common mode of communicating knowledge. Students traditionally listen in silence until the end of the discourse, with the material followed up in seminars and tutorials. Learning in schools and universities is developmental. To progress to a new level, students should have a familiarity with the knowledge, skills and context of the previous one.

The earliest learning takes place long before nursery or first school. "Research on early learning suggests that the process of making sense of the world begins at a very young age. Children begin in preschool years to develop sophisticated understandings (whether accurate or not) of the phenomena around them... Those initial understandings can have a powerful effect on the integration of new concepts and information."[10] Some learning is based upon comprehending incomplete knowledge and erroneous thinking: "Sometimes those understandings are accurate, providing a foundation for building new knowledge. But sometimes they are inaccurate... In science, students often have misconceptions of physical properties that cannot be easily observed. In humanities, their preconceptions often include stereotypes or simplifications, as when history is understood as a struggle between good guys and bad guys."[11] In this stage, information or raw data becomes valuable knowledge when it is memorised by the student: abler students prove themselves by assimilating the

---

[10] Bransford, J. D., Brown, A.L. & Cocking, R.R. (eds.)., (2000). *How People Learn: Brain, Mind, Experience and School.* Washington DC: National Academy Press, p.15.
[11] Ibid.

knowledge more quickly than others, and by being able to retrieve it more speedily from their memories. The agency of a human teacher can be helpful in memorising knowledge: it is not always vital.

2. *Applying the knowledge.* Merely memorising knowledge is of little value in itself. Students might 'know' a whole series of facts and be able to recall them in tests and quizzes. They might even win competitions or gameshows on television, such as the BBC's *Mastermind*. But our intelligence and understanding is very limited until we learn how to *apply* knowledge with discrimination and in context. This can be explained by an example from human biology: "people who are knowledgeable about veins and arteries know more than the facts... they also understand why veins and arteries have particular properties. They know that blood pumped from the heart exits in spurts and that the elasticity of the arteries helps accommodate pressure changes... Because they understand relationships between the structure and function of veins and arteries, knowledgeable individuals are more likely to be able to use what they have learned to solve novel problems—to show evidence of transfer."[12]

Active subjects, such as sports, music, drama or aspects of science, become more meaningful when the student applies or tests out the knowledge that they have learnt merely in theory. A student may have memorised a Beethoven piano concerto but, until they play it

---

[12] Bransford, J. D., Brown, A.L. & Cocking, R.R. (eds.)., (2000) Op. cit. p.9.

themselves on an instrument, that knowledge is incomplete. Golfers might know everything there is to be known about the perfect swing but, until they hit a ball, this learning is of limited value. An understanding of science is significantly improved by the conducting of physical experiments in school and university laboratories, which explains why they came to be built from the late nineteenth century onwards. The experience of mixing chemicals together under fixed conditions permits the student to comprehend with their own minds the application of theory, which allows the knowledge to become more deeply embedded. As one researcher wrote: "When students have a physical experience moving the wheels, they are more likely to activate sensory and motor areas of the brain... known to be important for our ability to make sense of forces, angles and trajectories... Those students who physically experience difficult science concepts learn them better, perform better in class and on quizzes the next day, and the effect seems to play out weeks later, as well."[13]

3. *Turning knowledge into understanding.* "Where is the knowledge we have lost in information" wrote poet T.S. Eliot. Knowledge needs deepening to extract its full potency. Learning is not just a solitary experience. The

---

[13] Ingmire, J., (2015). 'Learning by doing helps students perform better in science'. *UchicagoNews*, 29 April 2015. [Online]. Available at:
https://news.uchicago.edu/article/2015/04/29/learning-doing-helps-students-perform-better-science/
http://journals.sagepub.com/doi/pdf/10.1177/0956797615569355

benefits of learning in association with other students in class is most obvious in the humanities and social sciences. But in mathematics and science too, the learning of students can be powerfully deepened by participating in a class or seminars, when they listen to the contributions of fellow students asking and answering questions. It allows them to measure their own understanding against that of others and to gain in confidence that they are acquiring mastery.

In a literature class, the teacher might speak about a poet and the background to a particular poem studied. It might then be read out by members of the class with questions asked. It is in the asking of questions by students and the answers that teachers and other members of the class give that understandings are clarified and deepened. This process of discussion translates a transitory knowledge about a poem into a deeper understanding of what the poet was trying to say. A parrot technically could learn to repeat a poem perfectly but has no understanding. Neither does a computer, although it might be able to speak the lines of a poem. Much teaching is based upon rote learning, which is the memorising of facts through the mere act of repetition. But it is when it is opened up for a class to challenge, question and criticise, that insight and knowledge grows.

4. *Self-assessment and diagnosis*. Students need to gain an objective understanding of the progress they are making in each subject and what they need to learn better to improve. Self-assessment at best is undertaken by the students themselves. Self-aware students will be

44

constantly monitoring their own progress, testing their knowledge and reflecting upon what they are learning. But we cannot rely upon the younger and less experienced student alone, and teachers are necessary to ensure that they have their progress monitored, and to give feedback and encouragement that reinforces effective learning.

5. *Reflection and the development of autonomous learning.* "Where is the wisdom we have lost in knowledge", Eliot also wrote in *The Rock* (1934). The highest objective of learning is for students to develop their own *curiosity* in a subject, and gain confidence in their own ability to find out how to obtain answers. A successful school will help students to become independent learners, in preparation for the more autonomous learning environment in FE and HE. Learning academic subjects and performing to the best of the students' ability, as measured by exams, is necessary for a good education. But it is not *sufficient.* The student his/herself should grow as a human being and be changed for the better in the process. A medical student might come top of their entire year group at a medical school but, unless the learning of the subject has taught them to be reflective, empathetic and emotionally intelligent, they will never become good doctors in front of patients. They will not become fully human, the best version of themselves. Education is about more than making us into speedy and accurate processors of information; computers have for many years been able to outwit humans at the acquisition and use of data. What makes us fully human is, crucially, what computers will *never* be able to replicate, which is empathetic

understanding, the ability to reflect and to respond sensitively and personally to another human being. The best maths students at the highest performing maths university department in the world will remain only half educated, or less, if they haven't learnt how to be a fuller, or more rounded human being. This is what Eliot meant by 'wisdom'.

These are the principal stages of teaching and learning. The question that will be addressed in later chapters is how AI might help in some or all of these stages. Breaking down the components of teaching and learning in the way that we have is indeed suggesting already how AI might usher in the fourth education revolution to compensate for the deficiencies of the factory model.

What is an Educated Person?

Societies across the world tend to equate highly-educated individuals with the university degrees they have been awarded, the ranking of their *alma maters* and the classifications they have received. But no degrees from Harvard, Oxford or Beijing Normal universities will of themselves make for a fully educated person.

Let us return to the notion of the *journey* from birth until death, which can be considered on the continuum below:

Ignorance ⟶ *Fully Educated*

We might now begin to answer who a fully educated person is by asking how many people have been able to say on their deathbeds that they have fulfilled their gifts and talents, and have led a life in tune with their deepest ideals and aspirations. The highest achievers, who might say they are the most educated, may have made immense sacrifices in order to achieve excellence in their chosen fields, whether economics or playing the flute, but often to the detriment of wider ideals, responsibilities to others and fulfilment. The lives of the highest achievers can be strewn with the debris of human suffering, to themselves, to family and to colleagues.

Howard Gardner's work is pertinent again here. We might want to reframe notions of achievement and posit that the person who is most fully educated in life (i.e. furthest to the right-hand side of our diagram above) is one who has had a fulfilled, happy life and has developed all of their aptitudes. A philosophy teacher at my university comes to mind: intellectually brilliant and extraordinarily kind, but worryingly deficient in many wider intelligences in life, including the personal intelligence required to live a happy life. Schools and universities across the world can all too easily, if unintentionally, narrow students down, placing undue attention on the intellectual intelligence and the mind, to the detriment of the heart, creativity, the body, and the spirit. Taking just the intellectual intelligence, universities often narrow learning down to one subject, and to an ever narrower part of that subject the more the student advances. Ultimately, the system can render academics unable to communicate with the general public, or to recognise that their ability to describe the real world has often been lost in an imaginary world of academic debates and specialist language. Too much research, especially outside STEM, is guilty of just this.

Higher ideas and visions for what it means to be an educated person do exist. One such was the report in 1945 from Harvard: *On General Education in a Free Society*. It suggested that education at both school and university should regard social and moral development as just as important as academic learning. The accumulation of knowledge in just one area, it said, can be: "...positively dangerous if it is not grounded in a broad, deep and humane understanding of the human condition and a well-grounded moral sensibility." It went on to say that "the modern university had an obligation to require all students to take at least a third of their course selections from courses specially designed by teams of top faculty, not to advance students in their march toward specialization but rather to involve them in the study of complex issues, systems, big ideas from the full realm of human experience which, when taken together, would expose them to that experience in a way that would serve to help them lead the good life as the Greeks would have understood that phrase: to be decent, capable, concerned, involved contributors and thoughtful citizens."[14]

The Harvard report proposed a radically different and more humanistic vision of education than that which emerged in post-1945 universities across the world. It sought to furnish students with life-long skills and curiosity. Changes in the job market, most notably with the advent of digitalisation, have, ironically, highlighted the need for the very skills that the document advocated. "Thus the fruit of education is

---

[14] Tucker, M., (2015). 'What Does It Mean to Be an Educated Person Today?' *Education Week*. [Online]. Available at: http://blogs.edweek.org/edweek/top_performers/2015/10/what_do es_it_mean_to_be_an_educated_person_today.html

intelligence in action," the report states. "The aim is mastery of life; and since living is an art, wisdom is the indispensable means to this end."[15]

Albert Sloman, vice-chancellor of the then new University of Essex, gave the BBC Reith Lectures in 1963 on 'A University in the Making'. He recognised the need for universities to specialise, but cautioned that "specialization should come only after some acquaintance with what the Spanish philosopher, Ortega, called "the system of vital ideas which every age possesses and by which it lives", a sense at least of the whole range of human achievement. The greater the cult of specialization, the greater the need to give it a solid basis of general culture. And only with the experience of different subjects can anyone make an intelligent choice of specialization in the first place, let alone be able to see his subjects in any kind of perspective."[16]

A fully educated person will therefore have a thirst for knowledge and a curiosity that will last until their final breath on earth. Equally, the best teachers are those who are as excited and passionate, and as eager to learn, on their final day in their profession as they were on their first. As the classical author and educationalist Richard Livingstone said more than 70 years ago: "The test of successful education is not the amount of knowledge that pupils take away from school, but

---

[15] Bryant Conant, J., (1950). *General Education in a Free Society.* Cambridge, MA: Harvard University Press, pp.72–9.

[16] Sloman, A., (1963). 'The Training of Minds'. BBC Reith Lectures. [Online]. Available at:
http://downloads.bbc.co.uk/rmhttp/radio4/transcripts/1963_reith3.pdf

their appetite to know and their capacity to learn."[17] The contemporary philosopher of education Guy Claxton agrees: "being an effective, powerful real-life learner is a useful thing to be; and that twenty-first century education should be aiming to help young people develop this generic capacity to learn."[18]

Returning to the mediaeval notion of the *trivium* and liberal arts, education should be designed to help people to think independently and to develop free will, thereby possessing the ability to make decisions in tune with their own and society's interests. Learning the subjects of the *trivium* and then the *quadrivium* helped students acquire these tools. Broad and challenging curriculums today, with philosophy or critical thinking as an essential ingredient, can achieve similar benefits. Marry that freedom to the optimising of each person's human potentialities, and to the fulfilment of the person's ideals, and here we have a fully educated person. How did the third education revolution model succeed in leading students *en masse* to achieve this ideal? Were there inherent difficulties with it that means it could never achieve these ambitions? This is the subject of the next chapter.

---

[17] Claxton, G., (2006). 'Expanding the Capacity to Learn: A new end for education?' [Online]. Available at: https://docs.wixstatic.com/ugd/84a7e9_7c2c7b0cb542445cb3e972 c2f7180709.pdf,
[18] Ibid.

The third education revolution became an increasingly frustrating experience for teachers and lecturers, weighed down by the burden of administration and by repetitive tasks that prevented them doing their teaching and research jobs properly. As a result, teacher workload, stress and retention became problems the world over.

Chapter Three:

Five Intractable Problems with Conventional Education

The first three education revolutions conferred inestimable benefits on humankind. They made human life safer, more comfortable, more civilised and more enjoyable. Without education, human beings would still be wandering around in nomadic tribes, struggling to find food and water, threatened by a wide variety of disease and predators, and with poor quality of life.

But how complete were the three education revolutions? The third revolution may have given the masses a structured education until their teenage years in better-off countries across the world. But did it overcome a number of intractable problems, all of which affect the quality and extent of the educational experience, and render the journey towards a holistic, grounded and profound education incomplete?

It is not that these problems have not been regularly and tirelessly addressed by governments and private institutions over the last 100 years and more. We may conclude that while marginal improvements have been made, fault lines in the very engineering of the industrial model of education have stood in the way of more profound change. The problems are all *systemic;* they may be ameliorated but they cannot be solved without a new – fourth – revolution.

The Five Intractable Problems with the Third Education Revolution Model

Failure to defeat entrenched social immobility
Inflexible progress through the education system
Teaching overwhelmed by administration
Large class sizes inhibit personalised and breadth of learning
Homogenisation and lack of individuation of personality

We need to analyse them in depth now. What precisely are these problems? Might the deficiencies be able to be ameliorated or even solved by the advent of AI? We begin by diagrammatically displaying the five problems with the third education revolution model. The fourth education revolution model equally throws up inherent problems, which we will air in later chapters.

1. Failure to overcome entrenched social immobility

For millions of years, our *hominid* predecessors organised themselves into leaders and followers. Whether by dint of superior physical strength, gender, membership of a dominant family, greater intellect or powers of oratory, all groupings had some who claimed authority for making decisions affecting the many, and who enjoyed an unequal share of the material possessions going. When, during the last 7,000 years, civilisation became more sophisticated, with permanent settlement in towns and cities, new forms of elites emerged: political, financial, legal, business and cultural. Dynastic rule by families reinforced and served to perpetuate the tendency for power to remain in the hands of elites. The 'masses', tended to retain their lowly status; the children of the powerful, however, were very likely to retain their superior position.

While the first two education revolutions entrenched and perpetuated elites, the third education revolution, with schooling for the first time available for all, offered at least the prospect of moving beyond a self-perpetuating *status quo*. But the 'factory school model', as the third education revolution can be termed, barely addressed fundamental social mobility problems across the world. The elites paid for their children to have a privileged education or ensured that they secured places in academic, high-powered state schools. In communist countries, rooted notionally in a commitment to equality for all and the redressing of the inherent inequalities of the capitalist model, elites found unique ways to ensure that their children enjoyed the most highly regarded and aspirational education. This was as true of the Soviet Union as of China.

Many explanations have been given for the tendency of elites to self-generate. One of the clearest was given by Robert Michels in his *Political Parties* (1911), who argued that the power of the oligarchy was an inevitable 'iron law' within society. However democratically high-minded the intentions of the founding fathers of any new country or organisation might be, all of them will evolve eventually into oligarchies. Power within one organisation or society, he said, will always be delegated to individuals, elected or otherwise, who will become a 'leadership class', able to control access to information and power, helping to ensure that their own hegemony continues. Information in this model was power.

The third education revolution model could have changed all this. In the era of mass education, elites might have been swept away, replaced by a 'meritocracy' (derived from the Latin word *merio* or 'merit' and the Greek word *kratos*, meaning strength or power but coined in 1958 by sociologist Michael Young), where the ablest and hardest working, not the most powerful, rose to the top. A meritocracy helps ensure fairness and justice but also efficiency, because authority is conferred on the most proficient, rather than those who enjoy the benefits of inherited privilege. So why did the third education model fail to combat Michels' iron law of oligarchy and not result in a meritocracy to a greater extent? Leaders full of moral zeal for decades tried to fix the unfixable. President Barack Obama was one of a vast number. He said in his 2010 State of the Union address: "In the 21st century, the best anti-poverty program around is a world-class education." If the drive and the money were there, why was poverty not defeated, and such optimism remained unrealised?

Social mobility can be defined as the "ability of individuals from underprivileged backgrounds to climb the socioeconomic ladder".[1] It is grounded empirically, optimists

---

[1] van der Berg, S., 'Social mobility and education'. [Online]. Available at:

believe, on secure if disputed foundations. Children from less advantaged backgrounds are born with similar abilities to those from high-income homes, albeit allowing for inherited intelligence. A March 2018 report from Robert Plomin and Emily Smith-Woolley of King's College, London,[2] found that because of the import of genes, selective school makes little difference to academic results. Not all academics agree on the importance of inherited intelligence, but the evidence is overwhelming that making too much allowance for children of lower ability/income parents can become a self-fulfilling prophecy, consigning such children to low educational expectations.

A 2013 report by the Brookings Institute in Washington is unequivocal: "Controlling for age, number of siblings, race, and other environmental factors, the effects of socioeconomic status are small and statistically insignificant [in children between 8 and 12 months]. A child born into a family in the highest socioeconomic quintile, for example, can expect to score only 0.02 standard deviations higher on a test of cognitive ability than an average child, while one born into a family in the lowest socioeconomic quintile can expect to score about 0.03 standard deviations lower – hardly a measurable difference and statistically insignificant. By contrast, other factors, such as age, gender, and birth order, have a greater impact on abilities at the earliest stages of

---

http://blogs.worldbank.org/futuredevelopment/social-mobility-and-education.

[2] *The Economist*, 26.03.18.

life."[3] The jury is out, but genes are clearly an important factor explaining the self-perpetuation of elites in meritocracies. AI will have its work cut out if it is to compensate for this in the fourth education revolution.

Why else do children from better-off homes generally flourish better in society? The answers include: they eat more nourishing food; they benefit from more stable child care; they experience greater parental interest in their education; they participate in more intellectually enriching conversations at home; and they forge more useful social connections. These benefits begin to manifest in children before they even enter formal schooling. By the age of 4, children in the highest income quintile score in the 69th percentile on literacy and numeracy while children in the lowest income quintile score in the 34th percentile for literacy and in the 32nd percentile for numeracy.[4]

Programmes such as 'Head Start' in the USA and 'Sure Start', launched in the UK in 1998, were designed to address this problem head on "by giving children the best possible start in life".[5] Early research findings in 2005 on the impact of Sure Start found that any difference made was less than expected. Despite the inconclusive evidence, governments in the UK, as well as in the USA, Australia and elsewhere, have continued to invest heavily in early interventions.

---

[3] Greenstone, M. *et al.,* (2013). 'Thirteen Economic Facts about Social Mobility and the Role of Education'. [Onlline]. Available at:, https://www.brookings.edu/wp-ontent/uploads/2016/06/THP_13EconFacts_FINAL.pdf

[4] Ibid.

[5] Wikipedia. 'Sure Start'. [Online]. Available at: https://en.wikipedia.org/wiki/Sure_Start.

Once children are in formal schooling, the differential performance between children from various social backgrounds grows significantly. Parents in high-income households across the developed world spend far more on their children's education than lower-income families. In the 30 years from the early 1970s, high-income families increased their expenditure from slightly more than four times as much as low-income families to nearly seven times more.[6]

Mothers with a college degree spend on average four and a half hours a week more engaging with their children than mothers with only a high school diploma or less, according to a 2008 study.[7] One impact is that children from working-class families have much narrower vocabularies, in part because the parents are spending less time engaging with them and are using less sophisticated language. Children from better-off backgrounds, in contrast, have smaller class sizes and are given more work, and have made very significant gains while at school, which are reflected in much better terminal exam results upon leaving. This helps explain why they disproportionately gain access to higher education, especially those universities which provide access to the top end and best paid jobs.[8] In the UK, the Office for Fair Access (OFFA) was set up in 2004 to address this very issue in order to enhance access to HE in England for those from less advantaged backgrounds. Despite criticisms that OFFA 'levels down'

---

[6] Greenstone, M. *et al.,* (2013). Op. cit.
[7] Ibid.
[8] Ibid.

rather than raises standards, there has been some success from these initiatives.[9]

Children from better-off backgrounds going on to the top-paid jobs has, ironically, been facilitated by the narrowing down of the curriculum in state schools to boost academic results, squeezing out broader enrichment of the timetable. Expectations of high exam results for their schools has driven many heads to devote disproportionate resources to the achievement of good grades, above all at GCSE. Yet it is the young from disadvantaged backgrounds who are precisely those who most need non-cognitive skills, including confidence building, social and emotional learning and character education, as we saw in the last chapter, which is more in evidence overall in private schools and in the homes of middle-class parents. Children from less advantaged backgrounds might perform well in final exams at university, but can be at a disadvantage in job interviews. Sociologist John Goldthorpe has written persuasively about how employers can prefer candidates who display more socially developed skills at interview: "in more high-value sales and personal services, employers may regard it as important that employees have some familiarity and indeed empathy with the mores and lifestyles of the social groups from which customers or clients are chiefly drawn." He continues, "children of parents in the professional and managerial salariat who have obtained only lower-level qualifications do in fact have clearly better chances of accessing the salariat

---

[9] Office for Fair Access (OFFA). (2017). 'Outcomes of access agreement monitoring for 2015-16'. [Online]. Available at: https://www.offa.org.uk/wp-content/uploads/2017/06/OFFA-Monitoring-Outcomes-Report-2015-16-Final.pdf

themselves than working-class children with similar qualifications."[10]

The verdict of a report by the Social Mobility Commission in Britain in 2017 is thus no surprise. It says a generation or more's worth of focussed initiatives to boost social mobility, many in education, have failed to make *any* significant impact on the level of social mobility. In significant ways, it argues that the problems have become worse: "The divide between the attainment of rich and poor children at the age of five has only just begun to shrink despite billions of pounds of investment... and it will take 40 years before it is closed; graduate employment for disadvantaged students has "barely improved", though widening access to university is a seen as a success for social mobility policies." The report detected a closing of the attainment gap between poorer and better-off students at primary school, although it found that the gap then increased again substantially at secondary school. Furthermore, it foresaw no prospect of the gap between poor and wealthy and children being eliminated at the age of 16 for GCSEs or at 18 at A Level. Particularly disheartening was what it said about performance in England outside London: "whereas attainment in schools in the capital has been substantially higher than the national average, showing that political will and targeted programmes with

---

[10] Goldthorpe, J. H., (2013). 'The Role of Education in Intergenerational Social Mobility: Problems from Empirical Research in Sociology and some Theoretical Pointers from Economics'. [Online]. Available at:
https://www.spi.ox.ac.uk/sites/default/files/Barnett_Paper_13-02.pdf

resources can make a difference, in large swathes of the rest of the country mobility was slow or stagnant."[11]

A similar verdict was provided in early 2018 by Becky Francis, Director of the Institute of Education in London, who points out that social mobility has not been solved by governments worldwide. She said that "provision in the state system is patchy and very poor quality in some areas... teaching quality has the biggest effect on student success rates and that is particularly true of children from disadvantaged backgrounds, so it is doubly important that they access the best teachers, but they are least likely to do so."[12] If Francis is right, and if teacher quality and availability is the key to solving the problem, what might AI have to offer fresh that the factory model could not?

2. Inflexible progress through the education system

In the third education revolution model, students travel through their education journey at school as if they are on a production line, beginning at the age generally of 3, 4 or 5. They recommence formal education every September, moving one year along the conveyor belt ready to receive

---

[11] Social Mobility Commission. 'Time for Change'. [Online]. Available at:
https://www.gov.uk/government/uploads/system/uploads/attachment_data/file/622214/Time_for_Change_report_-_An_assessement_of_government_policies_on_social_mobility_1997-2017.pdf
[12] UCL Sound (Jan 2018). 'How the UCL institution of education leave the national conversation on education'.

more advanced injections of knowledge. These 'insertions' of knowledge are made in different academic subjects as they move along day by day, week by week, term by term, until the academic year or production line grinds to an end every July. Educationalist Ken Robinson has deplored the practice where "students are educated in batches, according to age, as if the most important thing they have in common is their date of manufacture".[13]

A factory system works very well if one is building an inanimate object along a conveyor belt, when installations of new materials are required in a set order. It works less well in a school production line, when the children have human variability, and may not be ready or are overdue to have various new bits of knowledge added to them. For some children, the overall pace of the conveyor belt will be too slow and they will become frustrated because they will want it to move at a quicker rate; for others, it will be too quick, and they may become disheartened and rebellious; or the pace may be too quick in some subjects, perhaps mathematics and science, but too slow in others, perhaps English or history.

The conveyor belt approach was further embedded in Britain with the implementation of the Educational Reform Act 1988 to accompany the first stages of the 'National Curriculum'. The new approach was designed to consolidate structures which had emerged over the previous 100 years, doing so by banding all children into 'key stages' according to their ages on 1 September each year. 'Foundation Stage' was for ages 3 to 5, covering nursery and reception; 'Key Stage 1' for ages 5 to 7, for school years 1 to 2; 'Key Stage 2'

---

[13] Robinson, K., Ed Tech Now, 20.01.12.

for ages 7 to 11, covering school years 3 to 6. Key Stages 1 and 2 compromise primary schooling and each were concluded by exams known as Standard Attainment Tests or 'SATs'. Children move to secondary school for 'Key Stage 3' for most, ages 11 to 14, for school years 7 to 9, while 'Key Stage 4' is for ages 14 to 16, incorporating school years 10 to 11, terminating in GCSE. The final stage was optional, covering ages 16 to 18 or school years 12 to 13, culminating in A Levels, national vocational qualifications or the International Baccalaureate. Masterly thinking if children were automobiles on a production line, where 'one size fits all'. But they are not automobiles. They are human beings.

To try to address the problem of widely varying student abilities, different jurisdictions have developed systems so that those who are abler academically can move at a faster rate. The Education Act 1944 introduced a 'tripartite system' in England and Wales, whereby secondary state schools were divided into grammar, technical and secondary modern schools, with entry on the basis of 11-plus examinations. It became the accepted system by Labour and Conservative governments until 1965, when Labour began to dismantle it, formally abolishing it in 1976 (although some 164 grammar schools are still in existence today). The main justification given for this division was that able children could move ahead more quickly in an academic school, where they are destined for university. The principal objections were that the age of 11 was too young to differentiate between children's life chances on the basis of academic performance on the day of the test, and that those from better-off homes disproportionately gained places at grammar schools. Those entering secondary modern schools additionally were given a sense of academic inferiority, while late developers were deterred from reaching their full potential.

'Comprehensive schools' progressively dominated the tripartite system from the 1970s. They correspond to public high schools in the USA and Canada, and now constitute some 90 per cent of British secondary schools. Initially, they offered an academic education alongside more practical subjects, including art, design, and technology, but, in the last 20 years, the focus has increasingly been upon a common core of academic subjects for all, which has entailed a squeeze on a broader education, but without the anticipated gains in performance for the least advantaged.

To ensure that the more academic are stretched, some schools go in for *streaming*, where high-, middle- and low-ability students are banded together in all subjects, where the pace and demands on students vary. A principal problem with this is that it can become a self-fulfilling prophecy, with those in lower sets aspiring less and giving up. Some students moreover may excel in some subjects but not others. Yet, in streaming, all have to move at a common pace. Many schools therefore adopt *setting*, where students are grouped according to ability in *single* specified subjects, particularly in mathematics. Mathematics sees roughly twice the numbers setted than for English: one study found setting in maths rose from 53 per cent in Year 7 to 100 per cent in Years 10 and 11, while English rose from 34 per cent in Year 7 to 63 per cent in years 10 and 11.[14] Some schools manage to combine both streaming and setting.

Some schools eschew streaming and setting and opt instead for 'mixed-ability' classes: whether selection should be pursued or not is one of the most enduring debates in education worldwide:

> "Some studies indicate that grouping can damage students' self-esteem by consigning them to lower-tier groups; others suggest that it produces the opposite effect, by ensuring that more advanced students do not make their less advanced peers feel inadequate. Some studies conclude that grouping improves test scores in students of all levels, others that it helps high-achieving students while harming low-achieving ones, and still others say that it has little effect."[15]

Selection does seem to entrench existing divides in society along racial and class lines, which is another argument against it: the Right still tends to prefer it. This prompts the Left to be wary of it and to prefer 'mixed-ability', though proponents of each variant can be found across the political spectrum.

---

[14] Taylor, B. *et al.*, (2017). 'Factors deterring schools from mixed attainment teaching practice'. *Pedagogy, Culture & Society*, 25(3), pp. 327–345. [Online]. Available at:
http://www.tandfonline.com/doi/pdf/10.1080/14681366.2016.1256908?needAccess=true

[15] Yee, V., 'Grouping Students by Ability Regains Favor in Classroom'. *New York Times*. [Online]. Available at:
http://www.nytimes.com/2013/06/10/education/grouping-students-by-ability-regains-favor-with-educators.html

The clear advantage experienced by children who are older at the beginning of the academic year, i.e. those whose birthday falls on or shortly after 1 September, is one reason why streaming and setting can be unpopular, because older children are to be found disproportionately in higher sets. One study concluded "it is well-established that attainment-based grouping has little if any overall benefit in terms of student outcomes. Indeed, it has been demonstrated multiple times that, while small achievement gains may be made by higher attaining students, the impact on students in lower attaining groups is negative. This extends not just to academic attainment but also to the student experience, with students in lower-attaining sets reporting that they are unhappy with set placement and developing poor self-confidence."[16]

The arguments for and against setting serve only to highlight the inherent problems with the factory model; one student might gain from setting, but only at the expense of others who lose. For every child challenged by being in a top set or stream, or in a grammar school, others may be demotivated by being in a low set, or in a secondary modern school.

Thankfully, there is an altogether different way of approaching school setting, where students move not according to their age but according to their 'stage' of understanding and ability. And not just their stage overall but by stage in each and every single subject that they are studying. Can there indeed be a system where every child gains and none lose? Yes, but it will require a very radical

---

[16] Taylor, B., *et al.,* (2017). Op cit. pp. 327–345.

change in thinking about schools and universities that AI will demand.

3. Teaching overwhelmed by administration

Teachers should be able to devote their best energy to teaching students. But that doesn't often happen. The problem is not new, although many teachers all over the world may think it is. Even at the dawn of the third age of education, time was lost to classroom teaching because of the burden of preparation of teaching materials, organisation of the classroom, noting and following up on attendance, dealing with misbehaviour, marking and commentary on student work, recording marks, and writing reports on progress.

The advent of computers into education from the 1980s was intended to reduce the administrative burden. Teachers were told that word processors, sophisticated reprographics and new technology would halve their repetitive labour, releasing them at last to give their energy fully to students. It was not to be. Of the 4,450 respondents to a 2016 survey in *The Guardian* about teachers' lives, "82% stated that their workload was unmanageable, with two-thirds saying that expectations had increased significantly over the past five years [up to 2016], and 73% of respondents said their workload was affecting their physical health and 76% their mental health. Almost a third of teachers reported that they worked more than 60 hours a week."[17] These findings were endorsed by research from the Education Support Partnership (ESP) which found that 80 per cent of teachers surveyed had

---

[17] *The Guardian*, 22.03.16.

suffered a mental health problem in the previous two years. A survey by the Association of Teachers and Lecturers (ATL) in 2014 similarly noted the widespread problems teachers were experiencing with workload and stress. So major has the problem become that the Office for Standards in Education (Ofsted), responsible for school inspection and standards in England, declared that for the beginning of the school year 2017/18, its inspectors should routinely ask head teachers how they intend to reduce the workload of teaching staff. New Education Secretary Damian Hinds said in March 2018 this would be one of his priorities.[18]

Enhanced demands for accountability in education systems across the world, in part in response to international comparative measures, such as the OECD's Programme for International Student Assessment (PISA), formed in 1997, have led to a greater burden of work for teachers, and unproductive pressure on them for their students to perform well in tests. Governance and inspection bodies worldwide have added to the administrative burden while not always adding to the effectiveness of teaching or learning.

Lesson planning has become inordinately burdensome for teachers under the scrutiny of the inspection body in England, Ofsted, and the demands of ever-expanding numbers of senior managers in schools, whose job is to monitor the performance of teachers, not always cost- or quality effectiveness. Lesson plans are one such burden. On top of having to prepare material for some four hours of teaching each day, a teacher will often have to write down a detailed lesson plan, outlining learning objectives, evaluation and content for the entire

---

[18] *The Guardian*, 10.03.18.

lesson. "These burdensome and unhelpful practices have arisen due to the real and perceived demands made by government and Ofsted, and how school leaders and teachers have reacted to them," a report from the Independent Teacher Workload Review Group in England said in 2016.[19]

Marking can be another overly-heavy burden for teachers, especially in subjects such as English, where they will be correcting not just content, but use of the English language. If a class has 30 students and the teacher has on average one set of marking per night, he or she might spend two hours marking, on top of time spent preparing lessons for the next day. "Marking is a vital element of teaching," a report for the Department for Education in the UK noted. "But when it is ineffective it can be demoralising and a waste of time for teachers and pupils alike. In particular, we are concerned that it has become common practice for teachers to provide extensive written comments on every piece of work when there is very little evidence that this improves pupil outcomes in the long term."[20]

---

[19] Independent Teacher Workload Review Group, (2016). 'Eliminating unnecessary workload around planning and teaching resources: Report of the Independent Teacher Workload Review Group', p.5. [Online]. Available at:
https://www.gov.uk/government/uploads/system/uploads/attachment_data/file/511257/Eliminating-unnecessary-workload-around-planning-and-teaching-resources.pdf
[20] Independent Teacher Workload Review Group. (2016). Op. cit. p.7.

Twenty years ago, a seminal article written by Black and Wiliam on 'assessment for learning'[21] argued for a much more instructive way to mark than merely 'summative evaluation', which evaluates and ranks students at the end of a programme of study. Assessment for learning comprises diagnostic comments initially to understand gaps in student knowledge, and then seeks to work collaboratively with them to help them become more autonomous learners. This approach is far more helpful to student learning than merely for them to discover they have been given certain marks with little idea how to improve. But it is also far more demanding of teacher time than just slapping a mark or grade at the bottom of a piece of work. Every extra hour that a teacher works in the evenings and at weekends consumes their finite energy, and means that they will have less to give in the classroom the following day. The senior leaders in schools and governors can spend a disproportionate amount of time vexing over the capture and interpretation of data. "Too often the collection of data becomes an end in itself, divorced from the core purpose of improving outcomes for pupils... This increases the workload of teachers and school leaders for little discernible benefit," the earlier-cited report stated.[22]

Teachers overall can easily end up spending more time on administration than standing up in front of a class teaching. The burden also impacts on the head teacher. Rather than being an inspiring and reassuring presence around school,

---

[21] Black, P. and Wiliam, D., (1998). 'Assessment and Classroom Learning', Assessment in *Education: Principles, Policy and Practice*, Vol. 5, Issue 1.

[22] Independent Teacher Workload Review Group. (2016). Op. cit. p.5.

they far too often retreat into their offices and become bureaucrats. This is not desirable because they need to be a visible presence around their schools, helping students and their staff perform at their best. The problem of teacher workload is utterly integral to the third education model and has become steadily worse over the years rather than better. AI promises total transformation.

4. Large class sizes inhibit personalised and breadth of learning

The third education era of mass education saw class sizes grow. Renaissance humanist Erasmus believed the teacher performed better if student numbers were kept small.[23] In the UK, it is uncommon to see class sizes larger than 30, but in the developing world they can be 60 or more. Decisions on class sizes are in part down to money as Erasmus himself acknowledged; teachers are expensive and it is uneconomic for class sizes to be too small. Overly small class sizes further can inhibit students 'speaking up' and can mean a narrow range of viewpoints being expressed. Students learn greatly from listening to the views of their peers, from offering their own contributions, and from noticing 'how they land'.

Equally, class sizes can be too big, and can pose a whole series of problems for the teacher and students. Individual pupils can be lost in large groups, especially the diffident and less secure. Fewer students have a chance to offer their comments in large classes, and the teacher has less time to diagnose and attend to individual needs. The setting of

---

[23] Erasmus, (1529). *De Pueris Instituendis*.

personalised work targets is harder in larger groups, and the authority of the teacher can be diluted. Routine administration takes up more time, and the teacher will have less opportunity to devote to the work of individual students. Educational theorist John Dewey at the start of the last century suggested a class size of 8-12 would be ideal.[24] Research has tended to support the notion that smaller class sizes are not the panacea.[25] But such findings seem counter-intuitive to teachers who have to spend time in overly large classes. It seems much more likely that there is an optimum class size for each age, level of ability and complexity, sufficient to secure diversity of opinion, but not so big that the teacher cannot come to know every student individually and be able to involve them meaningfully in every class.

The 'Holy Grail' would be for every student to have the benefits of personalised tuition for at least part of every lesson, which would ensure that their own needs were individually addressed, and then to have time for group work, when the student can offer contributions and listen to those made by fellow students and by the teacher. This will never happen fully under the factory model. But personalised learning will nevertheless be possible should entirely new elements be introduced into education, as AI is already beginning to offer.

---

[24] Boydston, J. A., (2008). '*The Middle Works of John Dewey, 1899-1924*', Vol 1. Carbondale IL: Southern Illinois University Press.
[25] Chingos, M. M. & Whitehurst, G.J., (2011). 'Class Size: What Research Says and What it Means for State Policy'. Brookings Institute. [Online]. Available at:
https://www.brookings.edu/research/class-size-what-research-says-and-what-it-means-for-state-policy/

5. Homogenisation and lack of individuation of personality

"Education is what society does to you, learning is what you do for yourself," says Joi Ito, Director of the MIT Media Lab.[26] Formal education we saw emerged and expanded in the second and third revolution stages of education in response to the political, commercial or religious authorities that set them up and funded them. The purpose was primarily utilitarian. Schools and universities today are seen by governments as primarily intended to develop cognitive skills, defined as the "ability to understand complex ideas, to adapt effectively to the environment, to learn from experience, to engage in various forms of reasoning, to overcome obstacles by taking thought." Such qualities are traditionally seen as the most useful to students for future employment. In contrast, non-cognitive skills are defined by Zhou as the "patterns of thought, feelings and behaviours that are socially determined and can be developed throughout the lifetime to produce value."[27]

It is right that a focus on cognitive skills should be central to the mission of every school. But as the UK's Social Mobility Commission has pointed out: "The important role of non-cognitive skills... in improving life outcomes is well established. Evidence shows that these outcomes include better mental and physical health, secure relationships,

---

[26] Joi Ito, 'Society-in-the-Loop', MIT Media Lab, 12.08.16.

[27] Zhou, K. (2016). 'Education for people and planet: Creating sustainable futures for all'. Paper commissioned for the Global Education Monitoring Report.

contentment, educational attainment, access to higher education and better careers."[28] Non-cognitive skills are also those that employers have become more vocal about, stating they have value above purely academic skills.

Despite this, non-cognitive skills have tended to be marginalised in schools worldwide in the last 25 years. In the UK, Prime Minister Blair's Labour government from 1997 put a strong premium on 'literacy and numeracy' across the country. Increasingly, schools, for the best of reasons they thought, began to narrow down what children experienced and learnt. Brave individual head teachers still had some leeway to buck the system and offer their students a more rounded education. But they were swimming against the tide. The mechanistic model of education, the only possible logical conclusion of the factory era, was carrying all before it. Academic success depended more and more on memorisation and mastery of data rather than reflection on it and personalised responses.

The model is inherently flawed. With the exception of some fee-paying schools, and the very best of government schools, education became a narrow experience of the acquisition of skills and knowledge. It was as if the government and academic elites wanted to make all students into homogeneous bots, rather than the opposite, i.e. to give them the opportunity through free expression to become the

---

[28] Social Mobility Commission. 'Time for Change, p. 45. [Online]. Available at:
https://www.gov.uk/government/uploads/system/uploads/attachment_data/file/622214/Time_for_Change_report_-An_assessement_of_government_policies_on_social_mobility_1997-2017.pdf

person who they uniquely are. I was so excited at the prospect of studying Philosophy as part of PPE as an undergraduate at Oxford. Rather than exploring philosophic ideas that interested me, such as consciousness, aesthetics, authority, theism, we were offered a diet of and texts exclusively by male, western, empirical thinkers. The academics were not interested in what I thought, but only in their right answers. The experience crushed my interest in Philosophy for many years.

We need to see the paring back of the arts and creative subjects in this context. These very subjects do not have a 'right' answer: nor do they admit to standardised quantitative tests with right answers. Rather, the individual response of each student, drawing on pools of talent deep inside them, helps them to discover who they are. Suppression can lead to insecure identity-formation and mental health problems. We should be expanding, not cutting back, on creative budgets in schools. All too often education has become a soulless as well as a numbing experience for the student.

It does not have to be like this. School can help every young person to discover their own unique identity and to grow in efficacy by letting their unique character progressively unfold. But the factory model has been especially poor at nurturing individuality for the least well off. The AI or fourth education revolution will assist here, by helping the young to understand that they have not one intelligence but many; a subject to which we now turn in the next chapter.

Howard Gardner of Harvard University. No single figure did more to show how flawed and limiting to education and humanity were the third education revolution's various attempts to define intelligence in ever more mechanistic ways.

Chapter Four:

What is Intelligence? The narrow vision of the factory era

We now turn to probing the nature and meaning of intelligence, and to asking if it is a uniquely human attribute, when machines "impart information to the growing mind at a speed hitherto unimaginable."[1] We will explore how intelligence has been assessed in the third education era and why its vision of intelligence was so narrow. We look at whether intelligence is an absolute or a relative quality, and whether it exists in one form as defined by a dominant culture, or in diverse forms. Unsurprisingly, we find that, the more we explore intelligence, the more 'slippery' the concept becomes.

A Meditation on the Subjectivity of what we term Intelligence

Everyone knew the clever child in school. For those who didn't, it was probably them. But what did it mean to be the 'clever kid'? That they did their homework and got top marks in their exams. In general, when we describe someone as 'clever' or 'intelligent', it reflects a judgement on our part

---

[1] Lawson, D., 'Man Versus Machine'. *The Sunday Times*, 28.05.2017.

about that individual's mental ability. It's an assessment we make through interaction with that person and seeing how they react to stimuli; it's something most of us believe we are able to intuit.

Were we to meet someone on a long train journey and strike up a conversation, we might, by the time we reach our destination, have come to a judgement about that person's intelligence. What would factor into our judgement? We might be convinced by an ability to pick apart a complicated subject, whereas others might be more impressed by someone who is sharp-witted and compelling when they tell a story. No view is wrong – they are indirectly products of the subjective way we habitually view 'intelligence'.

We may all agree that an intelligent person is easily adaptable, quickly absorbs ideas, makes links to other areas of knowledge, has a novel way of looking at facts and possesses an ordered mind. We might judge an intelligent person to be one who displays these abilities to a greater extent than what we might expect. In the context of our train journey, we might be impressed by such qualities compared to what we generally have come to expect from strangers during train rides.

Expectations are subtly baked into this notion of intelligence. Whatever criteria we select for intelligence, they are shaped by our prior understandings. The people we consider to be intelligent reflect the activities and attitudes of others who we consider to be intelligent, or who connote intelligence through their academic status. Our realisation of the subjectivity of our understanding of intelligence leads us to search for more grounded measures or definitions. Will this give us more certainty, or are we hunting a chimera? We can say with certainty that all concepts of intelligence involve applied 'knowledge'; the term we discussed in Chapter Two. Knowledge is not intelligence until actioned in some way towards the fulfilling of an 'objective'. We return to this definition later. But we are left with the nagging suspicion that subjectivity is very powerful and subtle in our assessment of intelligence.

Origins of the 'Measurement' of Intelligence

We can trace the attempt to quantify human intelligence objectively back to the Imperial Han Dynasty (206 BC–AD 220) in China. Following the advice of Confucian scholars, the emperor established an imperial 'university' by 124 BC with the intention of training a bureaucratic elite to administer the empire. Young 'mandarins' were given a range of tests. The better they performed, the higher up they would be assigned within the hierarchy of the Han government. Up to that point there existed an informal system of recommendation, with officials identifying those they felt most suited to work in the sophisticated bureaucracy required for the smooth governance of such a large nation, relying on gut instinct first and foremost.

The meritocratic system in China reached what is arguably its apex during the Song dynasty (AD 960–1279), with the establishment of public feeder schools for the poor throughout the empire. This early experiment in social mobility saw the poorest of Chinese males theoretically rising through the ranks. The prize was that the best administrators were able to navigate and control imperial China's complex and sprawling civic system. For the government, it was essential to keep business running smoothly across the Middle Kingdom. The system lasted until it was abolished by the Qing dynasty, in 1912. Like our own crude assumptions, it would be impossible to say whether the top bureaucrats were the most intelligent without question. But the attempts at measurement, like our exams, had some value as an instrument for assessing skill.

The attempt to quantify intelligence was developed in Britain by polymath Francis Galton at the time when the third education era was becoming most industrialised. A cousin of Charles Darwin, and one of the many who were inspired by the publication of his famous 1859 work, *The Origin of Species,* Galton is credited with the creation of the concept of 'correlation' and the law of 'regression to the mean'. Following Darwin's lead, Galton dedicated his life to applying his statistical methods to human beings and studying the variation between individuals. He concluded that there existed a general mental ability and that it was a 'natural gift' or a heritable trait, like those Darwin proposed, that bounded an individual's cognitive potential. Galton himself became frustrated in his quest for causation. His focus on psychometrics and the study of head size and other observable traits, such as reflexes and muscle grip as correlates of inherited intelligence, proved a blind alley. But his pioneering work inspired others and led to new research into intelligence, how to assess it and how to make use of measurements.

The first 'intelligence' test in Europe was devised by the French mathematician Alfred Binet and his partner Théodore Simon in 1905. Asked by the French government to find a way to differentiate between intelligent and challenged children, he struck upon the idea of mental age, a measure of intelligence that was based on the average ability of children of the same age. The new measure was greeted with enthusiasm in the USA, as elsewhere. The term 'IQ' was first used in German – *Intelligenzquotient* – at the University of Breslav (now the Polish University of Wroclaw) from 1912.

In 1916, the Stanford psychologist Lewis Terman took the original test, standardised the results for American participants and converted the result into a single number, which represented the child's intelligence relative to their age group. Mental age was divided by actual age and multiplied by 100 (i.e. 12/10 x 100 = 120). Studies showed that the new measure was relatively consistent across age groups. Those with the higher IQs tended to be the same as they progressed through education. Terman took this as an indication that his measure captured an innate stable ability that 'determined' a child's intelligence – an idea that Binet himself had explicitly warned against. The theory not least was blind to the impact of environmental factors that make a significant impact on a child's school performance. Elaborated IQ measures and their variants nevertheless became widespread and remain an important assessment tool up to the present day.

Enter Charles Spearman, another researcher, who observed that, as long as any two tests involved cognitive skills of some kind, those who did well in one test tended to do similarly in the other. While the correlations were not always of the same magnitude, they remained positive, or simply, getting one answer right indicated that the same person was likely to get the other one right regardless of which two items were considered. Spearman reasoned that the correlations were positive because the items were measuring the same general trait and that the magnitude of correlation varied because some items were more closely related to this general trait than others. He would name this general trait 'general intelligence' or g for short.

The understanding of g has evolved since it was first proposed by Spearman. Today, g is a well-established statistical artefact, although there is no consensus as to what actually causes its presence. It has been shown to be a reliable predictor for educational achievement and employee performance, and has been shown, to some extent, to be heritable. But the idea of g is not without its opponents. The arguments against it are generally variations on the same objections: the centrality of g risks making us reliant on what is still an approximation; and g underrates the importance of environmental and chance factors.

We must therefore be cautious in attempting to attach significance to g's findings.[2] Consider that ability in one sport is a good predictor for the ability to perform well in other sports. If we ran a factor analysis on scores of abilities across sports, we would probably conclude that there exists a general Athletic Factor a, and that this factor can be measured by an Athletic Quotient (AQ). Those with higher AQ will be more proficient across a range of physical activities. But we also know that this observed general ability is the product of multiple factors. Diet, lung capacity, hand-eye co-ordination and many other qualities indicate excellence in some sports, not others. Messi and Roger Federer might be outstanding footballers and tennis players, but there is no guarantee of merit if they played each other's sports. Any read across from

---

[2] Darlington, R., (n.d.) 'Factor Analysis'. [Online]. Available at: http://node101.psych.cornell.edu/Darlington/factor.htm

AQ to IQ also falls short because we can physically observe the body. We cannot do the same for the mind. Grave errors are therefore possible when abstractions are treated as scientific fact, especially if these 'facts' are then used in the formation or proposal of policy, without proper consideration of ethics, context or history. The effort to measure intelligence as a purely cognitive quality has been fraught with such impatience for results that they are not sufficiently grounded or reliable. We cannot escape the conclusion that human intelligence was often given a spurious objectivity in the factory era, and that it was used to measure only a narrow range of ability, and that subjective judgements often predominate when evaluations of individuals occur. Might machines do better?

Machine Intelligence

The earliest computational or counting devices can be dated back to the origin of the second educational revolution, with the abacus in use in Babylonia as early as 2400 BC. The earliest analogue computer designed to calculate astronomical positions that has been found can be traced to the Greeks in 100 BC. The slide rule was developed in the 1620s following the discovery of the concept of the algarithm [sic] by John Napier.

The first mechanical computer was devised by Charles Babbage, the British inventor described as the 'father of the computer' in the early nineteenth century. The machine used punch cards and had an integrated memory. Analogue computers using a mechanical or electrical model as the basis for computation reached a high point in the 1920s. By the late

1930s, the first digital computers were in use. Modern computing was first proposed by Alan Turing in his famous 1936 paper 'On Computable Numbers', which showed that machines could be programmable. This opened up the possibility of 'machine learning' or artificial intelligence. Up to this point, computers merely executed human instructions quickly and reliably. They were not 'thinking' nor were they in any sense 'intelligent'. We look at what happened in computing and machine learning in the next chapter, and what it means for machines to 'think'.

Collective Intelligence

Individual human intelligence may have significant predictive power when it comes to individual lives. IQ can be a useful guide to performance in school and at work. But individual IQ does not contribute much insight to understanding large-scale outcomes. The simplistic approach would be to assume that more units of 'raw intelligence' always leads to better collective results. But there exist myriad organisations chock-full of highly intelligent people that display what might be considered unintelligent behaviour. The proposed release in Britain of multiple rapist John Worboys in 2017-18 by the Parole Board after only ten years in custody is a recent example of a decision from bright people which seemed foolish to most.

Hari Seldon (no relation) is a central character in Isaac Asimov's 'Foundation' series. A professor of mathematics, he develops the theory of 'psychohistory', which he uses to chart the entirety of humanity's future in probabilistic terms. This theory is derivative of what is termed 'Brownian motion': the motion of individual particles in a gas is random, but it is possible to predict the behaviour of the gas as a whole. In the same way, the theory goes, it is difficult to predict the actions of individuals, but it is possible to predict the cumulative effect of those actions.

The explosion of the internet has resulted in greater interconnectivity than the world has ever known, with people desperate to find new ways to collaborate. Advances in technology have transformed utterly the ease with which information can be accessed, proliferated and processed. Might this offer new opportunities for humanity to collaborate in intelligent ways? The theory of 'Collective Intelligence' (CI) seeks to explain the emergent phenomena as individuals collaborate and compete exploiting the advantages of these new environments. As social entrepreneur Geoff Mulgan writes in the introduction to *Big Mind* (2018), "In its narrow variants, it's mainly concerned with how groups of people collaborate together online. In its broader variants, it's about how all kinds of intelligence happen on large scales. At its extreme, it encompasses the whole of human civilisation and culture, which constitutes the intelligence of our species, passed down imperfectly through books and schools, lectures and demonstrations, or by parents showing children how to sit still, eat, or get dressed in the morning."[3]

At its best, the operation of the US Supreme Court for much of its history, the British Cabinet or the French Academy of Sciences, show that bringing very able people

---

[3] Mulgan, G., (2018). *Big Mind: How Collective Intelligence Can Change Our World.* Princeton, NJ: Princeton University Press. eBook Collection EBSCOhost.

together can result in wise decisions. But the theory of CI nevertheless reminds us that, regardless of the magnitude of an individual's intelligence, there is no guarantee that an aggregation of high IQs, be it in a company, university, or government, will necessarily result in highly intelligent decisions emerging. The voice of the more reflective, considered and thoughtful individuals can all too easily not be heard. But at best, new opportunities for solving our common international problems are now possible because of the internet and video conferencing. In a later chapter, we foresee a top tier of 'global' universities will emerge dedicated to solving just such problems. In the Conclusion, we also assign major responsibility to the United Nations in overseeing AI in the future.

'The Abilene Paradox' is a vivid example of how intelligent people collectively can decide on a course of action which is neither intelligent nor in tune with what they want, as described by teacher and researcher Carl Hendrick.[4] The paradox describes how a professor in Texas and his family and friends went on a 53 mile road trip on a hot day to a restaurant which none enjoyed, because no-one questioned the strategy. It led to the professor concerned, Jerry B. Harvey coining the Abilene description "to explain a curious aspect of group dynamics in which the opposite of what everyone wants is tacitly created by the group who thinks they are agreeing with everyone else".[5]

---

[4] Hendrick, C. and Macpherson, R. (2017) *'What does this look like in the classroom? Bridging the gap between research and practice'*, Woodbridge UK: John Catt Educational.

[5] Watson, P. 'The Abilene Paradox: why schools do things nobody actually wants'. Montrose Blog, 19.03.18.

More forms of intelligence: EQ, CQ, SQ and NQ

The all-pervasive and undeserved sway of 'IQ' is being challenged from many too. 'Emotional' intelligence, the capacity for recognising our emotions and those of others, has been called the 'emotional quotient' or 'EQ'. It first appeared in a paper by Michael Beldoch, and gained popularity when the American science journalist Daniel Goleman wrote his best seller *Emotional Intelligence* in 1995. The theory, criticised by some academics, highlights the qualities or traits needed to live a more emotionally intelligent or happier life. Some of the criticism at least came from those antagonised by the attempt to dethrone IQ from its pedestal. We will see at the end of the book how central *happiness* is to the notion of living as humans in the age of AI in the twenty first century. In this, the work of psychologist Martin Seligman is a more reliable guide.[6]

'Curiosity intelligence', or CQ, has far less literature behind it, but merits serious attention. As Tomas Chamorro-Premuzic writes, "CQ … concerns having a hungry mind. People with higher CQ are more inquisitive and open to new experiences. They find novelty exciting and are quickly bored with routine. They tend to generate many original ideas and are counter-conformist."[7] CQ has grown in popularity in part

---

[6] Seligman, M., (2018). *The Hope Circuit: A Psychologists Journey from Helplessness to Optimism*. London: Nicholas Brealey Publishing.

[7] Chamorro-Premuzic, C., (2014). 'Curiosity is as Important as Intelligence'. *Harvard Business Review*, 27 August 2014. [Online]. Available at:

in reaction to the information overload of our contemporary time; an overload that was troubling philosophers Gottfried Wilhelm Leibniz and Denis Diderot nearly three centuries ago when they wrote of the "horrible mass of books". Cognitive psychologist Daniel Levitin has added his weight to the case for taking CQ seriously in his *The Organised Mind: Thinking Straight in the Age of Information Overload* (2014). CQ provides us all, including students, with the skill to negotiate through too much and too often incorrect fact, and to develop the ability to ask the right questions.

CQ can lead to greater 'wisdom'. So too can 'spiritual intelligence', or 'SQ'. James Fowler described the 'six stages' of development of SQ in 1981, and this has been developed by psychiatrist Larry Culliford, who writes that it "links the deeply personal with the universal."[8] Curiosity and spiritual intelligence need embedding in our education systems far more deeply in the fourth education era.

Finally, 'natural intelligence', or 'NQ', claimed to be the inherent intelligence in nature which has allowed humans to evolve and our bodies to function day by day with little input from our minds. Equally, NQ is responsible for mutations in cells and in viruses which can damage humanity. In many ways, NQ, over which we have next to no control, exhibits far higher intelligence, ensuring we survive and flourish more than our IQs.

---

https://hbr.org/2014/08/curiosity-is-as-important-as-intelligence
[8] Culliford, L., (2011). *'The Psychology of Spirituality'*, p.20. London: Jessica Kingsley.

'State' intelligence

The word 'intelligence', specifically drawing on the word's derivation from the Latin *intelligere* (to understand) was purloined early on by political and military systems to aid their own security and to advance their mission. With the emergence of the first states some 6,000 years ago, leaders sought to acquire intelligence about their enemies abroad, and among their own citizens, to ensure their own survival. Intelligence gathering emerged in many forms and often as an instrument of coercion and punishment. The medieval Christian church garnered intelligence to ensure that people were holding to the true faith, while the Mongols were renowned during the twelfth and thirteenth centuries for adopting a particularly ruthless intelligence apparatus to coerce the population.

The emergence of nation states after the Treaty of Westphalia in 1648 saw the beginning of modern intelligence gathering. Ascertaining by overt or covert methods the intentions and plans of other states was considered to be essential. 'Spying' to gather intelligence was closely interwoven with the tasks of overseas diplomats and ambassadors. The spread of mass national armies during the nineteenth century, and industrial militarisation by the great empires towards the end of that century, provided a powerful boost to the need for contemporary intelligence. High-quality intelligence could make the difference between survival and disaster. By the eve of the First World War, Europe was covered with a vast network of intelligence gatherers. It did nothing, however, to avert war, and they may have precipitated its arrival by heightening suspicion.

Throughout the twentieth century, developments in radio communications, rapid travel and computing considerably enhanced the role of intelligence. In Britain, MI5 (known as the Directorate of Military Intelligence) or home security, was founded in 1909. MI6, or the 'Secret Intelligence Service', which spies abroad, was also founded in 1909, although the names became used only from the 1930s. 'MI' stands for 'military intelligence' and the number suffixes stand for the sections in which their offices were first housed, though neither MI5 nor MI6 have ever been part of the military. Their equivalent in the USA, the Federal Bureau of Investigation (FBI) and the 'Central Intelligence Agency' (CIA), were formed in 1935 and 1947 respectively.

The use of the word 'intelligence' in these contexts is very specific; concerned with the acquiring of 'accurate' information which is considered to be 'valuable', which others have reason to keep 'secret'. This particular world of intelligence is fascinating to many, and grips vast numbers in its portrayal in novels, non-fiction histories, films and computer games. The appetite to engage with this form of intelligence is notably higher than some students have for acquiring knowledge as part of their formal education. The advent of AI has made the world of state intelligence simpler and more complex at the same time. This is how AI works. It also reminds us that intelligence should be for the advantage of all humanity, not just a section of it.

Controversies in the study of intelligence: eugenics

Since the first attempts to measure intelligence, the term has been mired in controversy. Galton's measurement of intelligence led him in 1883 to a crude idea of eugenics, the attempt to improve the genetic quality of the human race. Differences between individuals suggested the possibility of manufacturing 'super-intelligent' children by borrowing the practices of animal husbandry for humans. This was the formula: encourage more desirable specimens to breed together; breed young and breed often; discourage the less desirable from doing the same.

Mention of eugenics today evokes images of forced sterilisation, euthanasia and segregation in the service of creating a 'stronger, more perfect' race. Galton's proposals, although ethically dubious, did not advocate any of this explicitly. But it is not difficult to draw a direct line between his ideas and the practices implemented in Germany under the Nazis. The vagaries that obviously exist in the conceptualisation of intelligence lead all too easily to the appropriation of intelligence theories and measures to terrible ends. All we need to do is to introduce a corrupting agent.

The prospective eugenicist must first answer: what traits are desirable? Defining what is necessary carves out the opposite: what is not. The task of the eugenicist is then to determine a way to stymie the proliferation of what has been labelled 'undesirable' and, if possible, eliminate it. It is in this determination and the subsequent elimination of what has been termed undesirable that Galton's ideas descend from noxious curiosity into something altogether different. Many supposedly 'objective' tests have been created that reaffirm race and class supremacy. It is another reason why any mention of intelligence together with class and genetics must proceed with care. This suspicion is not without justification. History is marked by the terrible consequences of eugenics that have run out of control.

However, there should be no attempts to sanitise Galton. Large-scale human genetic engineering is an unequivocally unethical position. It would be mendacious to label his connection to the atrocities committed in the name of his idea a coincidence. If AI machines do acquire general artificial intelligence, what use may this have for humans deemed not intelligent or useful *to them*? But we get ahead of ourselves. AI is the subject of the next chapter, and we have another controversy to consider first.

Controversies in the study of intelligence: the Bell Curve

In 1994, Charles Murray and Richard Herrnstein co-authored a book called *The Bell Curve*. These two researchers, "anchored so securely in the middle of the scientific road"[9] in their views on intelligence, set out to explore the relation between a person's IQ and their socio-economic status, with a view to making sensible and useful policy recommendations. The pungent outcome was not foreseen by them.

---

[9] Murray, C., (n.d.) 'The Bell Curve' and its Critics'. *Commentary Magazine* (blog). [Online]. Available at:
https://www.commentarymagazine.com/articles/the-bell-curve-and-its-critics/

The Bell Curve was a book perfectly suited to incite frenzy. Its subject matter was sensitive and, although the language was moderate, the conclusions proved explosive. Murray and Herrnstein argued that intelligence is the greatest driver of socio-economic outcomes in the USA, that there are persistent gaps in the aggregate IQ of different races, and that it stands to reason that these gaps are genetically determined.

In the 25 years since its publication, the argument the book makes has been taken apart and put back together many times over. The task is made no easier by the book's length (850 pages, depending on edition) and its numerous detailed statistical appendices. Anyone seeking to discredit the argument completely must first pick holes in pages of largely accurate data. Furthermore, it is made no easier by the book's style, which straddles serious academic tome and popular science book. Its key ideas have been uncomfortably exaggerated by those with a clear political agenda. And it has become difficult to tell if vocal objections are directed at the contents of the book or simply what it has come to represent in an urgent political moment for race in America.

Intelligence is, as we have seen, a charged concept. Ideology intervenes where the evidence stops. An op-ed in the *Wall Street Journal,* signed by 52 eminent scientists,[10] sought to illuminate what the book's critics got wrong and "promote more reasoned discussion of the vexing phenomenon that the research has revealed in recent decades." Good point, but we can legitimately be sceptical about the prominence that the book accorded to *g* as a proxy for intelligence, in view of its limitations: that it did not entertain that alternative

---

[10] *Wall Street Journal*, Dec. 13, 1994, p. A18

conceptions are explanations; and that the authors specifically overstate the extent to which intelligence is inherited, overstate its utility as a predictor for socio-economic well-being and understate the value of significant other contributory factors.

The Bell Curve is uniquely challenging because its data are so correct. There *does* exist a gap between black and white IQ scores. Where it fails is in the authors' commitment to limiting possible interpretations for the data, to whatever confirmed their own previously held notions. When introducing notions of intelligence into machines, we must be careful to make sure that their programming does not similarly reflect our bias.

Machines are impolite because they cannot self-deceive or flatter; neither can data. This is not to say that data cannot be falsified or biased, but to make the point that the bias inherent in the data cannot be prevented from affecting results in some way. Therefore, in selecting the data we feed into machines, we must seriously question the process of its collection, the variables contained within it and what those imply.

A stark example of this phenomenon is the 'sexist' or 'racist' translations that machine learning algorithms produce, typified by 'the Gorilla Incident', when Google's indexing systems described a photo containing black men as 'gorillas'. There was nothing technically wrong with the algorithms themselves; they simply describe a problem solving process. However "AI models hold a mirror up to us; they don't understand when we really don't want honesty. They will only tell us polite fictions if we tell them how to lie to us ahead of time."[11] If the data fed into them reflects human bias, it becomes difficult to retroactively address the biased conclusions drawn. Again, we are fast-forwarding into the next chapter on AI, but the conclusion here stands. IQ evaluations might well tell us much about who excels at tests prepared by white, predominantly middle-class men, but little about wider evaluations or intelligence. Again, we see the slipperiness of the term 'intelligence'.

Dethroning the sovereignty of thinking

Guy Claxton, in his book, *Stronger than we Realised* (2017), presents a critique and partial rejection of 'Cartesian duality'. This notion is grounded on the primacy of thinking in the work of seventeenth-century philosopher, René Descartes, specifically in his Latin proposition *cogito ergo sum*, or "I think therefore I am". In its place, Claxton offers an explanation for a unified understanding of intelligence that acknowledges the importance of the human body. We can refer to this as the 'extended mind' or 'embodied' intelligence. This is the view that cognition is not purely the result of brain function. Instead, it is a mixture of the experience of having a body which senses and makes changes

---

[11] Zunger, Y., (2017). 'Asking The Right Questions about AI'. *Medium*. [Online]. Available at:
https://medium.com/@yonatanzunger/asking-the-right-questions-about-ai-7ed2d9820c48

to the world, and which is in turn embedded within a larger "biological, psychological and cultural context."[12]

This argument can seem remote or otiose. It is of central importance though. Claxton and fellow travellers, among which we count ourselves, argue that thinking or mental intelligence is highly important, but not all-important. The theory implies that the body, its health and our awareness of it, must remain integral to any conversations we have about intelligence and, by extension, to the way in which we are educated in the fourth era. Indeed, we would go further than Claxton and assert that more attention in the fourth education era needs to be given to consciousness, and less just to cognitive thinking, which so dominated the first three eras, and which struggles to answer the question *Why*? Or to translate Descartes' maxim differently, "I am, whatever I think".

Revisiting Gardner's theory of multiple intelligences

Howard Gardner is another academic to give attention to physical intelligence. His theory of multiple intelligences arose out of his dissatisfaction with the widely held belief that there exists a single capacity for intelligence and that it can be measured meaningfully by means of short answer papers or written tests. This view he considers to be narrow and untenable:

---

[12] Rosch, E., Thompson, E. & Varela, F.J., (1993). *The Embodied Mind: Cognitive Science and Human Experience*. Boston MA: MIT Press.

In my view, if we are to encompass adequately the realm of human cognition, it is necessary to include a far wider and more universal set of competences than we have ordinarily considered. And it is necessary to remain open to the possibility that many—if not most—of these competences do not lend themselves to measurement by standard verbal methods, which rely heavily on a blend of logical and linguistic abilities.

With such considerations in mind, I have formulated a definition of what I call an 'intelligence'. An intelligence is the ability to solve problems, or to create products, that are valued within one or more cultural settings—a definition that says nothing about either the sources of these abilities or the proper means of 'testing' them.[13]

Gardner's thinking has, as we have seen, not been universally popular. By his own admission, "most psychologists, and particularly most psychometricians, have never warmed to the theory."[14] From a more mystical

---

[13] Gardner, H., (2011). *Frames of Mind: The Theory of Multiple Intelligences*. New York, NY: Basic Books. [Online]. Available at: http://ebookcentral.proquest.com/lib/duke/detail.action?docID=665795

[14] Gardner, H., (2016). 'Multiple Intelligences: Prelude, Theory and Aftermath', In Sternberg, R. J., Fisker S. T. & Foss D. J. (eds.), *Scientists Making a Difference*. Cambridge: Cambridge University Press, p.167.

perspective, theologian Richard Rohr has written "Deep knowing and presence do not happen with our thinking minds. To truly know something, our whole being must be open, awake, present".[15] Criticisms focus on a paucity of tests to measure the categories that Gardner has identified, and charges of lack of empirical rigour. But we must also consider the difficulty of devising useful tests and whether empirical testing is ultimately necessary to give value to a theory which is essentially experiential and intuitive. As with any theory for intelligence, we must of course proceed with caution in applying it. The theory has found application in education in part because it supports the belief held by many teachers that education systems currently are overly narrow, that it disparages some student talents, and diminishes overall achievement. We share this belief.

Gardner's theory allows us to escape some of the challenges posed by more rigid conceptions of intelligence. It acknowledges that it is a social construct determined by cultural context and bias. It de-emphasises the centrality of measurement and therefore the need to find ideal and objective means of measurement. Finally, it allows us consider a range of abilities that are deemed to be valuable to the individual or society, or both, that deserved to be 'drawn out' and educated. This gives us new tools to consider how education might need to be re-imagined in the fourth education era to help develop those attributes that a changed culture would consider most valuable, and it suggests a different path with which to address inequity in society.

---

[15] Rohr, R., 'Bodily Knowing', *Daily Meditation*, 04.04.18.

Gardner defines seven different types of intelligences: musical-rhythmic, visual-spatial, verbal-linguistic, logical-mathematical, bodily-kinesthetic, interpersonal, and intrapersonal. But neither he nor we are especially wedded to a specific number. Indeed, in interviews after the publication of his seminal book, Gardner has suggested that he would add 'naturalistic' – the ability to recognise flora and fauna and to make productive use of nature – to his original seven intelligences, along perhaps with 'existential' intelligence or spirituality, and 'teaching-pedagogical' intelligence. We prefer the four couplet model of the 'eight aptitudes' built at Wellington College in the UK from 2008: namely, 'logical' and 'linguistic', 'personal' and 'social', 'cultural/creative' and 'physical', and 'spiritual' and 'moral'. But there is no perfect model.

The now considerable literature on 'twenty-first century skills' stresses similar breadth of abilities. Charles Fadel, founder of the Center for Curriculum Redesign in Boston, Massachusetts has said three kinds of education are needed. 'Knowledge' i.e. what we know and understand, including traditional subjects like maths, 'modern' subjects like entrepreneurship and themes such as global literacy. 'Skills' i.e. 'how we use what we know' includes creativity, communication and critical thinking. Finally, 'character' which is 'how we behave and engage in the world', including mindfulness, curiosity, ethics and leadership. Taken together, these produce 'Meta-learning', or 'how we reflect and adapt'.[16]

---

[16] Center for Curriculum Redesign website, with thanks for drawing our attention to this to Nick Kind, interview, 29.01.18.

The third education era model did not easily adapt to teaching students about multiple intelligences and twenty-first century skills. But this new technology has the potential to develop our intelligence and remedy our deficient understanding of intelligence to date as never before in human history.

Alan Turing (1912-54), mathematician, computer scientist, logician, code-breaker in World War 2 and theoretical biologist, was the father of AI. The mechanistic mindset of the factory model capitalised on his intellect but could never comprehend his humanity.

Chapter Five:

What is AI and what is its History?

AI is coming. To understand the stage we are with its arrival, we can draw an analogy from the car industry in 1886. Karl Benz had just invented the internal combustion engine. People had no idea how the invention would take off, or that it would transform human life across the planet. The comparison is wrong though in one respect. AI is far more wide-ranging than the car, and will carry humans much further. Yet public discourse is still too often resorting to woolly approximations and leans too much on examples from popular culture. We all know the kind of thing but which is the more accurate analogy: the sinister Skynet Corporation from *The Terminator* or the perpetually depressed and existential Marvin from *The Hitchhiker's Guide to the Galaxy*?

A common misconception is that AI necessarily involves robots. Robotics and AI are distinct, but related disciplines. Robotics is concerned with physical movement and human interaction; AI with thought and human impact. AI can have a robotic interface with the world, but a robot is only one of many possible interfaces.

Speculation around AI reveals more about our cultural anxieties, fears and hopes than it says about the technology itself. Yesterday's visions of the future all too often seem risible when viewed from the present. But we should not use fear of scorn as an excuse not to interrogate what *might* happen and what AI *can* be. For this is no frivolous matter. Informed imagining of the future will help us craft policies that minimise the most undesirable outcomes and maximise the best prospects from AI for education and the future of humanity.

An attempt at a definition

AI or Machine Intelligence (MI) is a digitally controlled process by a human-created machine which 'perceives' its environment and adapts to it in order to achieve its objectives. A formal description comes from the Engineering and Physical Science Research Council: 'Artificial Intelligence technologies aim to reproduce or surpass abilities (in computational systems) that would require 'intelligence' if humans were to perform them. These include: learning and adaptation; sensory understanding and interaction; reasoning and planning; optimisation of procedures and parameters; autonomy; creativity; and extracting knowledge and predictions from large, diverse digital data.[1]

AI is at least as effective already as humans at some tasks (or classes of tasks) which require the application of intelligence. It has often been the case that when AI has

---

[1] Quoted in O'Harain, K. Hall W. and Pesenti, J., (2017). 'Growing the Artificial Intelligence Industry in the UK', Department for Digital, Culture, Media & Sport and Department for Business, Energy & Industrial Strategy. p. 8.

'solved' a problem, the goalposts are shifted. Since merely a machine has solved it, the problem could not have required intelligence: it's not AI, it's just a phone. This solipsistic approach confines intelligence to the ever shrinking group of problems that machines cannot yet solve. And as we know from history, what is not yet possible does not always remain that way.

The term given to AI when it can perform any intellectual task that a human can is 'Artificial General Intelligence' (AGI), known also as 'full AI' or 'strong AI'. In contrast, machines that perform just a specific or set tasks such as playing chess or 'Go' are known as 'weak AI', 'narrow AI' or 'applied AI'. Since the Second World War, researchers have sought to develop AGI to match and even outdo human intelligence not in specific but in broad applications: Margaret Boden describes it as "the goal of most of the AI pioneers".[2] How did this fascination begin and develop?

A brief history of AI

Humans have long been interested in creating beings which can function equally and independently on human intellectual planes. History is littered with the dreams of proto-AI creations. In the *Iliad*, Homer describes the golden attendants of Hephaestus as "in appearance like living young women. There is intelligence in their hearts, and there is speech in them and strength, and from the immortal gods they have learned how to do things." Medieval alchemists, it was

---

[2] Boden M. in Al-Khalili, J. (ed.), (2017) *What's Next?*, p. 120.

claimed, fabricated bronze heads that could correctly answer any question put to them, 800 years before IBM's Watson.

The derivation of the term 'Machine learning' can be traced to Ohio State Psychology Professor Sidney Pressey in a series of devices from the 1920s. His early machines offered students a multiple-choice menu, which did not move on to the next question until the right answer had been given. He sought to demonstrate that machines could indeed 'teach' students, and that knowledge of results encouraged good learning.[3] The self-teaching aspect drew inspiration, if not consciously, from the work of one of the great education thinkers, Maria Montessori (1870-1952), who believed each child should drive their own learning.

The roots of modern AI can be traced to the publication of Norbert Wiener's book, *Cybernetics* (1948) which provided the theoretical foundations for the discipline of AI and the creation of self-regulating mechanisms. Two years later came a seminal paper written by computer scientist and code-breaker Alan Turing, *Computing Machinery and Intelligence* (1950).[4] In it, he proposed a test (which has become known as the 'Turing Test') to answer the question "Can machines think?" A computer and a human are separated from a third human party. If this human arbiter, communicating with both of the other parties by typing messages, cannot distinguish between the two, the machine 'passes' the Turing Test. This places the emphasis on purely

[3] Pressey, S.L., (1932) 'A third and fourth contribution towards the coming 'industrial revolution' in education'. *School and Society*, 36, pp. 668-672.
[4] Turing, A. M., (1950) 'Computing Machinery and Intelligence'. *Mind* 49: 433-460.

verbal communication, but is still used as a key waypoint by researchers eager to reach the Holy Grail.

The formal field of research into AI began in earnest soon after at a series of meetings between academics at Dartmouth College in the USA in the summer of 1956. It was there that the term 'Artificial Intelligence' was coined by computer and cognitive scientist John McCarthy. The researchers' shared vision can be found in their historic request for a grant from the Rockefeller Foundation:

"We propose that a two-month, ten-man study of artificial intelligence be carried out during the summer of 1956 at Dartmouth College in Hanover, New Hampshire. The study is to proceed on the basis of the conjecture that every aspect of learning or any other feature of intelligence can in principle be so precisely described that a machine can be made to simulate it."[5]

The group that gathered that summer in New England and did not perhaps fully anticipate what they were getting themselves into. They were not so carried away however to imagine that the problems that they had gathered to explore could be satisfactorily solved over the course of one summer. But they probably did not think that their questions would become the defining subject of their academic careers, and the age we are entering.

---

[5] McCorduck, P., (2004). *Machines Who Think: A Personal Inquiry into the History and Prospects of Artificial Intelligence.* 25th anniversary update. Natick, MA: A.K. Peters.

Many powerful minds contributed to the evolving field, but we should mention polymath Herbert Simon, who won the Turing Award in 1975 and a Nobel Prize for Economics in 1978. A pioneer in AI, and its application in education, he created the Logic Theory Machine in 1956 with Allen Newell, and the 'General Problem Solver' in 1957, which separated problem-solving strategy from information about particular problems. That year he predicted that a computer would beat humans at chess within ten years. He was wrong only in his timing.

Even in the earliest days there were questions whether the hype surrounding AI would match the realities. Government interest was driven in part by military imperatives too during the Cold War. In the early stages of concerted AI research, the US government was a key backer too for foreign language projects such as 'Machine Translation'. After a decade during which the returns on investment did not match expectation, and the Automatic Language Processing Advisory Committee (ALPAC) reported that, for the foreseeable future, it would be considerably cheaper to use human translators, interest dried up. In the UK, the influential and dismissive 1973 Lighthill Report into AI came to a similar critical conclusion: "in no part of the field have discoveries made so far produced the major impact that was then promised".[6] The British government stopped funding AI research except in a small group of universities, Edinburgh, Sussex and Essex. The burst bubble in the 1970s, led to what became known as the 'AI

---

[6] Lighthill, J., (1973) 'Artificial Intelligence; A General Survey', Science Research Council.

winter', which lasted to the flowering of the internet from the mid-1990s.

The cycle is familiar. The development of complex but exciting emerging fields sees an initial surge of interest, driven by unrealistic expectations, followed by a period of disillusion and withdrawal of interest. Those of the true faith regroup and often rebrand, and good days often return. In this case the AI scientists plugged away at 'Informatics' and 'Machine Learning'. With each cycle, some progress was made. AI systems 'HiTech' and 'Deep Thought' first defeated chess masters at their own game – the ludic representation of human systemic and strategic genius – in 1989. But it took till 1997 for IBM's 'Deep Blue', the descendant of 'Deep Thought', finally to beat reigning world chess champion Garry Kasparov. Chess became the latest domain to be mastered by the seemingly all-conquering machine, albeit we must remind ourselves this is only 'weak AI'. Still a very long way from AGI.

Key to understanding the potential of AI in education is the difference between 'supervised' and 'unsupervised' learning. The former follows known patterns, the latter thinks for itself, and can thus be said to be creative. AlphaGo and Alpha Zero illustrates the difference.[7] 'Generative AI' can similarly be said to be creative and challenges those who say imagination is uniquely human. It uses AI to make something either completely new, or with Google's Deep Dream artwork, or 'inspired' by existing works of art, e.g.

---

[7] Interview with Peter Read, 21.03.18.

Shakespeare.[8] After all, Turing himself famously said: it is not altogether unreasonable to describe digital computers as brains'.[9]

The computer that beat Kasparov was a vast black obelisk of circuits and wires. Since then AI technology has become smaller and far more powerful. Advances have followed the exponential path laid out by 'Moore's Law', the theory first put forward in 1965 by Gordon Moore, co-founder of chipmaker Intel, that states that the speed and memory capacity of computers doubles every two years. This does not mean that the development of AI will follow the smooth arch of a curve on a graph; like most technologies, AI progresses along a drunken, lurching, rising path and pulses driven on by leaps of invention and imagination big and small. Some say it may soon even power its own development.

The innovation that has paved the way for the current surge in AI, Big Data, discussed at the end of the chapter, has made possible 'deep learning'. It needed extremely powerful computers to learn from the great mines of data that we create using technology, within which we can find patterns and meaning.

In education, researchers in fields ranging from computer science to psychology have invested considerable efforts since the 1960s to try to find breakthroughs, utilising knowledge-based and rule-based systems to deliver tailored systems for schools and universities to use, but without

---

[8] Interview with Martin Hamilton, 04.04.18. See
http://Karpathy.github.io/2015/05/21/rnn-effectiveness/
[9] Alan Turing, 'Can Digital Computers Think?' BBC lecture, 15.05.51.

conspicuous success. "What changed in the last ten to fifteen years", says Nigel Shadbolt, "is the very large scale of analysable data".[10] This helps explain why we have seen such little impact so far in AI on education. But the three chapters following, reveal we are on the cusp of a revolution, the fourth education revolution.

The computer and the overcoming of tedium

The history of AI and the computer are inextricably linked. The computer was invented in part to ease the tedium of computation. This seems like a meek ambition given the vast array of tasks to which computers are applied today. But the simplicity of the claim belies its true power. On some level, no one who uses a computer is unappreciative of how much easier they make our lives. It may be that a more important effect that the rise of the digital computer will have had is the minimisation of 'boredom' in the expansion of human knowledge.

To illustrate, consider two numbers each ten digits long. Proceed to multiply those numbers together in the manner we learned at school. We are not allowed any shortcuts or aids besides pen and paper. We quickly become disenchanted by this exercise, because long multiplication requires the repetitive execution of elementary operations, and close attention to detail. The constituent operations may be simple, but any slip will result in the wrong answer, and multiple mistakes will render the result completely unusable.

---

[10] Interview with Shadbolt, N. 16.03.18.

Imagine that the year is 1614 and your name is John Napier. You have discovered the logarithm: a powerful arithmetic tool derived from the Greek words *logos* and *arithmos* meaning word and number respectively. It makes it possible to reduce multiplication to addition by means of a transformation. A computation that would require hundreds of elementary operations for ten digit numbers now requires only a fraction of these.

Clearly, this is a much more efficient and accurate means of multiplication. But here is the catch; for you and others to benefit from a decrease in complexity, you must first somehow manufacture the logarithms for a significant subset of the numbers that you may need to multiply. And you must also do so by hand. You must repeatedly apply the same process of generation, demanding crisp attention to detail. Napier is reported to have taken twenty years to publish his *Mirifici logarithmorum canonis descriptio*[11] which contained ninety pages of his derivations. Today, Napier's algarithm is a few lines of code. The common word *algorithm* we should note is merely a defined set of instructions that a computer can process, derived from a ninth century Persian mathematician. Two close-sounding words that have little or nothing to do with each other which can be confusing, at least to non-mathematicians.

The study of the laws of the physical universe, and the axiomatic exploration of the abstract structures that we use to understand those laws, are challenging intellectual pursuits. Manual computations required to do it are less so. And while it is impossible, or perhaps even undesirable, to eliminate the

---

[11] Napier, J., (1614) *Mirifici Logarithmorum Canonis Descriptio.*

mundane completely from the ways we learn and discover, the mundane can stand in opposition to learning and discovery. Imagine the impact that Napier's logarithms could have had on scientific discovery if he could have published his work without long delays.

It is nearly three centuries since philosopher Leibniz penned words that set out the core need for computing:

> "... astronomers surely will not have to continue to exercise the patience which is required for computation. It is this that deters them from computing or correcting tables, from the construction of Ephemerides, from working on hypotheses, and from discussions of observations with each other. For it is unworthy of excellent men to lose hours like slaves in the labour of calculation which could safely be relegated to anyone else if machines were used."[12]

At the heart of computing lies the ideal that humans should be free of tedium and drudgery to pursue more intellectual goals. It is not difficult to see how this ambition leads directly to the creation of AI, which is even more adept at circumventing tedium. This philosophy also underpins the future of education, which is concerned with shaping individuals to live rewarding lives. Teachers were the key drivers of learning in the third revolutionary age but were deeply handicapped by the tedium of administration. They

---

[12] From Leibniz's celebrated 1685 description of his machine, quoted in Eugene Smith, D., (1984). *Sourcebook in Mathematics*, New York: Dover Publications.

need a more perfect and complementary aid if they are fully to educate our young people in this new era. We will also need to be mindful, that some of the perspiration of tedium, of trudging thought the foothills of knowledge, is necessary, if students are to enjoy the more sophisticated heights.

A word about programming and language

There is a myriad of coding 'languages'. Some approximate English syntax and structure, while others borrow heavily from mathematics. Languages also vary by purpose and the precision with which a programmer wishes to instruct a computer. Programming has proven very effective but we cannot ignore the barrier they present to communicating with the computer. It would be much simpler if a computer could understand instructions in plain English such as "move this byte to that memory address" or "sort these dogs in alphabetic order of breed". We're coming closer to this being a reality. Smartphones, and ubiquitous digital assistants, can already process a subset of what we say. They can already respond satisfactorily to humans speaking, as long as the question is within certain defined domains.

The benefits are thrown into sharper relief when we consider the use of computers in an educational context. Speech is an integral part of the way in which knowledge is transferred and students communicate: even if lacking 'true' intelligence, having computers that can respond appropriately when spoken to would be a significant pedagogical aid. This is where AI comes into its own: it provides the opportunity to build unique educational experiences for each learner. Because such flexibility would be impossible without the integration of speech, 'natural language' must figure prominently in systems that will interact with students. Natural language processing (NLP), as it is called, the interaction between computers and humans using natural languages, started in the 1950s, with Alan Turing again a pioneer in his *Computing Machinery and Intelligence* (1950).

The process of problem solving requires movement between varying resolutions of abstraction and detail. A student-facing AI should be able to move seamlessly between these levels, identifying which is more appropriate according to the capabilities of the student. Such an AI should further be tasked with learning about how students optimally learn. Do they prefer auditory or visual information? Do they need regular breaks? Are they stimulated or distracted by interesting tangential information? They must be able to distinguish between deficiencies that are the result of idiosyncrasy, disability and external disturbance. In short, the new technology must be capable of learning how teachers and students interact with others. NLP is opening doors in education unimaginable just ten years ago. Especially, as we shall see, when 'quantum computers', still in their infancy, succeed current computers with vastly enhanced powers of computation.

Trying to understand what an AI is or will look like quickly brings us to some of the deepest philosophical questions and existential musings. Alan Turing did not shy away from these questions. He acknowledged that it may never be possible to believe that entities separate from the self are intelligent. But he thought that was beside the point. "The original question," he noted, "I believe to be too meaningless to deserve discussion."[13] We cannot in the course of our lives definitively say whether other humans are intelligent or just high-fidelity simulacra: we accept the fact of their intelligence. If an entity is able to convince a human of its intelligence, we must either accept that this entity is in fact intelligent, or find a new way of defining intelligence. What does it matter if the machine is intelligent in an absolute and objective sense, if it is satisfactorily able to convince persons that we have already assumed to be intelligent, of its own intelligence?

If we accept this, then the questions that remain are ethical. Can we treat intelligent machines the way we currently treat computers? Will computers be interested in working for and with us if they become intelligent? We return to these questions in the final chapters.

At one cutting edge: DeepMind

AI research has always been fascinated with complex board games. In one reading, the history of AI is the history of computerised chess, based perhaps on the old assumption that skill at complex board games is indicative of high intelligence. As we make refinements to our understanding of intelligence, and as AI has mastered these games, this assumption has been challenged. But our framework also provides a very compelling reason for studying these games.

---

[13] Turing A. M., (1950). Computing machinery and intelligence. *Mind* 59, 433–460.

Winning complex board games falls within the "indirect goal, deterministic environment" class of problems. What makes these games so challenging is a phenomenon called 'combinatorial explosion'. To illustrate, consider a game of chess where we play as white. There are sixteen possible board states after our first move. Once our opponent's seventh move is complete, there are almost eleven million possible board states. Searching for all paths to victory takes some brain power, storing all possible board states along with an efficient way of recalling them. This is where AI enters the picture.

The numbers involved may be impressive but the application of AI to these games, even though AI has been instrumental in better understanding these games, is ultimately not about the games themselves. Far more important are the by-products of the process of creating AI to win these games. Enhanced theoretical frameworks for AI are re-examined or invented. Faster, more efficient, dedicated hardware is designed and built. The process might bring us even closer to creating AI that can generalise to solve 'indirect goal, deterministic environment' problems or an AGI.

At the 'bleeding edge' of this type of research, and research into AI full stop, is the London based firm 'DeepMind'. Founded in 2010 and acquired in 2014 by Google, but determined to maintain its independence, its mission statement, emblazoned across its website home page to: "Solve intelligence. Use it to make the world a better place." Mission statements are what they are, but there is serious intent here. Indicative of their ambition is the 'Differential Neural Computer' (DNC), described thus:

"A machine learning model called a[DNC], which consists of a neural network that can read from and write to an external memory matrix, analogous to the random-access memory in a conventional computer. Like a conventional computer, it can use its memory to represent and manipulate complex data structures, but, like a neural network, it can learn to do so from data. When trained with supervised learning, we demonstrate that a DNC can successfully answer synthetic questions designed to emulate reasoning and inference problems in natural language."[14]

This is a game-changer. The DNC is an extension of a neural network but it is one which is able to solve even more complex problems because its 'knowledge' is not limited to what is contained within the nodes of the neural network. The extent to which this constitutes a breakthrough in the study of AI is disputed. But DeepMind's credentials are undeniable.

Towards the end of 2017 a wave of articles appeared declaring "DeepMind AI needs mere four hours of self-training to become a chess overlord"[15] and "AlphaZero's Alien Chess Shows the Power, and the Peculiarity, of AI". Lost in the breathlessness was the most important claim the DeepMind team was making. It can be found in the abstract of the paper *Mastering Chess and Shogi by Self-Play with a General Reinforcement Learning Algorithm.*

---

[14] Graves, A., Wayne, G., Reynolds, M., Harley, T., Danihelka, I., Grabska-Barwińska, A., Gómez Colmenarejo, S., *et al.*, (2016). 'Hybrid Computing Using a Neural Network with Dynamic External Memory'. *Nature* 538 (7626): 471. https://doi.org/10.1038/nature20101.
[15] Mattise N.-*ArsTechnica* 12 July 2017.

"In this paper, we generalise this approach into a single AlphaZero algorithm that can achieve, tabula rasa, superhuman performance in many challenging domains. Starting from random play, and given no domain knowledge except the game rules, AlphaZero achieved within 24 hours a superhuman level of play in the games of chess and shogi (Japanese chess) as well as Go, and convincingly defeated a world-champion program in each case."[16]

In other words, AlphaZero achieved human being potential in just 24 hours starting with nothing more than an understanding of the rules of the domain. It can self-teach 'superhuman' performance in bounded move games where it already knows the rules. We need to be aware of such cutting edge work now, and remind ourselves that we are still in the age of Karl Benz. He had no clear understanding either of the impact his invention would have.

VR, AR and MR

Other emerging technologies are beginning to transform education: Augmented Reality (AR), Mixed Reality (MR) and Virtual Reality (VR) can be used in conjunction with AI and on their own to great effect.

VR is a computer generated reality which can challenge our notions of what is 'real'. It allows an immersive

---

[16] Silver, D., Hubert, T., Schrittwieser, J., Antonoglou, I., Lai, M., Guez, A., Lanctot, M., *et al.,* (2017). 'Mastering Chess and Shogi by Self-Play with a General Reinforcement Learning Algorithm'. ArXiv:1712.01815 [Cs], December. [Online]. Available at: http://arxiv.org/abs/1712.01815.

environment to be created and maintained through control over the user's sensory experience, most often focusing on their visual feed. To reinforce the reality being presented, VR can include 'haptic' or kinaesthetic communication, typically through a series of targeted vibrations, to mimic the sense of touch and space to the user. The traditional gloves and suits to provide feedback to the wearer are being superseded by 'mid-air haptics' which use ultrasonic to create the sensation of touch in mid-air, produced for example by Ultrahaptics, a spinout from Bristol University.[17]

Overall, VR has proven challenging to scope, despite its history being almost as old as modern computing. Laurence Manning's 1933 short stories *The Men Who Awake* depict people who wish to have their senses replaced by electrical impulses. Then in the 1950s, Morton Heilig developed an *Experience Theatre*, a very early example of immersive, multi-sensory technology, which he later prototyped in a 1962 *Sensorama*. Later that decade, Ivan Sutherland and Bob Sproull are credited with producing the first head-mounted display (HMD), named 'The Sword of Damocles'.

In the 1990s, consumer grade headsets were on widespread release such as 'Sega VR' and 'Virtuality'. Today there are some 250 companies developing and delivering VR-related products, including Google, Apple, Amazon, Microsoft, Sony, and Samsung. In January 2018, Sky became the first media company to announce that "it would use the Jaunt XR Platform to deliver immersive content to customers, taking film and television to altogether new levels of reality and accessibility." VR is fundamental to modern day gaming,

---

[17] Interview with Martin Hamilton, 04.04.18.

by seeking to bring users as close as possible to real-life experience. In education, VR is popular in training scenarios, because it can provide trainees in various fields with a risk-reduced reality to gain experience. In cultural fields, the British Museum and the Guggenheim have transferred large portions of their content onto VR, in an effort to make the humanities and fine arts more accessible and lifelike to all.

AR offers a view of the physical world overlaid, or 'augmented', by computer generated elements. We might consider AR to be the middle-ground, allowing for and relying on a framework of the physical world while providing virtual enhancements. The origins of this idea can be traced back to E. M. Forster's science fiction short story *The Machine Stops* (1909), which predicted a world enhanced by an augmented sense of reality. Fast forward 90 years, and the Canadian investor Steven Mann submitted a patent in 1999 for what he entitled "Contact Lens for the Display of Information such as Text, Graphics, or Pictures", or what are currently being called 'bionic contacts' by developers.

In 1986, 'Virtual Retinal Displays' (VRD) had been pioneered in Japan by Kazuo Yoshinaka of Nippon Electric Co., a technology which shares a similar concept but augments the 'screen' directly to the user's retina. AR has not had the easiest time finding markets in commercial spheres, but the effort continues unabated. Google Glass produced its optical head-mounted display in the shape of eyeglasses with a small camera and computer which enjoyed little success, underlining that AR is still in its infancy.

AR is being deployed successfully, however, by several fields of training such as within the US military for navigation, flight training and real-time communications. In healthcare, near-infrared vein finders such as 'VeinViewer' and 'AccuVein' are used to aid medical providers in finding veins by mapping them out. Archaeologists, architects and interior designers utilise AR for the same reasons: visualising space as it is and could be simultaneously. However, in education specifically, AR has yet to be seen making large strides. It is a question of time. The Google-funded start-up 'Magic Leap' announced in 2018 a release date for an AR headset which promises a single tool which will enable users to experience a completely augmented reality.

MR, or hybrid reality, as the nomenclature suggests, is a blending of real and virtual objects to create new realities, interacting in real time. The current applications and innovators are largely the same as for AR and VR, with the distinction between AR, VR and MR depending on the extent to which virtual elements are privileged. In a wholly VR environment, virtual elements are the only ones in use. In a MR environment, virtual elements have the same status as real elements and in an AR environment, virtual information is clearly auxiliary. We can thus conceive of these categories as existing on a "virtuality continuum".[18] On one end is a totally real environment and on the other end is a totally virtual environment.

What is certain is that these technologies, in conjunction with and independent from AI, will form an integral part of the fourth educational revolution. They are already beginning tentatively to transform learning opportunities in schools and universities, as we explore in the next chapter.

---

[18] 'IEICE Paper on MR', (n.d.) Accessed 11.02.2018.
http://etclab.mie.utoronto.ca/people/paul_dir/IEICE94/ieice.html.

What else is coming?

We close this chapter with a consideration of six related innovations which will, to differing extents, make an impact on education in the fourth revolution.

1. Transhumanism

We begin with one of the more outlandish possibilities. Or is it so outlandish? Since tools were first discovered at the start of the first education evolution, humans have been in search of ways to enhance themselves. Transhumanism is one of the logical extrema of this search for enhancement. "Transhumanists believe that we should use advanced technologies, such as pharmacology, genetic engineering, cybernetics and nanotechnology, to radically enhance human beings. In other words, we should be trying to create new types of humans – sometimes referred to as 'post-humans' – who are significantly improved when compared with us",[19] writes Mark Walker.

In his book on AI, Toby Walsh speculates that by 2050, it will be common to leave behind after we die an AI chatbot: "it will talk like you … it will comfort your family after you die".[20] This claim immediately begs several questions, including, what constitutes an improvement? We might answer, humans who are more happy, more virtuous, who live longer and are more 'intelligent'. We can readily imagine

---

[19] Walker, M. 'Transhumanism' in *"What's next?"* Al-Khalili, J. (ed.) 2017, p. 80.

[20] Walsh, T., (2017). *Android Dreams: the Past, Present and Future of Artificial Intelligence*, London: C Hurst & Co.

drugs that could permanently improve our mood without negatively impacting cognition, or engineering away the genes that increase a disposition towards depression. We might extend the length of years that we can live. Advances in medical science have already led to a significant increase in the average lifespan, mostly by reducing infant mortality, and hence we live longer before disease or ailment kills us off. Imagine if it became possible, supposing we even chose it, to engineer us to live for hundreds, thousands even, of years. We already modify and improve our bodies after all. It is just that the modifications that are culturally permissible are mostly seen as 'necessary'.

Repairs and improvements to the human body are made steadily more possible by new technology. Prosthetics, artificial devices to replace missing body parts, were pioneered by the Egyptians and have been in use ever since. The sophistication grew rapidly last century, enhanced by new technology and advances in medical advance, and by the needs of the two world wars. In Britain, Stoke Mandeville Hospital became a specialist at rehabilitation during the Second World War: and out of their belief that those with prosthetic limbs could compete at sport, the first Paralympic Games were held in Rome in 1960. After 1945, the National Academy of Sciences based in Washington DC began to advance better research and development overseeing dramatic improvements and enhancements to the lives of those without limbs.

These ways by which the human body was transformed caused no consternation. Illness or incapacity was being aided by a return to mobility and a sense of well-being; chronic pain and limited movement was consigned to the past. No one viewed this as threatening our sense of self-identity; the intrusion of the artificial into the human body being regarded in these instances as an adjunct to what might be termed the normal body. 'Intelligent', AI-enhanced, leg and arm prosthetics can be viewed in this light. "The artificial help aids rather than challenges the body, both structurally and functionally."[21]

But what happens when we move to AI-enhanced ears, or eyes, or parts of our brains? Enthusiasts have already implanted RFID chips into their bodies to open cars and doors.[22] Some progress has indeed been made on restoring vision to the partially blind.[23] When South African cardiac surgeon Christiaan Barnard performed the first human heart transplant in 1967, a frenzy of moral debate ensued. Where exactly is a line crossed? How transhumanism will actually work in our future is hard to predict. Many of the technologies required, at least in primitive form for the modification of the human, and the surpassing of a Darwinian evolution, already exist. What remains to be seen is how well we will tune it to the benefit of humanity. This will be our measure: the benefit to humanity, all humanity, not just the elites and the powerful, not the big tech companies alone. Everyone.

---

[21] Molloy, C., Shakespeare, S., and Blake, C., (2011). *Beyond Human: From Animality to Transhumanism.* London. UK: Bloomsbury Publishing PLC. http://ebookcentral.proquest.com/lib/duke/detail.action?docID=894596.

[22] https://popsci.com/my-boring-cyborg-implant

[23] *The Independent*, 22.12.16.

2. Robotics

Robots have been with us a long time and are wrongly synonymous with AI in the eyes of many. We are cautious about the centrality of the need for robots, which may always be cumbersome and less dexterous than humans, in the classrooms and lecture halls of the fourth education revolution. Maybe the popular belief in the centrality of robots owes something to the BBC *Dr Who's* Daleks, to *The Day the Earth Stood Still's* Gort or the *Forbidden Planet's* Robby. Or perhaps the creators of these fictions were responding to a need in the human psyche. But these all date back fifty or more years. The world has moved on.

When robots came into the factories in the 1950's and 1960's, they were doing static, repetitive, simple tasks. But once they step outside the shop floor, "they are unable to deal with the chaos of unpredictability and vagueness of human interactions", in the words of BBC Science Correspondent Pallab Ghosh.[24] Amazon though added 75,000 robot employees in 2017 alone, and cut its human workforce by 24,000. Are we on the verge of change? Noel Sharkey believes so. 'Service robots' are he says becoming commonplace.

> "These are robots that operate outside the factory to work on everything from healthcare to the care of children and the elderly; from cooking and preparing food to making and serving cocktails; from domestic

---

[24] Ghosh, P., 'What happens when AI meets robotics?', BBC News, 11.03.18

cleaning to agriculture and farming; from policing, security and killing in armed conflict to monitoring and repairing climate change damage; and from robot surgery to robot intimacy and protecting endangered species."[25]

Sharkey should know what he is talking about: as emeritus professor of AI at the University of Sheffield and chair of the International Committee for Robot Arms Control, he has made the field his own. Robots may well as he says have a prolific, if essentially mechanical future. Most optimistically perhaps, we would hope, robots could play the decisive role in cleaning up our oceans, rivers and lakes, our cities and villages, our air and wild areas, from the garbage and pollution that human beings have wrought on them. Indeed AI robots are already helping.

Researchers at the University of Texas (UT) are trying to incorporate AI into robots, to see how far they can go in making them more capable of human behaviour. Making them understand as opposed merely to recognising human speech is one challenge. "The problem is that robots have to be able to deal with the dynamics and noise and unpredictability that people bring into the environment, and so we have to think about perception, control and learning", said Andrea Thomaz at UT. This is difficult, as she admits.[26] More ambitiously still, robots are being engineered to play football, part of an international 'RoboCop' initiative. The

---

[25] Sharkey, N., 'Robotics' section from "*What's next*" Al-Khalili, J. (ed.) p. 176.
[26] BBC News, 12.03.18.

ambition is to build a team capable of beating the men's World Cup winners by 2050. Computers can win at chess and Go. Why not football? Will the robots spit and demand vast salaries? Will they exceed the prowess of today's Messi and Ronaldo? Will we want to watch robots play sport?

What about robots in education? As with AI in general, education is the Cinderella subject of the vast robot literature. It is rarely mentioned. We remain sceptical about it having a significant need or role in teaching. As Sharkey wrote: "Looking into the future, we will see many robots *assisting* in the tasks of care. But we must be careful to leave the *practice* of care to the humans".[27] Herein lies a clue to how the future will unfold, a foretaste to which we will return.

3. Voice and face recognition

Voice and face recognition are further technologies promising to transform education. Voice recognition work began in the 1950s but was limited initially to single-speaker systems with vocabularies of some ten words. Progress was uneven over the next 20 years until the late 1980s, when speech recognition products began to appear on the market, including Dragon Dictate and then AT&T's Voice Recognition Core Processing service in 1992, with the ability to route telephone calls without the intervention of a human operator. The economic, defence and security possibilities are enormous, and early in the 21st century, the Defense Advanced Research Projects Agency (DARPA) and the National Security Agency had both become heavily involved in developing the

---

[27] Sharkey, op cit, p. 182.

technology. Google's first foray into speech recognition came in 2007, with other companies following. The last decade has seen dramatic progress facilitated by a deep learning method called 'Long Short-Term Memory' (LSTM), which was easily able to outstrip traditional speech recognition. By 2015 it was available to all smart phone users through Google Voice.

An indication of how voice recognition will help in schools and universities comes from examining the progress of voice-controlled personal assistants. 'Siri', the virtual assistant in Apple products, was acquired by the tech giant in 2010, and has been standard in the iPhone since 2011. Google and Microsoft followed soon after with their own personal assistant technology using voice recognition, joined subsequently by Amazon with 'Echo' and Facebook with its own virtual assistant, 'M'. We are still in the very early stages of personal assistants. 'Viv', developed by an AI company of the same name based in California, is one of the more sophisticated developments. Dag Kittlaus, CEO of Viv, says the system will be able to perform thousands of tasks, and will not just be rooted to phones, but available in a range of devices from cars to fridges. He envisages rapid development: "what happens when you have a system that is 10,000 times more capable [than current personal assistants]? … It will shift the economics of the internet".[28] Before long, we will have personal assistants "every bit as sophisticated as the most knowledgeable hotel concierge".[29] For 'concierge' read teacher and lecturer. For 'hotel', read school and university.

---

[28] Kittlaus, D. in *The Observer*, 31.01.16.
[29] Etzioni, O. in *The Observer,* 31.01.16

Facial recognition takes us one step further forward still. As Woody Bledsoe, one of the early pioneers, noted fifty years ago "[facial] recognition is made difficult by the great variability in head rotation and tilt, lighting intensity and angle, facial expression, ageing, etc … in particular the correlation is very low between two pictures of the same person with different head rotations."[30] The earliest research can be traced back to the 1960s with Stanford pioneering much of the early developments.

The last decade has again seen very rapid progress in technology, driven in part by the opportunities it offers to state security and/or corporate gain. China's government has a record of the faces of all of its citizens, while the FBI has photographs of half of the adult population in the US. Welsh police in 2017 used face recognition to arrest a suspect outside a football ground. Already the technology is being used to unblock home screens on smart phones. Churches in the US are using it to track attendance of worshippers and retailers in Britain to identify those with a history of shop lifting. In Russia, an app called FindFace compares photographs of strangers with pictures on VKontakte, a social network, identifying people with a 70% accuracy rate. Before long we will be able to pay for our purchases in shops, and gain access to restricted areas including schools and universities, just by looking briefly at a camera.

A dark side of the technology is that it could be used by corporations and governments to detect those who it might not like. Researchers at Stanford have shown that face recognition can identify human sexuality correctly 81% of the time,

---

[30] Bledsoe, W. (1966), 'Facial Recognition System', Wikipedia.

compared to human beings at an average of only 61%.[31] Google has claimed it is turning its back on matching faces to identities for fear of misuse, but other companies, including Microsoft and Amazon, are continuing to use their Cloud services to develop opportunities in face recognition.

The technology has considerable potential in education with sophisticated applications already beginning to identify and interpret human emotions and understand when a student is surprised, confused, excited or bored. This will be of considerable value for schools and universities diagnosing students' problems early on, as well as for AI 'teachers'.

In Sweden, 'Furhat Robotics' is developing robot-style machines which can not only read faces but portray faces with emotions as well. The face can appear on a screen or, in time, on a hologram. Samer Al Moubayed, the founder of the company, says "we ae trying to capture the subtle head nods, the blinks, the eye gazes, so we can have a richer conversation with computers".[32] Already the company has held conversations with the Metropolitan Police in London about how the technology can train officers to detect and question potentially dishonest suspects. With voice and facial recognition, possibilities of personalisation in the fourth revolution era are transformed.

4. Quantum computing

The emergence of quantum computing was predicted by physicist Richard Feynman in the 1970s. There are still

---

[31] *The Economist*, 09.09.17.

[32] *The Times*, 27.11.17.

doubts about whether it will be able to work commercially, but Google claimed early in 2018 that it was on the brink of demonstrating 'quantum supremacy'; the ability to use the technology to solve problems that traditional computers with their more limited power could never achieve.[33] Quantum technology can tackle thousands of complex problems simultaneously because the 'qubit' or quantum component can harness the ability of sub-atomic particles to be in a super-position of multiple possible states. "We expect commercially valuable uses of quantum computing within the next five years ... in 10-15 years, every major organisation will use this technology", said Madhav Thattai of Rigetti Computing in California in 2018.[34] Professor of Computer Science at the University of Texas, Scott Aaronson, agrees that its potential is huge "not only for designing new drugs, software and financial analytical tools but also for new material, super conductors and photovoltaic [solar powered technology]".[35] Yet again, we find little mention of education applications from these prophets of the future, but the speed of the technology and its sophistication will be felt within the next decade in the subtle applications required to help machines understand individual students and their personalised learning needs. Tech investor Peter Read sees quantum computing being utterly transformative in education, as elsewhere. "Traditional computers solve problems as we do. Quantum solves them as nature docs".[36]

---

[33] 'Quantum Leap', *The Times* 03.002.18.

[34] *New Statesman*, 04.01.18.

[35] Wes, J. 'A post-digital world', *Prospect*, January 2018.

[36] Interview with Peter Read, 21.03.18.

5. Cloud Computing and Collaborative Working

Our schools, universities and our world are being transformed by the cloud and by 'collaborative working'. Cloud computing, which provides access to a shared pool of storage, processing and service resources, pre-dates even the arrival of the Internet in the 1980's. Reference to 'cloud computing' began to appear more widely in the 1990's though the term only become popularised when Amazon released its highly flexible 'Elastic Compute Cloud' in 2006. Leading computer scientist Schahram Dustdar says this about the significance of this technology:

> "In the past few years, cloud computing has transformed the IT landscape for both individuals and enterprises – from the way we access, store, and share information to how we communicate, collaborate, and process data. This has led to unprecedented levels of R&D and spawned numerous academic and industry conferences".[37]

A whole new world of living and working has been opened up. Broadcasting engineer Naomi Climer puts it nicely: "You can pick up your g-mail in Paris or Cairo, you can work in Chicago and Tokyo staying connected to the office HQ and watching Netflix in your downtime".[38] For

---

[37] Dustdar, S., 2016. "Cloud Computing", *Computer* 49(2): 12-13. https://doi.org/10.1109/MC.2016.46.
[38] Climer, N., in *'What's next'*, Al-Khalili, J. (ed.) p. 95.

teachers, academics and researchers, the implications are enormous. Our world is forever changed. Again.

So too is it because of the impact of 'collaborative learning', facilitated by the cloud. In brief, it permits individuals to 'meet' in real time anywhere on the planet. We're used to the 'black-and-white' technology of today's conference calls, the stop-start, the over-talking and the embarrassing pauses. Collaborative technology will permit us to move from the frustrations of the present-day 'Space Invader' level of basic provision to a world of communication akin to the sophistication of the latest computer games. It is transforming MOOCs, school-to-school exchange globally, university collaborations and international research programmes.

6. The Internet of Things and Big Data

The Internet connects people in vast numbers. It allows inanimate *objects* also to connect, the so-called Internet of Things or 'IoT'. While estimates suggest some 4 billion people are on the Internet in 2018, they indicate some 50 billion 'things' will be connected in 2021. The pace of change is rapid even for the digital world. Back in 2013, one assessment of big data said this: "Google has more than 1 billion queries per day, Twitter has more than 250 million tweets per day, Facebook has more than 800 million updates per day, and YouTube has more than 4 billion views per day. The data produced nowadays is estimated in the order of zettabytes, and it is growing around 40% every year".[39] Who knows what these numbers will have become by the time you read these words.

As leading AI philosopher Margaret Boden memorably put it: "In the future it won't be Big Brother watching you, but rather a trillion of little brothers, and each talking to each other non-stop".[40]

The IoT facilitates the collection of big data on a scale we are still unable fully to assess or exploit, as the sheer volume can militate against sifting the quality from the unreliable evidence and forming solid conclusions. We have had mass data for some years, as Nigel Shadbolt said above, but only recently has Cloud storage and computer power allowed us to analyse and learn from the ocean of information. Already we can see some early trends and uses emerging in education.

We will see 'smart schools' and 'smart universities' develop, akin to smart cities, which are working to connect on-line services which are currently separate, including transport, hospitals, police, refuse collection and social care. Smart cities include Bristol and Glasgow in the UK, and San Francisco in the US, which has sensors to guide visually impaired people. Smart schools and universities will ensure deliveries of learning resources and food are optimised, students and staff are kept safe, temperature and humidity optimised, the environment is kept clean, and the IT never goes wrong. Well maybe.

---

[39] Wei, F. and Bifet, A., (2013). 'Mining Big Data: Current Status and Forecast to the Future', *SIGKDD Explor Newsl* 14 (2): 1-5. https://doi.org/10.1145/2481244.2481246.
[40] Boden, M. Op. cit. p.118.

The IoT will assist VR, AR and MR to deliver learning to students ever more effectively. It will bring to these applications the latest research and information from across the globe, ensuring that students need never lag behind, wherever on the planet they are, access to the technology and connections permitting. As Climer writes "VR and AR are still relatively young, but their potential to become an everyday part of education ... is massive".[41]

Student and staff well-being will also be enhanced by the IoT. Body sensors will monitor physical, mental and emotional well-being, giving early warnings of problems and helping us monitor ourselves better. British EdTech company 'Stucomm' is one of those which is already integrating sensor networks with existing university resources. Students suffering from depression may be identified by observing how much time they spend alone in their room or by other health indicators. Students themselves can learn more which activities, relationships and spaces at school or on campus they find most congenial to their well-being and learning. The Internet of Things will leave no thing unturned.

We are still living in the car equivalent of 1886. But change is already coming. We turn in the next chapter to studying what the impact of AI is already, as the third education revolution draws to an end on our schools and universities.

---

[41] Climer, N. Op. cit. p.99.

Schools and universities in 2018 are little changed from 1600, for all the ubiquitous (non-AI) technologies. The teacher or lecturer address rows of students from the front of the class, who advance at the same pace. Learning is not personalised, and the teacher is weighed down by the burden of preparing material, setting and marking assignments, and reporting on student performance.

Chapter Six:

The state of AI in the USA and the UK

AI in the world today

We stand in the middle of the road, transfixed by the headlights of a fast-approaching AI juggernaut and in education, it is uncertain if we will be entranced and transformed for the better, or fall under its monstrous tyres. The cusp of the AI technological revolution is a dizzy place to be. The major players, Amazon, Apple, Facebook Google and Microsoft are ubiquitous, and the Chinese are coming, rattling their technology just on the other side of the hill. Here they come: Tencent (in Facebook's territory), Baidu (in Google's) and Alibaba (Amazon's). They're hoovering up the talent from other companies and HE offering high salaries and big visions. Who knows which competitors will emerge in the next decade to disrupt and sweep away today's powerhouses? AI is already beginning to help us do things quicker, with greater safety, more bespoke, reliably and efficiently than we have ever achieved without it. The largest tech companies are in an ever fiercer race to integrate AI solutions to keep ahead of their rivals. Smaller tech companies are trying to outdo the Goliaths in niche markets. It's silicon-rush frenzy out there.

Most telling are the uses being found for AI in sectors where technology is not at the core of the services on offer. From the classification of tumours to spotting credit card fraud, or finding survivors after terrorist attacks or natural disasters, the same techniques are being put to powerful use. The reason is simple: AI can adapt what it is doing to new stimuli to augment and de-risk human experiences and actions. As Andreas Schleicher, head of the Programme for International Student Assessment (PISA) has said "Our education system was very effective for the industrial age. Now computers will always be quicker than humans. We need a new vision for education".[1] Education must not remain the Cinderella domain of AI for much longer.

The early history of educational technology

From the earliest days of the third education revolution, printed books and articles became common tools in schools and universities. To facilitate learning, teachers wrote on large boards with chalk at the front of the classroom (whiteboards began to replace blackboards from the later twentieth century), while students wrote on slates and then, as paper became cheaper to produce, in 'exercise books'.

From the early twentieth century, mechanical technology began to make an impact, with duplicating machines including Gestetner, and stencil devices allowing for duplication of learning materials for students. Films soon appeared to aid instruction, training soldiers during the First and Second World Wars. Slide projectors began to appear in

---

[1] Interview with Andreas Schleicher, 23.1.2018.

the classroom from the 1950s, and the earliest computers in schools from the 1960s. The Open University was set up in the UK by Prime Minister Harold Wilson in the late 1960s, to exploit the arrival of television into most homes that decade. James Redmond was a pivotal figure; he had himself obtained qualifications at night school and had a passion for adult education, which drove him to overcome the technical difficulties of using television to broadcast teaching programmes across the country. Cognitive psychologist Aldwyn Cooper reminds us that in the US, the Computer Curriculum Corporation was founded at Stanford in 1967 to offer student-personalised instruction while the Plato system developed at Control Data Corporation sought to change the role of teachers through technology from the 1960s to 2006.[2]

The 1970s saw computers making a significant impact in education, with a particular impetus coming from the mid-1980s. 'Smartboards' were introduced in the USA from 1991. They consist of an interactive whiteboard, a computer, a projector and software which allows the teacher to move material around the board with fingers or electronic pens. The technology was expensive and it took several years for most schools to have one in classrooms. Evidence not least in primary schools, questioned whether the millions spent were justified.[3] The simpler technology of data and video projectors, however, began to be used widely in the classroom from the 1990s, allowing the teacher to write at their desk and display material on the board at the front of the class, to show video extracts and project material from their tablets and

---

[2] *The Times*, 12.09.2017.
[3] *The Guardian*, 26.06.06.

laptops on to a screen. This was seen as superior to teachers showing videos to classes on portable televisions, the lot of a whole generation of students in the 1980s and 1990s. It was inherently unsatisfactory because the television screens were small and involved the students often in just passive observation and learning. All these technologies enhanced the teacher's abilities to put over material in a more contemporary, arresting, time-efficient and active way. But it was still essentially the third education model, with the teacher at the front of the class and students participating in the same lesson at the same speed.

Before AI: a journey back to 2012

My interest in the subject of digitalisation in schools and higher education dates back to 2012, when I was asked to present on the subject at a seminar at Number 10. I conceived the idea of dividing the 'school journey', from Year 1 to Year 13 in Britain (or 'K-12' in much of the rest of the world) into two halves. The model entailed an education 'hard core' above a central line, and a 'softer' or broader aspect of learning below that line. The line itself represented the 13-year journey along the factory of schooling, as shown in the diagram below. I equally devised a 'university journey' for higher education, from matriculation to graduation, with again, the hard learning or academic core above the middle line, and the broader university benefits below it.

My quest was to discover where digitalisation was already making an impact and where AI impact might be made in the future. Where a transformative impact had by 2012 already been made, the rectangular boxes on the two diagrams are shaded in dark grey; where there was a lesser but still significant impact, the areas are shaded in light grey, and where there is little or none, the areas remains white. The ovals indicate the effect that digitalisation is having on administration as well as communications within and externally to the institution being discussed.

a) The school journey

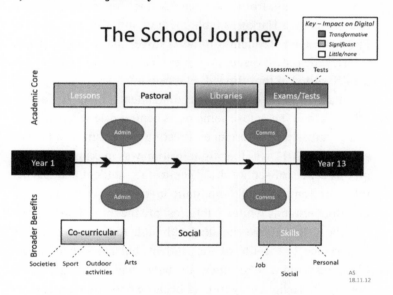

'Lessons' or classes are at the heart of schools worldwide. The journey to increased independence in students' learning continues throughout school and accelerates very considerably in the final two years. But the core activity in school is the teacher addressing and questioning the students. The 'Lessons' box is thus lightly shaded on the diagram because technology had made little impact on the core activity of teaching, for all the widespread use of Smartboards and other technologies. The slow take-up has been widely criticised: leading Ed Tech thinker Stephen Heppell has said "teachers are in fact bad at asking questions. They for example ask struggling students easier questions. It becomes a self-fulfilling prophecy. An AI machine would push them and engage them better".[4] Teachers often asserted that technology had changed everything about teaching, but they were wrong. Ironically, many schools missed bringing in one device, the Harkness table method, initially developed at Phillips Exeter Academy in the US over many years, which prioritised student discussion over teacher monologue, and is ideally suited to the 'flipped' classroom.[5]

'Pastoral' care of students is fundamental to the life of any school, albeit it can lose some of its central role when schools overly stress the importance of testing and exam results. The position by 2012 was that digitalisation was making no impact on this aspect of school life. Face-to-face student and teacher relations remained all important in pastoral care. The box therefore remains white. 'Libraries' are the third 'hard' aspect of school life above the line, although they rarely had the importance in the life of the student that heads and school librarians might like them to have had. This aspect is portrayed in a light grey format, because books and magazines in physical rather than digital form were still common at the time. In 2011, at Wellington College, we opened what we believed was the first 'bookless' or digital school library in Britain. With the number of titles reduced from some 60,000

---

[4] Interview with Stephen Heppell, 4.01.2018.
[5] They were introduced at Wellington College in 2010.

to fewer than 10,000, the move was prompted by a desire to stimulate more autonomous reading and research, by encouraging students to research and read their material online, to help preparation for life at university. The main call for physical books after the switch was reading for pleasure as well as core textbooks. The announcement of the change produced a predictable outcry that it heralded the 'death' of reading; it is a common misconception by those wedded to the idea that the only legitimate form of reading is print on paper.[6] The change in reading habits at schools to digital, not the least for capital resource reasons, has been slow to come, and many new school libraries have been built since 2012 with large shelf areas for books, some of which space will become redundant.

'Exams and Tests' are the final area above the line; again shaded in a light grey to suggest that little impact had been made by digitalisation. Exams were still being set on paper, and with answers written in ink or pencil, and with students sitting usually in large school halls watched over imperfectly by invigilators. Multiple choice questions, which date back to the mid-twentieth century, saw the greatest use of digitalisation in marking, but few other systematic developments in technology had been introduced to assessment.

'Administration' within schools is shaded heavy grey, because computers and digitalisation had made an enormous impact by 2012; not least with the introduction of the 'SIMS' school management information system from 1984. The innovation transformed the handling of data, which is core to

---

[6] BBC Education website, 17.05.2011.

the running of any school. The use of digitalisation became steadily more sophisticated but remained essentially about saving staff time and enhancing efficiency rather than finding altogether novel applications. 'Communications' within schools were equally transformed (hence heavy grey) by the spread of 'information and communications technologies' from the 1980s; the decade when we first heard the term 'ICT' being used by academic researchers. Emails, which can be dated back to the 1960s, saw a rapid increase in schools from 1995 when restrictions on carrying commercial traffic over the internet were lifted. Mobile phones began to be used widely in schools from the mid-1990s. ICT made communications within schools and between schools, parents and external bodies, speedier and more efficient, but expected savings in staff administration costs did not transpire.

Digitalisation had made little or no difference to the three aspects of the broader aspects of school life by 2012, which can be seen below the line. For many schools, 'Co-Curricular' activities that take place outside the classroom are almost as important as the academic subjects themselves. Sport and the arts are the two principal activities. Computers assisted in the administration of these activities, but the actual taking part in individual and team sports, playing music, acting in plays, dancing, clubs and societies, and outdoor activities, including hikes and weekends in tents, were barely affected by digital.

'Social' life, vital to the very nature of schools and the emotional development of children, was similarly untouched by digitalisation, with the exception of social media; hence the white colour. Social media can be dated back to the arrival of The Advanced Research Projects Agency Network (ARPANET), developed as a military communications network, which first came online in 1969, allowing for new methods of communication, particularly in business. Bulletin Board Systems (BBS) went online in 1978 and spread swiftly among school students from the 1980s.

b) The university journey

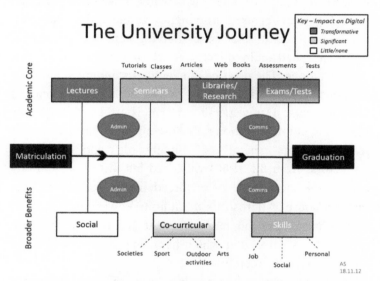

The internet from the mid-1990s enormously expanded the reach for social media among the young. Friendster started in March 2002, and LinkedIn the following year, along with MySpace. Facebook started in February 2004, Bebo in 2005 and Google+ in 2011, with mixed fortunes. Our final heading, 'Skills' saw a greater role for digitalisation particularly those skills required for employment and, to a lesser extent, social and personal skills. Learning about how digitalisation was transforming employment, and its many practical applications, was equally vital to students' learning in the skills for life category.

Universities by 2012 had been far more affected by digitalisation than schools. 'Lectures' (from the French *la lecture*, meaning 'reading') have been core to university education from the very outset; medieval universities in Europe saw the teacher reading aloud their pre-prepared lectures to a class of students who would make notes. Original textual sources featured prominently in the earliest lectures, which evolved into the lecturer giving students summaries, which morphed again to lecturers offering students their own interpretations. The practice of a lecturer standing at the front and reading out their script has continued largely unchanged for 700 years, despite persistent criticism that this one-way method of communication relied merely upon passive student learning. The advent of whiteboards and 'overhead projectors' from the 1960s enhanced but did not essentially change the inert mode of lecture delivery. Neither did the introduction of Microsoft's ubiquitous PowerPoint in 1987, which has dominated more than 90 per cent of software presentations since, and which has done little to help weak lecturers improve their art.

When studying to be a teacher during the early 1980s, the lecture format was widely criticised. A wry joke at the time was about a lecturer who became so bored and resentful having to read out his own pre-prepared lecture to each new factory cohort of students for the nth time, that he decided to pitch up at the beginning of the academic year and to place a tape recorder on the table at the front, which then delivered his lecture. When he turned up the following week to follow the same routine, he was disconcerted to find banks of tape recorders on the students' desks which were switched to 'record' left behind by the students. An apocryphal story no doubt, but one which highlights the inherent limitations of the lecture format. Not the least of the weaknesses is that students are unable to pause and think about a particular idea in a lecture that they find stimulating, or difficult to assimilate. The mono-speed pace is determined by the lecturer at the front of the class and by the rigid format. As students the world over have often remarked: "why must we attend lectures when we can read what X or Y has written about the topic in books and articles?" A genuinely inspired academic can bring the lecture to life, but how many manage to do so? In my life I recall many good but just one truly scintillating lecture, by historian AJP Taylor in 1972, and that was at a schools conference before I even arrived at university. At Oxford, no. At the London School of Economics, no. I tried.

The writing had thus been on the wall for many years before the advent of 'online lectures' and the arrival of the idea of 'flipped classrooms' challenged the tired format to the very core. A key text here was the publication in 1993 of *From Sage on the Stage to Guide on the Side* by Alison King,[7] which suggested that time in class or a lecture could be used better to gain understanding than merely passive information transmission. In 1997, Harvard psychologist Eric Mazur published *Peer Instruction: A User's Manual,* which specifically advocated shifting the absorption of knowledge outside the classroom and focussing classroom time instead onto assimilation and debate, i.e. 'flipping'.

The establishment in 2006 by American educator Salman Khan of 'The Khan Academy' was another key moment.

---

[7] Alison King, A. (1993) *From Sage on the Stage to Guide on the Side,* London: Taylor & Francis Ltd.

Khan, a bright and gifted science teacher, found himself regularly besieged by his family members asking for advice on their academic subjects. Because he found himself replicating the same advice, he decided that his words should be filmed on video and placed on the internet, later to be published on YouTube. In 2007, the US company Panopto was founded as a spinout from Carnegie Mellon University. After just one year in operation, 100,000 lectures online had been viewed by students using its technology, and in 2009, it partnered with Moodle's open sources project to provide its lecture software worldwide.

The spread of online and distance learning university courses has been prodigious ever since though the progress has not been even: the Open University saw student numbers halve after funding charges from 210,000 to 125,000 between 2010 and 2016. Some 25 per cent of university lectures nevertheless by 2018 were being recorded in Britain and available online; a figure which will exceed 50 per cent in the next five years in the UK and the USA, according to the CEO of Keypath Education, Rajay Naik.[8] Aston University has worked with Keypath to deliver its Aston Online postgraduate programmes. Deputy VC Helen Higson, one of the country's leaders in the field, reflecting on the exercise one year on in 2017, wrote "Ironically, I find online to be a much more personalised type of learning; you learn what you want, when you want".[9] Online lectures powerfully enable flipped learning, although, as long as lecture halls are constructed for

---

[8] Interview with Rajay Naik, 1.02.2018.
[9] Helen Higson, H. (2017). 'What online can teach on-campus', *Wonkhe*, 6.12.

serried ranks of students and not with 'clusters' to facilitate small group discussion, opportunities for lectures to involve active learning will be inevitably restricted.

'Seminars' had been partially transformed in universities by 2012 – hence the light grey colour – in particular by the introduction of mass open online courses (MOOCs). The first use of the term dates back to 2008, where the University of Manitoba set up a course called 'Connectivism and Connective Knowledge', recruiting more than 2,000 students online. The MOOC idea is an evolution of distance learning via 'correspondence courses' dating back to the 1890s, and later to distance learning via radio and television broadcasting. A benefit of digitalisation is that students could be drawn from all over the world, with cameras and voice recorders allowing them to participate interactively in the same forum at the same time. In 2011 Stanford University launched three MOOC courses. The first, "an Introduction to 'AI'", led by Sebastian Thrun, saw an enrolment of an extraordinary 160,000 students. The *New York Times* dubbed 2012 itself as 'the year of the MOOC', with the three major brands named as Coursera, Udacity and edX. In 2013, Michael Barber, then with Pearson and now head of Britain's Office for Students, said middle-ranking universities might merge or close if they didn't embrace the new technology.

Since those heady days, some of the initial enthusiasm has dwindled, with concerns over MOOC completion rates at less than 10 per cent have dampening spirits. '[MOOCs] came, they conquered very little; and now they face substantially diminished prospects' said University of Pennsylvania's Robert Zemsky in his ironically titled 2014 paper 'With a MOOC MOOC here and a MOOC MOOC there, here a

MOOC, there a MOOC, everywhere a MOOC MOOC'.[10] Seattle Pacific University's Rolin Moe was damning in early 2018: "despite the earnestness of most MOOC professors, the efforts of development, implementation and assessment have not been shown to be worth the time."[11] Inherent problems with the format, including reliance upon students to self-regulate, difficulties for the teacher to interact with such vast numbers, lack of digital literacy from disadvantaged groups in particular, and language barriers, all need to be better resolved. Nevertheless, the higher education environment will forever be changed by MOOCs especially with the technology improving rapidly.[12]

'Libraries' feature much larger in the life of undergraduates and post-graduates than they do for students at school. Students are older and more independent at universities, and a far higher proportion of their learning takes place independently and often in libraries. By 2012, digitalisation was already transforming research in them. Many academic journals, newspapers and books were already online. Students no longer needed to waste hours travelling to libraries, ordering books and articles to find the material they needed. Increasingly, everything they needed was available via search engines at the press of keys on their laptops. Libraries became places where students could study in quiet, while experiencing a social and communal atmosphere.

---

[10] *Times Higher Education*, 8.03.2018.
[11] Moe, R., (2018). 'The MOOC is not dead, but maybe it should be', Wonkhe daily blog, 03.04.
[12] 'MOOCs and Distance Learning', Montrose blog, 7.11.2017.

'Exams and Tests' had also begun to change more significantly than at school. Assignments were increasingly written online and sent electronically to academic staff, but exams still mostly took place in halls under invigilation. Every aspect of administration and communication had been revolutionised in universities by digitalisation by 2012, much as in schools. The internet was ubiquitous. The UK's JANET network which originally connected universities to colleges linked them to schools from 2003.

'Below the line' activities, i.e. the broader range of benefits of university life, had as yet been little affected by digitalisation. For many students attending university, the wider enrichment of student life was more important than it was at schools. Social life had been barely affected, beyond ubiquitous social media. But, for all the new platforms, students still derived the greatest satisfaction from meeting each other face to face: universities unsurprisingly reported no decline in social activities among its students. Co-curricular activities and skills were affected to a limited extent by digitalisation, much as they had been at school. The principal difference between school and university was that, at the latter, students were using digital technology more for themselves, whereas at schools it was more teacher-led.

But 2012 was a very long time ago. In the intervening years, AI has begun to make an impact on education, albeit to a limited extent compared to what we will see in the next few years.

An original spark for AI in education

Why is AI 'qualitatively' different to all that has happened before? A book, described by Ed Tech entrepreneur Henry Warren as 'the bible' in Silicon Valley on the development of AI in education,[13] helps explain the difference. In 1997, American science fiction writer Neal Stephenson published a novel *The Diamond Age: or, A Young Lady's Illustrated Primer*. The subject is a young girl named Nell from a humble background. At the age of 14, she received a stolen copy of an interactive book, *Young ladies' illustrated primer: a Propædeutic Enchiridion*. Intended for a wealthy child, it enables Nell to develop a more rewarding life by adapting its lessons to her and her environment. The key is the promise of a personalised education and life that technology in the near future will bring all regardless of wealth.

In Chapter Two, we defined the educated person as one able to think for themselves independently, to make decisions for their own good and the benefit of society, and to be capable of fulfilling all their human potentialities. Taking a cue from Neal Stephenson, the 'Holy Grail' in the application of AI to education (or AIEd) would be a comprehensive education system capable of adapting to the needs and talents of each individual student, and, by so doing, offering them the opportunity to become optimally 'educated' through the use of adaptive learning that tailors itself to their needs.

We now look at how this approach has already been making an impact on the ten stages of teaching and learning we have identified.

---

[13] Interview with Henry Warren, 2.02.2018.

Our Ten-Part Model of Education Revisited

Impact of AI on Teaching and Learning

We return to the analytical model outline in Chapter Two where we broke down the elements of the teacher's and the learner's tasks.

Five Aspects of Teaching	Five Aspects of Learning
1. Preparing materials	1. Memorising the material
2. Organising the learning spaces	2. Applying the knowledge
3. Presenting the material to engage students	3. Turning knowledge into understanding
4. Assessing student learning and giving feedback	4. Developing self-assessment ability
5. Preparing students for terminal assessments and write reports	5. Becoming an independent learner

Our approach makes a distinction between the roles that a teacher must undertake and the responsibilities that the student must fulfil in the course of becoming educated. Already the most sophisticated adaptive learning techniques are making an impact through their understanding of the learner, their strengths, idiosyncrasies and needs.[14] Because the technologies that aid the teacher also support the student, we will consider the impact of AI on them below in tandem. We should remember that many of the AI technologies being employed to date under the 'AI' are barely using machine learning at all. It is commercially advantageous for the term 'AI' to be deployed liberally and loosely.[15]

The early years since 2012 of AI's impact on education

1. Preparation of material/memorising knowledge

At university level, the material to be presented to students is typically determined by academics in consultation with their head of department or faculty. In schools, learning outcomes and subject content are often centrally defined by government and the requirements of external examining agencies. The head of department or faculty in particular has responsibility for deciding on the 'programme of study' and for outlining what each class will be taught week by week over the course of the school year to cover the content determined by others. The individual teacher has some leeway though in curating the information they put across in the class or lecture and in what formats.

---

[14] Luckin, R., Holmes, W., Griffiths, M. and Forcier, L. B., (2016). *Intelligence Unleashed: An argument for AI in Education.* London: Pearson Education.
https://www.pearson.com/content/dam/corporate/global/pearson-dot-com/files/innovation/Intelligence-Unleashed-Publication.pdf
[15] Email from Martin Hamilton, 04.04.18.

AI can, and is already, helping here by recommending material to meet the individual needs of learners. Technology scans the profiles of students and their progress in order to personalise learning content for them. London-based company Century Tech is one of the providers producing software to integrate with the SIMS school management system to select material for students with special education needs and disabilities (SEND). AI is being used to suggest changes to designated texts where the subject matter is unclear or confusing to students, helping them understand how source material relates to assessment results. In September 2017, another foretaste of the future came when the IBM Foundation launched 'Teacher Advisor', designed to help teachers select optimal resources and students to learn by "finally fulfilling the promise of personalised learning".[16] The technology has been trialled across the US, offering 'the ability to adapt to both teacher's and the student's needs. The more the teacher uses it, the more it begins to recognise what they're looking for'. But in 2018, this technology is still a long way off helping select individualised material for students in most schools and universities.

2. Organisation of the classroom/applying the knowledge

If students are to learn optimally, teachers need to be in command over their classroom, making it clear that they are in charge, even when - especially when – adopting more consensual pedagogical approaches. AI has made little impact

---

[16] Morrison, N., (2017) 'Will AI be the next big thing in the classroom', *Forbes*, 18.09.

on this area of classroom management to date, though it is beginning to be used to create personalised acoustic, lighting, temperature and seating positions to optimise learning. Learnometer, designed by a team led by Stephen Heppell, is a combination of hardware and software and data analysis allowing students to perform better by optimising their physical environments. In 2014, 'Google classroom' was launched, which promised more than it has so far delivered. It allowed students to submit work electronically using Google's products, for teachers to grade and monitor progress, and return work with comments. It was still the factory model, with a fixed number of students gathering together in a classroom with a teacher to study particular topics. Much more age than stage.

More has been happening in self-directed learning helping students apply knowledge using their own resources. In schools, the BBC launched 'Bitesize', its online study support resource for students as long ago as 1998. It became popular rapidly, and in March 2018 at the launch of the BBC's new education strategy, its head of strategy and digital James Purnell said 80% of school students reported it helped them in exams.[17] In Britain also, the Duke of York established the inspiring Digital Enterprise Award (iDEA) to equip the young with digital skills and awarding digital badges. Kerensa Jennings, who runs it, says "we need to make digital learning more 'gamified' and less 'eat your greens'". Its fast take up shows the formula works.[18]

---

[17] BBC online, 8.03.2018.
[18] Interview, Kerensa Jennings, 12.02.2017.

Moving to university level, MOOCs may have had mixed success but the numbers using Coursera, Udacity and edX, as well as universities offering their own online courses and the UK's FutureLearn platform, are vast. Answering student queries in online seminars correctly and promptly remains a major problem for MOOCs, especially given the large and diverse numbers of students in classes. The minimal impact of AI-based processing on MOOCs to date means they are still only able to offer students 'broad-brush' guidance. But Georgia Tech professor Ashok Goel deployed an AI system in 2016 called 'Jill Watson', based on IBM's Watson platform, to help solve this problem. Jill answers students' more routine questions, freeing up Goel and his assistants to focus on more conceptually challenging enquiries.[19] Jill Watson is a harbinger for how AI will allow MOOCs to overcome problems of scale.

'Chatbots (also known as 'chatterbots' or 'talkbots'), are widely assisting students to discover answers for themselves without asking the lecturer or teacher. Coined in 1994, students access them today via virtual assistants like Amazon's Alexa, Apple's Siri, Google's Assistant, or via messaging apps like WeChat or Facebook Messenger. Many like Jill Watson simulate humans and will be used increasingly widely in the future. Cambridge professor of information Zoubin Ghahramani predicts these virtual assistants will be 'superintelligent' by 2025, when we will have much more natural conversations with them on our

---

[19] http://pe.gatesch.edu/blog/meet-jill-watson-georgia-techs-first-ai-teaching-assistant

"priorities, what it should remind [us] about, clever recommendations it could make."[20]

3. Presentation of material to optimise learning/deepening understanding

Science practicals, which are particularly important for the teaching of science, are often expensive, difficult to set up or pose safety concerns for students. Drawing on the inspiration of flight simulators, products like Labster and Oculus Rift have developed VR in virtual lab technologies to serve as an alternative to practicals undertaken in class.[21] "VR comes into its own when scenarios are dangerous", says Henry Warren, "like students exploring the rim of volcanoes".[22] But he believes AR will become much bigger than VR in education, with companies like Blippar overlaying content onto the real world, and Microsoft's HoloLens using MR to allow even nursery children to engage with digital content and engage in holograms in the real world around them. Smartphones plugged into headsets allow students to conduct experiments guided by virtual technicians. Economists can model a whole series of financial futures. A limited application for robots has been found assisting teachers in delivering STEM subjects via Lego's EV3 robots, which can help students it is claimed understand their learning objectives better.[23]

---

[20] *The Times*, 01.01.16.

[21] Bodekaer, M. (2015). 'The Virtual Lab will revolutionize science class!' TEDxCERN.

[22] Interview with Henry Warren, 2.02.2018.

[23] Sage, R. and Matteucci, R. (2018). '*The Robots are Here*', University of Buckingham.

A very different use of AI has been developed in English assisting reading in primary schools. 'Bug Club' is a phonics-based scheme developed by Pearson, which has produced some 300 fully digitalised books. They are assigned by teachers to students in a personalised way, allowing them to read them at home as well as in school, meaning they can move at their own pace. Rod Bristow, President of Pearson UK, believes such technologies show that "it isn't true that universities have to be ahead of schools on AI and digital".[24] In Finland, one product challenges the normal hierarchy in education. 'Student Agents' helps students show their teachers how to get the most out of the technology. "In one Finnish school, instead of hiring consultants, they made kids teach teachers how to use different digital tools".[25] We are only in the earliest foothills though of seeing AI impact on the presentation of material across schools and universities.

4. Setting and marking assignments and assessing/self-assessing progress

'Adaptive assessments' allow students to take the right assessments at the optimal time for their learning, rather than at a time to suit their institution or an external agency which has set the exams on a date decided months in advance. Computerised adaptive testing (CAT) uses an iterative algorithm and adapts to the student's ability level: if the student performs well on earlier questions, more difficult ones are asked. This technology is already in use in the USA, as in the Graduate Management Admission Test, and estimates

---

[24] Interview with Rod Bristow, 1.02.2018.
[25] Josh Worth, J. (2018). 'What next for Ed Tech', *Times Educational Supplement* Guide to Ed Tech.

suggest that some 25 per cent of schools in the UK have begun to use some form of adaptive assessment. It is a world apart from the blunt instrument of a rigid test for all. Machine marking also reduces or eliminates teacher bias. Amos Tversky and Daniel Kahneman long ago shed much light on the many biases teachers are subject to in their assessment of students.[26] Bias and unfairness by teachers in assessing students, whether or not personally known to them, is an inescapable problem with the factory model. Plagiarism and cheating is another inherent problem which AI is beginning to address.

The teacher is constantly making assessments of their students during each class or seminar. A good teacher adapts the lesson they planned to deliver according to the overall mood of the class and other environment factors, and they try to personalise the learning for individual students. AI will assist in allowing personalised assessments throughout each class, with accurate real-time information being fed to them on the progress that each student is making. Early products helping in this area by using simple AI are already on the market. They include Reading Eggs, which will not allow a child to unlock the next level of difficulty until they have demonstrated proficiency in an end-of-level test, while Skoolbo allows teachers to understand better where their students are finding difficulty.[27]

---

[26] Tversky, A. and Kahneman, D. (1974). 'Judgement under uncertain ties; Heuristics and Biases', *Science*, Vol 185, No 4157
[27] Jarmin, L. (2018) 'Will you survive the AI Revolution?', *Times Educational Supplement* Ed Tech Supplement.

5. Setting exams and reporting/the development of autonomous learning

The end goal of traditional education is for students to succeed in a terminal examination at the end of a predefined course of study. In the UK, students may sit end-of-term and yearly exams to prepare for GCSE and, for those staying on after the age of 16, many take A-levels or International Baccalaureate (IB). At university, students sit regular tests and examinations. Traditionally, university staff are responsible for setting internal exams, for marking them and for reporting on students' performance, while exams with marks going to final degree classifications have to be validated and assessed by outside bodies.

Terminal exams do not always present a true picture of student ability but, rather, their performance on a given day on questions in a particular exam paper. Students who are perfectly capable of passing an exam well may do poorly because of many factors which exams cannot take into account. "Decades of research have shown that knowledge and understanding cannot be rigorously evaluated through a series of 90-minute exams", writes UCL's Rose Luckin.[28] AI is already beginning to allow for truly continuous assessment, with the collection, analysis and reporting of data built in. It is beginning to allow for a tighter integration of metacognition into assessment; student confidence is being measured directly, for example, by asking how students assess questions and by measuring response time. All of these are beginning to help students reach a state where they can perform at their

---

[28] Luckin. R., (2017) 'Towards artificial intelligence-based assessment systems', *Nature Human Behaviour*, March.

best, and where the assessment of their performance, including terminal assessments, is far fairer, more accurate and more comprehensive than bald exam grades.

Numerous products came onto the market from 2012-2018 to help students with autonomous learning. Duolingo which had been developed at Carnegie Mellon University was launched to the public in June 2012. It offers language learning support and a digital proficiency assessment exam. By 2017, it had 200 million registered users worldwide, learning 23 different languages.

By 2018, AI is beginning to make an impact in some of these defined areas in some countries. Many mistakes and false starts have bene made, and will continue to be made, before AI comes fully into its own in the fourth education revolution.

Case study: Arizona State University

In the UK and the USA, companies more than educational institutions are at the cutting edge of innovation in AI learning. However, it is schools and universities that directly serve students and understand them best. Too often the Ed Tech industry has designed products and assumed education will want to purchase them. This is in evidence every year at the annual British Educational Training and Technology show (BETT), which started in 1985. The conclusion is that the implementation of AI and adaptive learning in any context requires closer collaboration between established institutions of learning and the Ed Tech companies driving these innovations.

Arizona State University (ASU) is at the forefront of such partnerships, driven by its visionary president, Michael Crow, who wanted to convert it into a 'New American University', markedly open and inclusive. Stephanie Marshall, author of Strategic Leadership in HE, believes no simple university head has done more to lead the sector into the new technology.[29] Since 2011, ASU has been using adaptive learning to enhance comprehension, retention and access. Its track record highlights the potential for AI and adaptive learning in general. Universities are faced with a raft of problems, which include, but are not limited to, falling government funds, political pressures, falling enrolment, affordability, concerns over value for money, and a growing number of students who arrive on campus inadequately prepared for university level work or able to cope mentally.[30] AI can already help with some of these. In time, it will help with all.

The essence of the challenge at ASU is encapsulated in the words of the head of its mathematics department Al Boggess: "There is a sea of people we're trying to educate that we've never tried to educate before. The politicians are saying, "Educate them. Remediation? Figure it out. And we want them to graduate in four years. And your funding is going down, too". With more than 70,000 students, ASU is the largest public university in the USA. This scale infuses existential immediacy to problems that other smaller institutions can take more time with which to find solutions."

---

[29] Interview with Stephanie Marshall, 09.04.18.

[30] https://www.scientificamerican.com/article/how-big-data-taking-teachers-out-lecturing-business/

In 2011, in collaboration with adaptive learning start-up Knewton, the university "placed 4,700 students into computerised mathematics courses".[31] Knewton has since suffered setbacks, including criticisms that it overhyped the capabilities of its software.[32] But ASU has continued to expand its use of adaptive learning,[33] and began working with CogBooks in 2015, a UK-based company supported by the Bill and Melinda Gates Foundation, which offers digital textbooks, lectures, videos, assessments and collaborative tools. ASU offers adaptive learning sessions in a variety of subjects and according to CogBook CEO Jim Thompson, pass rates increased from 70-90% after the new technology was adopted. He says that it will offer the world's first adaptive degree, in Biology, in 2018.[34] Although it has been hampered in controversy, ASU shows higher education what a leader-led vision of technology innovation can achieve.

Robots are a red herring

Robots (from the Slavic language meaning 'foreign labourer') are not new: in some forms, mechanical devices imitating human activity have been with us for 1,000 years. As early as 1928, a humanoid robot, 'Eric', made of aluminium, delivered a speech in London. The first programmable robot was

---

[31] https://www.scientificamerican.com/article/how-big-data-taking-teachers-out-lecturing-business/

[32] https://www.edsurge.com/news/2017-05-12-pearson-an-investor-in-knewton-is-phasing-out-partnership-on-adaptive-products

[33] https://www.edsurge.com/news/2017-11-30-hitting-reset-knewton-tries-new-strategy-competing-with-textbook-publishers

[34] Interview with Jim Thompson, 23.12.2017.

invented in 1954, and were used first on a car production line, for General Motors, in 1961.

Their indispensability in the 'education' production line, however, has been exaggerated. Robots are unnecessary to the application of AI to education: "they are stupid. You don't need them", says Ed Tech guru Donald Clark. "Google is the greatest pedagogical success and it is a piece of AI".[35] Robots will not be replacing teachers in schools, lecturers in taught university courses, or doctoral supervisors for research students. Some successes with robots teaching students should be noted. London Design and Engineering UTC school uses the Pepper robot to help teach students about robotics, while many schools use simpler technologies like the Bee-Bot to teach coding.[36] AI does not need the moving embodiment of a robot though to accomplish its tasks in education. We will see in the next two chapters that AI can interact with students and teachers through a computer screen, using voice and face recognition, through headsets and holograms. Eric, or Erica, will not be replacing John or Fatima teaching in the classroom yet, or indeed ever.

Why has AI not made more impact on schools?

AI will change the educational experience in the long term, however. Why has the way ahead on AI in education been so patchy? Why has it been the Cinderella application among AI? Martin Hamilton notes the paradox: "AI is impacting everyone, every day, but schools and universities aren't

---

[35] Interview with Donald Clark, 20.12.2017.
[36] Interview with Martin Hamilton, 04.04.18.

consciously using it to exploit teaching and learning or adequately to prepare their learners for the AI-driven workforce they will subsequently encounter".[37]

A major reason is that companies have seen quicker financial gains in other sectors – transport, health sciences and finance, while governments have been focussing on defence and security applications, and they have yet to be convinced that there is much value in AI improving test targets, which is what concerns them.

Another reason for slow take up is the baffling complexity of the new technology, and the state of uncertainty (still) about what really works in education. It is almost impossible to model all of the factors that might affect how a learner is learning. We can term this 'the breakfast problem', grounded on the research that indicates that a child who hasn't had breakfast will not learn very well. As Ed tech entrepreneur Nick Kind however puts it: "I haven't come across a single piece of learning technology that asks if a child has had any breakfast". Add to that the uncertainty about whether the billions of dollars and pounds spent on Ed Tech to date have been worthwhile. In 2015, the Organisation for Economic Co-operation and Development (OECD) found no link between what countries spent on IT in general in schools and their 15 year olds' performance in maths, science and reading. According to a 2016 report from George Bulman and Robert Fairlie of the University of California, the new technology "has little to no positive effect" on outcomes such as test scores. If the existing technology has been disappointing, why invest in the still more tentative AI in education?

---

[37] Interview with Martin Hamilton, 04.04.18.

Institutional factors are equally impeding the adoption of AI. Across schools, on boards, within leadership teams, and among parents and teachers, people are reluctant to embrace what is happening in AI. Few school groups are as respected by government in Britain as Ark. Yet it has pulled back on plans for using blended learning in one of its new schools opening in 2019, in favour of traditional methods.[38] Change happens slowly in Britain. The influential Education Endowment Found (EEF) has reported favourably on some Ed Tech innovations including Accelerated Reader, for example, which matches children to suitable books digitally.[39]

Parents are wary of the potential harm of digital machines to their children, and their apprehensions spreads to governments who across the world warmly embrace innovation in every sector except education, where they are relentlessly conservative. In 2015, the UK government set up an inquiry to investigate banning smartphones in the classroom because of their potential to distract and harm. Sugata Mitra is one of many Ed Tech professors to be outraged. Instead of trying to ban smartphones and return the classroom to factory-model rote-learning, he says we should be encouraging schools and universities to find out how the technology can be used to improve education and solve problems: "I am going from country to country", he says, telling them, "Try it!"[40] Sending the ICT teacher off to the BETT show or other similar ICT conferences, the stock response of many overburdened headteachers, doesn't do it.

---

[38] *Times Educational Supplement*, 06.04.18.
[39] *The Economist*, 31.03.18.
[40] *The Sunday Times,* 4.10.2015.

Our thinking needs to change. Ignorance of AI is not an excuse. Teachers need to engage with what is happening.[41] Digital crusaders are in part to blame. For too long, they have been telling us that digitilisation will change everything in schools. They have cried wolf too often. Now that real change is coming with AI, people are apathetic or suspicious. Universities are more alert than schools in general to what is happening, with leaders like Tim O'Shea, the pioneering Vice Chancellor of Edinburgh University.[42] Michael Spence at the University of Sydney, Michael Crow of ASU and others we will meet in Chapter 8, piloting their institutions into an unheralded future.

---

[41] Interview, Demis Hassabis, 7.04.2016.

[42] Tim O'Shea founded the Computer Assisted Learning Group and the Open University and has made a prodigious impact on our understanding of Ed Tech and AI.

Schools of the future won't have conventional classrooms, and each student will begin their day have with their personal work plan. If we use AI well, we will retain the best of the third education revolution benefits, e.g. the social experience, the positive interactions with staff, the stimulating careers for teachers, and the academic ambition and seriousness. But AI will help ensure the five inherent problems of the factory system will be swept away: gross social unfairness, the factory line not personalised education, teachers weighed down by administration, a very narrow range of student abilities developed, and each student homogenised not individualised.

Chapter Seven:

The future of AI in Schools

Schools do not know the future for which they have to prepare. This is difficult for them when they come to plan for the future. Doing nothing is not an option. Hard though it may be to peer into the future, and unsettling though some scenarios may be, not to prepare is to court serious risk. We are clearer of the ends than the means of getting there. But the mists are beginning to clear. British teacher Simon Balderson says "What we think of as a teacher's role is going to evolve ... AI will manage data for each pupil, ensuring that work is always pitched at exactly the right level for every student ... it will be possible for lessons to be delivered by the best teachers and most knowledgeable subject specialists in the world".[1]

Schools will change fundamentally in the next 15-25 years, as will the jobs for which schools are preparing their young people. This alone should be waking up schools to the need to change the curriculum more than it is. The coming AI revolution will differ from the earlier three because it will

---

[1] Quotation *Times Educational Supplement* Ed Tech Supplement, 2018.

disrupt the lives of the most privileged and academic, not just manual workers, as Richard and Daniel Susskind argue in their book *The Future of the Professions* (2015).[2] Venture capitalist Marc Andreessen has said there will be just the two types of jobs in the future: for those who tell computers what to do and for those who are told by computers what to do.[3] Yet schools the world over are just ploughing ahead, doing what they have always done, preparing their children for the twentieth century. "Wake up" is indeed a key message of this book. Smell the silicon.

Schools of the future: The 'School Journey' Revisited

To help us imagine what schools might look like by 2030, we return to the diagram of the school journey discussed in Chapter 6, where we saw only limited impact being made by existing digital technologies and emerging AI on education. Proper AI will change all this, as in the diagram below shows. The intensity of the shading again indicates the degree to which AI will impact on each of the activities that schools undertake.

---

[2] Susskind, R. and Susskind, D. (2015) *The Future of the Professions: how technology will transform the work of human beings*, Oxford: Oxford University Press.
[3] *Financial Times,* 04/05.02.17.

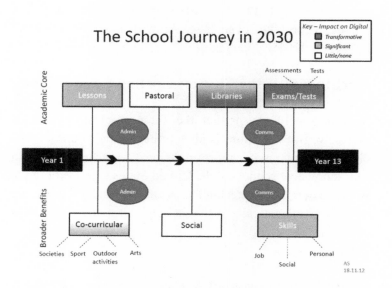

'Lessons' are shaded in light grey because adaptive learning technologies will fundamentally alter the way that learning takes place, and the role of the teacher. 'Pastoral' remains white, because AI will not significantly intrude into the key relationship between teacher/tutor/mentor and student, though we should not ignore the many ways that AI technology will assist in personal tutoring of the young, especially for those experiencing difficulty. Libraries and exams/tests are in heavy grey, because they will be transformed by AI. 'Libraries' will become the focal learning spaces in schools, but will contain few physical books, while 'Exams' is in dark grey because they will be superseded by online continuous assessment.

Below the line, 'Skills' and character is in light grey, as AI will make a significant impact on the development of each young person through interactions online and AI counselling and support. Only the 'Co-curricular' and 'Social' activities remain white, and, even here, AI will make an important impact on the development of the young in both areas.

Harbingers of the Future: Cutting Edge Schools

It is impossible to predict the future for AI in schools precisely. But the future is already beginning to unfold. For clues as to what may happen in the next ten years, we turn to four innovative schools in the United States and one in India, where emerging AI technologies and radical thinking are offering a dramatically different school experience to their students.

1. AltSchools

AltSchools consist of a number of 'lab schools' in California and New York where the students have the ability to organise their own learning in consultation with teachers. They do this by consulting two particular pieces of software on their tablets.[4] A 'portrait' provides a record for each student of their progress in both academic subjects and social skills, while the 'playlist' guides them in the work that they are to undertake that day and week, and assists them in completing appropriate assignments. Personalised learning thus lies at the very heart of each AltSchool.

They are considered 'labs' because the teachers and engineers designing the learning are expecting that the innovative approaches will extend to schools across the

---

[4] 'Machine Learning', *The Economist*, 22.07.17.

United States and then to the world beyond. Max Ventilla, formerly Head of Personalisation at Google, is the AltSchool Founder and its Chief Executive. He describes it as "neither a school nor a start-up, but a 'full-stack education company'",[5] full-stack being tech speak for comprehensive. A third of the staff are educators, a third are engineers while a third run the business. As the *Financial Times* observed, the location of the AltSchool head office is significant at the heart of the San Francisco start-up district, just doors away from other pioneering companies including AirBNB, Pinterest and Dropbox. Backers of AltSchool include the 'Omidyar Network', founded by eBay founder Pierre Omidyar.[6] With the market in Ed Tech set to grow to $120 billion by 2019, it is not surprising investors are watching what happens with keen interest.[7]

At the Yerba Buena AltSchool in San Francisco, teachers do not have to undertake fully any of the five core teaching tasks we have identified. They do not curate or plan lessons, neither do they organise the classroom, present the material, set tests or mark. Instead, they use the time freed up to give individualised attention to student progress, diagnose individual problems, and analyse student performance in far greater depth than was possible under the factory model. One AltSchool student told *The Economist*: "I feel like the teachers here really

---

[5] Kuchler, H. (2017), 'Can Silicon Valley Really Hack Education', *Financial Times* 04/05.02.
[6] *Financial Times,* 04/05.02.17.
[7] Estimated by Technavio, *The Economist,* 22.07.17

know me".[8] Significantly, students only spend some 20-30% of the day in front of their screens, which will be reassuring to many teachers today worried about the loss of the human element in education, as well as their own jobs. Parents and governments too should take note that only a quarter of the school day is 'screen time'.

The AltSchool experiment is still in its early stages, with advocates and critics hotly arguing its benefits, as well as its value as a guide to schools' future. Privacy issues have already emerged as a concern. With cameras mounted on walls used to review what students are doing, the potential for abuse of privacy is enormous. Fairness issues also arise as the algorithms are making judgements on students that the teachers do not always understand, and which they cannot explain to parents. But the AltSchools' project forges ahead and important markers are being laid down.

2. Summit public schools

Summit schools are a publicly-funded network of schools in California and Washington State serving mostly poor, often Latino students, which provide an answer to those who say the new technology only benefits the rich. The model evolved to several schools from a single school in Silicon Valley, and to a distance learning platform used by over 20,000 students across 27 states by 2017.[9] Diane Tavenner, Summit's Founder and Chief Executive, had been fired up by the possibilities of individualised

---

[8] *The Economist,* 22.07.17.
[9] *Financial Times,* 04/05.02.17

learning since her own days at school in the 1970s. No surprise then that personalised learning lies at the heart of the approach in the Summit schools, as it does in AltSchools.

"Children don't need to be walked through every step", says Andrew Goldin, Chief of Schools at Summit, arguing that students learn much more efficiently from personalised technology than they do when they all move at the same pace in the conventional classroom. He believes further that giving students more control over their own learning motivates them to learn the basics better, which is almost certainly correct in my experience. To those who worry that deep learning will be sacrificed, he responds that learning such core knowledge is essential if they are to participate in their signature projects. Two-thirds of pupils at Summit schools perform as well or better at maths tests nationwide, he says, than demography would predict, and 10% more students go on to graduate than from comparable neighbouring schools.

Time saved through technology at Summit schools is devoted to project-based learning which takes up to half the school day, mentored by teachers. Tahoe Expedition Academy is one of Summit's schools to use software developed by Facebook, which built the platform. At the beginning of each day, students log on to their 'personalised working platform' and examine their playlist of reading material, videos and tests, before deciding, in consultation with their teachers, which modules they will be studying that day, influenced by what they most enjoy and most need to master.

At Tahoe Expedition Academy itself, the students are privileged, and work on projects, from developing 3D printed technology to testing water quality, and understanding emotions that robots will lack. The school aims to combine an academic learning which is technology rich, with outdoor adventure. These experiences are designed to push students to the edge of their comfort zones to build character, like the famous 'Timbertop' term in the outback that students at Geelong Grammar School in Australia experience. At Tahoe Expedition Academy, year groups spend 40 or so days a year on 'constructive experience' projects as far away as Mexico and Syria in an effort to help them understand what makes human beings unique individuals in an age of digital technology.[10]

Mark Zuckerberg and his wife Priscilla Chan founded the Chan Zuckerberg Initiative (CZI) devoted to a similar quest. When their daughter Max was born in 2015, they announced they would donate their own Facebook shares (worth an estimated $45 billion) to CZI. They wrote an open letter to her declaring: "you'll advance quickly in subjects that interest you most and get as much help as you need in your most challenging areas. You'll explore topics that aren't even offered in schools today. Your teachers will also have better tools and data to help you achieve your goals". Within a decade, CZI aims for schools across the United States to adopt the emerging technologies, and hopes to see education across the world transformed.

---

[10] *Financial Times,* 4/5.02.17.

3. School of One (SO1)

This is a middle school mathematics initiative which began in 2009 and is operating in six schools in New York City. The philosophy, similar to AltSchools and Summit Public Schools, is for each student to use adaptive learning machines to move at their own appropriate pace. Its students all receive their own uniquely tailored daily learning schedule, using a learning algorithm, based on what will most help them according to their strengths, needs and optimum learning approaches.

Classrooms are open plan, with multiple learning stations with reconfigurable furniture, allowing students to work on their own or in collaboration with other students and teachers. Teachers are plentiful, which might arrest fears of disappearing teachers: indeed, the student:teacher ratio is 10:1. Founding CEO Joel Rose developed 'New Classrooms' to scale up SO1's instructional model, called 'Teach to One'. Wendy Baty, Head of Maths at New Classrooms, says the technology and approach allows students to receive feedback that "even the best teachers could not provide to all of the class".[11]

4. Khan Lab School (KLS)

Khan Lab School (KLS) is the brainchild of Sal Khan and is still in its experimental stage. It is an allied development of the Khan Academy, which has done so much to pioneer online tutorials. At the KLS in Mountain View, California, students do not spend all day in the

---

[11] *The Economist,* 22.07.17.

classroom, nor do they have homework nor conventional assessments, nor are they organised by age. Instead they share common spaces much like a modern, open-plan office, as they pursue their own individual learning objectives on their personalised platforms, using the software to help them advance at their own pace and in their own way.[12] Again, students are heavily involved in planning their own learning, (which inevitably works better for well-motivated students). They decide, in consultation with their teachers or mentors, in what subjects they are experiencing difficulty, and take responsibility themselves for transcending difficulties in those areas. KLS Mountain View had grown to only 100 students by its second year in 2016, and is aiming for an eventual size of 400.[13] The numbers are small, but could KLS be showing us what the future looks like?

5. Riverbend School in Chennai, India

This fee-paying school will, when it opens in 2020, offer a different vision again of the future.[14] The aim of Riverbend is to develop the personal fulfilment and happiness of its students, with innovative physical architecture based upon the idea of the village, which the school believes best fosters personal relationships and academic progress. The school's founders, SPI Incubator, believe that high student achievement requires emotional intelligence, personal happiness and strong relationships.

---

[12] *The Economist,* 22.07.17

[13] 'Khan Academy's Experimental School is Thriving', *Mountain View Voice,* 07.11.16.

[14] *Inhabitat,* 15.02.18

The architects, Kurani, say "The school centers around a public plaza and has spaces for studying, playing, reflecting, living, and farming. Every aspect – intimate walkways, outdoor pavilions, traditional courtyard housing – encourages socializing".[15] Inside, the school is built around interconnected pods behind glass. When the school opens it will be using the latest technology, including robotics, and sees no conflict between deploying the most advanced technologies and the essential proposition that social relationships lie at the heart of every school. We might add that sympathetic and natural architecture, as opposed to the depersonalised school buildings that often accompanied the factory era.

The cost of the technology and the skills required from staff mean that experiments such as these five examples will, without massive benefactor/corporate capital, remain for the privileged few whose parents can afford the high fees. But they all point to the future, especially once the technology becomes cheaper. The vision of the pioneers is clear: "Silicon Valley wants to move on from a 19th Century, artisanal model – where knowledge resides with each classroom teacher – to a 21st Century personalised experience that technology can replicate on a global scale.[16] We should take careful note of innovators such as these, and start working out ways to apply their learning rather than thinking of reasons for not doing so. It would be a brave voice to say the technology such as in

---

[15] https://kurani.us/riverbend/

[16] Kuchler, H. (2018). *Financial Times*, 04/05.02.

these experimental schools will not spread rapidly across school systems worldwide.

The Imperative to Change

Schools must thus change radically and quickly if we are to educate students ready to take on the unique challenges they will face in our rapidly evolving society and economy. The engine driving this change forward in education and in employment will be AI. This book is not a solitary voice arguing for the notion that a fourth educational revolution is inevitable, necessary and must be fashioned: we might be standing athwart history yelling "get on with it!" but we do not yell alone. In this chapter and the chapter that follows, we hear of the work of many pioneers, the good, bad and ugly, but mostly good, who are risking their reputations, money, or both, to bring the future into the present. A combination of expert opinion and an examination of current trajectories should we hope help us distinguish what is probable from fantasy.

Henry Warren, an EdTech and AI Expert, is an unashamed champion of the transformative power of EdTech. We do not see robots being at the heart of this transformation, as he does, believing other AI platforms will mostly be used to connect with learners. But there are aspects of his argument which are compelling: "there will be at one point two billion children in the developing world. We are never going to be able to train enough teachers to teach them all. There'll never be the money for it." He is one of those who see AI driving educational change for all children across the most deprived regions, and the heartening point is we do not have to wait indefinitely to achieve it. "You don't need AGI (Artificial

General Intelligence) for us to provide a majority of the roles of the teacher. If you break the tasks of teaching down, you discover we can achieve much of what teachers are doing', though as a caution he adds, 'there's not much happening in schools at the moment".[17] We return to this subject below when we consider 'One Laptop Per Child'.

Britain and the US both face severe crises in teacher recruitment. In the former, 47,000 extra teachers are required for secondary schools alone by 2024. Traditional solutions including raising class size and reducing entry qualifications for new teachers pose their own problems. Could AI be the solution here also? Warren think that problems in teacher recruitment in Britain as in the US will drive a change of approach from government: "necessity will be the mother of invention".[18]

It is precisely in our breaking down of the constituent elements of teaching that we believe we can begin to see how AI will make such an impact. In the previous chapter, we returned to our five stage model for the various elements of teaching and learning, to see how far digitalisation by 2018 had impacted on teachers and students. We revisit that model here and use it to examine the impact of AI on schools of the future, with a focus on 2030 as a meaningful timeframe.

In breaking down the constituent elements of teaching, we again use our shading device to see whether change due to AI by 2030 will be negligible, significant or transformative. The fact that each of the five boxes is shaded dark grey shows that the impact of AI will be seismic.

---

[17] Interview with Henry Warren, 02.02.18.

[18] *Times Educational Supplement*, 06.04.18.

The Five Phase Teaching Model

1. Preparation of material
2. Organisation of the learning spaces
3. Presenting the material to engage students
4. Assessing student learning and giving feedback
5. Preparing students for terminal assessments and writing reports

1. Preparation of material

Teachers throughout history have treated the curation of material for transmission to students as fundamental to their craft. They research existing material or create it themselves, deciding what is most appropriate for students to engage with at any particular level. It is one of the most creative and one of the most satisfying tasks for any teacher. AI will increasingly assist and even replace the teacher is identifying such material, with AI authored resources, and the tagging of material appropriate for a student's particular learner profile, as we have seen is already occurring at Summit and AltSchools.

For further sophistication, we must await breakthroughs in National Language Processing (NLP).

Judging how a particular source will impact on a student when the material has not yet been exposed to students, or authoring content in a way that is fully optimised to a specific student's preferences, requires the AI truly to "understand" the language in which material is presented. Natural language understanding (NLU) is not yet within the range of abilities of AI, and we may need the arrival of AGI to solve it, which begs the question whether we will achieve AGI. Continued research meanwhile will continue to optimise the roles that teachers currently play in material curation. Even education traditionalists like John Blake or London's Policy Exchange believes it is 'unhealthy' for teachers to still believe they have fully to 'plan and prepare and design' learning materials themselves.[19] Curation 'specialists' may well emerge whose jobs it is to work with AI machines to author and identify the most appropriate material for particular student profiles.

2. Organisation of the classroom/Absorbing the knowledge

Teachers often invest great care into designing sympathetic and attractive physical spaces for learning, and into structuring the classroom to help ensure the best potential for effective work and fruitful relationships. This is another creative and individual aspect of the teacher's craft, which is being affected by AI. Research shows that some of the most important factors affecting learning outcomes are fresh air, temperature, and seating

---

[19] *Times Educational Supplement*, 06.04.18.

arrangement. AI will increasingly help personalise each to maximise the prospects for learning.

Greater personalisation will force change on the traditional idea of the "classroom". If students are learning on their own for much of the day, is there still need for schools as they are currently configured? Classrooms are however still being constructed as they were in 2000, in 1900 and in 1850, with corridors and classrooms. "In a traditional school, since learning is monopolised by large-group direct instruction, all you need are cellular classrooms, with rows of desks focussed on a single instructor", says one recent analysis. "Since this habitat for learning is so culturally ingrained, it often goes unquestioned. Surveying articles about newly built schools, rarely throws up a photograph of a classroom. Why? Because they are considered boring and predictable: everybody knows how classrooms work."[20]

This third revolution era style of classroom worldwide is indeed a monument to unthinking conformity. But according to Michael Horn, the co-founder of the Clayton Christensen Institute, whose mission is "improving the world through disruptive innovation: In the future, we won't have 'classrooms.'" Students [in future] will learn in student-centred environments—perhaps we'll call them learning studios—where each student's learning is personalised to meet his or her precise needs. It will be

---

[20] 'Tear Down This Wall! A New Architecture For Blended Learning Success - Edsurge News'. (2015). *Edsurge*. Accessed February 19.02.2018. https://www.edsurge.com/news/2015-06-29-tear-down-this-wall-a-new-architecture-for-blended-learning-success.

critical to rearrange the physical space and furniture to align with the principles of student agency, flexibility, and choice that are the core of new learning models. Because these models will leverage multiple modes of learning, they will need spaces built for different activities, which can occur individually through digital media or in small interactive groups. The teacher's desk, if there is one, is pushed to the margins."[21]

So separate classrooms will disappear in time, and be replaced by pods and wide open, flexible spaces which can be configured for individual and flexible collective learning. Sensors will monitor individual students, measuring their physiological and psychological state, picking up on changes faster and more accurately than any teacher could. This information will be used to suggest interventions to the teacher and to head off concerns before they fully develop.

3. Presentation of material to optimise learning/deepening understanding

Another essential craft of the teacher is to be a performer, an actor and communicator, capturing and retaining students' interest by presenting them with learning material in an attractive and stimulating way, which allows them to comprehend at a deeper level than if left to their own devices. But AI changes the whole meaning

---

[21] Glatter, H. and Wong, A. (2016). 'The Classroom Of The Future'. *The Atlantic*. Accessed 19.02.2018.
https://www.theatlantic.com/education/archive/2016/09/reimagining-the-modern-classroom/498224/.

of a student being 'left to their own devices'. With AI, the information presented on a page, in an article or on screen is no longer inert. It becomes animated, in the same way that a teacher today animates it bringing it to life, by grabbing the student's attention and making it personal to them.

The flexibility of visual representation with AI allows material to be presented to students which renders much teacher exposition redundant. The real power and flexibility stems from digital text separation of content and its "display." Unlike printed text, where content and display are static, digital content can be put over in countless ways and in multiple modalities. Digital text can thus be "displayed" as spoken words (through modern text-to-speech technologies) and the words can be highlighted as they are spoken, making the connection between written and spoken forms more evident. The same digital words can also be displayed as tactile words through a refreshable Braille device.

For students who face barriers in language itself, a click on a word can bring up a contextually appropriate definition with graphics and in multiple languages. In these and many other ways, digital text can reduce barriers for students with disabilities, for struggling readers, and those learners unfamiliar with the English language. Digital content can be variably and reversibly "marked." With mark-up languages, the same content can be displayed on different computers and devices, in unique ways for different users, without losing the integrity of the original content. A single web page can be displayed on a large desktop, a small laptop, and a handheld device.

With 'extensible mark-up language' (XML), the tags are not only structural, but also semantic, enabling elements to be identified based on their meaning and not just structure or syntax. A body of text can thus be labelled as a summary or a question and then at a later time be selectively displayed for one student or a group of students, while hidden for others for whom it would be unnecessary or distracting. The same flexible power is also available for other digital media including video, audio, as well as virtual and augmented reality."[22] The possibilities of this new style of learning are only now beginning to be appreciated. A student can put on a VR headset and have a totally immersive experience of being in a classroom on the other side of the world: former British head teacher Mark Steed believes such innovations will happen inevitably "with increasing bandwidth and processing speed".[23]

4. Setting assignments and assessing/self-assessing progress

To do their job well, teachers need to be constantly checking and assessing what students are absorbing and whether they are understanding the material. Herein lies the difference between teaching and broadcasting, as in a

---

[22] Rose, D. and Dalton, B. (2009), 'Learning to Read in the Digital Age'. *Mind, Brain, and Education,* 3: 74–83. doi:10.1111/j.1751-228X.2009.01057.x

[23] *Times Educational Supplement,* 4.10.2017.

recorded lecture or television programme, where there is no opportunity for two way communication. But keeping alert to the progress of 30 or more students in a class is difficult for a single teacher. UCL's Rose Luckin has no doubt that by 2030, all teachers will have "an AI assistant that takes care of record keeping and marking".[24] Teachers need also to create environments where students can assess their own learning and build up confidence in it. In some cases, teachers may not always be the best people to assess their own students' learning. Diane Tavenner of Summit Public Schools highlights the problems that can arise from the dual task of a teacher coaching and testing students including grade inflation and bias, even if subconsciously. But "with technology, it doesn't have to be true".[25]

The factory model typically sees a significant time lag between students being assessed and them receiving feedback on their performance. According to Mark D. Shermis at the University of Akron in Ohio, "with increasingly large classes, it is impossible for most teachers to give students meaningful feedback on writing assignments."[26] The delay can be anxiety-inducing, as well as inefficient. Delays mean that learners may be unable to benefit from feedback before they move onto

---

[24] Quoted by Jarmin, L., *Times Educational Supplement* Ed Tech Supplement, 2018.

[25] *Financial Times*, 04/05.02.17.

[26] Markoff, J., (2017). 'New Test For Computers: Grading Essays At College Level'. *Nytimes.Com*. Accessed 20.02.2018.
http://www.nytimes.com/2013/04/05/science/new-test-for-computers-grading-essays-at-college-level.html.

the next topic on a course. Advances in real-time assessment enabled by AI will virtually eliminate this waiting period, and ensure feedback comes when most useful for learning.

The Hewlett Foundation introduced a prize in 2012 for the development of automatic grading systems, and EdX introduced one in 2013. Not everyone though is a fan of machine marking. Les Perelman at Massachusetts Institute of Technology (MIT) is one such critic and drew attention by crafting essays that were gibberish, but which scored highly on the automated graders. We are right to be cautious, but Mark D Shermis's thoughts are instructive too "often [criticisms] come from very prestigious institutions where, in fact, they do a much better job of providing feedback than a machine ever could [but] there seems to be a lack of appreciation of what is actually going on in the world."[27]

Improvements in technology will iron out the problems and mean that students will benefit from real time attention, with individually-tailored assessments, and personalised feedback on how to improve performance. Machines are a lot smarter too at spotting the students who are cheating on assignments. ProctorU is one product that helps ensure honesty and integrity in exams online worldwide. Teachers will in future still monitor their students' progress, but not be shaping their assessments nor marking them. The physical (or virtual) presence of other students though will remain central to student learning, as it is only by listening to how other

---

[27] Ibid.

students respond that students share and gain, assess their own progress against their peer group, and ensure insights and learning will be deepened.

5. Setting exams and reporting/the development of autonomous learning

The final task of the teacher is to prepare their students for exams and assessments at the end of each year, stage or level of study, to mark and grade the student (depending on the jurisdiction), and to write terminal reports and references for the next level of education or for a future employer. All this will be swept away by AI. The all-conquering cumulative exam is going to die and we should celebrate its death. Not because it has been wholly bad but because its ubiquity has been an inadequate good. In its place will be attention to continuous data reporting, and real time of feedback that will help students discover how to learn autonomously and how to address any deficiencies on their own.

In the factory model of education, students were given greater autonomy in their education as they progressed along the conveyor belt year by year. In the highly structured school environment, jumps in the degree of "freedom" though were so mild that it prevented many school leavers from acquiring the vital skills to become autonomous learners. It largely assumed that when it came to coping in FE, HE or work, students would just "figure it out". Many did eventually: but too many did not. With the aid of AI, however, students will be much better prepared to become autonomous learners. "Current exams" says Stephen Heppell, "are very blunt. Students learn nothing about how to do better. All this will change".[28]

Computer-based assessment could "displace" final exams: "the technology exists now", says Simon Lebus in February 2018, head of the UK's Cambridge Assessment exam company.[29] Zzish, a UK EdTech company, launched its plan in 2017 to use all the new data available to give governments round the world real time information on student and school performance to enhance achievement. The age of the monolithic exam is drawing to a spluttering end.

Turning now to developing autonomous learners, we see it as built on several tenets: "learning must be personalised, competency-based, accessible any time/anywhere, and owned by the student," according to one report.[30] The role of the school will equally change its approach from 'Here's your study guide and here's your answer sheet' to 'How do you want to learn the content, and how can we support you?'[31] Schools have always found it difficult to develop self-directed learners as universities demand: AI will help here enormously.

---

[28] Stephen Heppell, 4.01.2018.

[29] *Time Educational Supplement*, February 2018.

[30] 'Student-Centered Learning - Education Writers Association'. 2016. *Ewa.Org*. Accessed 21.02.2018. https://www.ewa.org/student-centered-learning.

[31] Richmond, E. (2014). 'When Students Take Over The Classroom'. *The Atlantic*. Accessed 21.02.2018. https://www.theatlantic.com/education/archive/2014/10/what-happens-when-students-control-their-own-education/381828/.

The wealth of data produced by students week on week will equally allow AI to produce fully tracked CVs on each student's performance, as well as link the student to optimal higher education courses and ideal jobs. Employers have already started creating their own training programs to identify and develop the most suitable talents among staff. In the future, it will matter much less whether a student has particular grades in school exams or a particular degree classification, as employers will be able to draw on considerably more comprehensive and forensic information about each candidate. An evolving record of every student's abilities and performance will be recorded on a distributed and immutable register, with Blockchain to the fore, which we return to later.

Will AI (VR, AR and MR) apply to all subjects?

It is widely assumed the new AI technologies will principally be applicable to STEM subjects, then to social services, and far less to the humanities. Because answers are (mostly) right or wrong in STEM, it is easy to understand why this thinking has taken hold. But AI and associated technologies will make its impact on all subjects in school, while helping develop some we have not yet seen.

English might be deemed the least accessible. Yet the software Unity allows the Anglo-Saxon poem *Beowulf* to be translated into a 3D reality, allowing students to wander around the setting of the poem and interact with the characters.[32] Sarah Ellis of the Royal Shakespeare Company (RSC) is working at the cutting edge of technology and creativity, to allow the plays to be performed by the RSC's actors in a school hall or on a table at home in 3D.[33] "It is designed in part to connect with the way the young see the world", she says. Languages will be taught by robots and chatbots, says Plymouth University's Tony Belpaeme: "If a robot explains something, you're going to take away more from it".[34] History will be transformed too. UCL's Valerio Signorelli speaks of "a step towards an immersive history ... that is close, shared and intimate".[35] The possibilities for bringing History to life, as well as the classics, are prodigious.

AI will not be, nor will ever be, replacing human's abilities in the arts and creativity, which is another reason why we see them as so central to schools in the future. "Children are good at using their imagination and creativity ... this innate human ability is fiendishly difficult to train software and computers to do ... luckily for us, robots are hopeless on that front".[36] The fact that digital machines find difficult tasks (e.g. winning at chess) easy and easy tasks difficult (e.g. walking across a room) has been termed 'Moravec's paradox'. But is walking really 'easy'.

Social, Emotional and Special Needs Learning

AI will help those too with special education needs and disabilities (SEND). These students, for all the dedicated

---

[32] *Time Educational Supplement* Ed Tech Supplement, 2017, p. 34.

[33] Interview, Sarah Ellis, 23.03.2018.

[34] *The Times*, 27.01.2016.

[35] *Time Educational Supplement* Ed Tech Supplement, 2017.

[36] Silva, R. (2018). *London Evening Standard*, 15.03.

work of many, were too often marginalised in the factory model, less through deliberate neglect than because the system was calibrated to the average student, and time as well as money was short.

SEND students are benefitting from emerging products including 'Branching Minds' which uses the latest developments in learning science and academic research to help respond to their differing needs. 'Education Modified' meanwhile is aimed specifically at students whose "diagnosis is there but it is not so bad that they need to be kept out of school".[37] It allows teachers to track students' behaviour and responses to tune interventions.

Robot-style AI learning devices have proved particularly successful in helping those with physical difficulties. A Swedish company No Isolation manufactures a robot, Bee that allows children unable to attend school to participate in the classroom and engage with the teacher and students by having a robot in the class that acts as their eyes and ears. It came to the UK in 2017.[38] Many general purpose applications currently in use are beginning to be applied to education such as the telepresence robot from Double Robotics.

How might AI help students with Social and Skills as referred to in our 'School Journey' diagram? Already, a number of holistic initiatives and products are coming onto the market which point the way. A harbinger is New York University's (NYU) Steinhardt School, whose EdTech programme 'StartEd' helps students develop their emotional intelligence. Managing director Ash Kaluarachchi extols the

---

[37] Ibid.
[38] *Daily Telegraph,* 31.08.2017.

virtues of students learning about concepts including empathy and integrity: "Such topics were traditionally reserved for the brightest students [but] are now getting scaled through technology".[39] 'Peekapak' is another company in this space: it uses research-based learning and digital games to teach students about gratitude, teamwork and respect. 'Panorama Education' is another: used already by some 10% of US school students, it surveys them regularly to assist in their personal growth and development.

'SchoolHack', based in Vermont, USA, is also spreading rapidly in the US, and encourages personal development through an on-line personal development platform. 'Hello Ruby' is a Finnish product that helps younger children think through creative and artistic programmes, while 'Emerge' in London, an Ed Tech accelerator, has invested in Pi-Top, which has built a desktop and laptop PC around the Raspberry Pi to help students develop tech skills. We are only in the foothills. Expect by 2030 AI-assisted learning to improve very significantly the lot of SEND students and in character and skills education.

An integrated Case Study: One Laptop Per Child (OLPC) and AI

New technology will have its most transformative education and hence life prospects of children in the developing world who do not at present benefit from sufficient good quality teachers. The controversial 'One Laptop Per Child' (OLPC) was founded in 2005 on the premise that though these children

---

[39] Worth, J., (2018). 'What Next for EdTech', *Time Educational Supplement* Guide to Ed Tech.

may lack opportunity and resources, they do not lack capability. It aims to provide "an ultra-low-cost, powerful, rugged, low-power" laptop to every child on the planet.

A recent OLPC initiative took place in two remote Ethiopian villages. The company dropped off a box containing android tablets preloaded with educational programmes and no instructions. Here's what happened next, according to David Talbot.

> "We thought the kids would play with the boxes. Within four minutes, one kid not only opened the box, found the on-off switch ... powered it up. Within five days, they were using 47 apps per child, per day. Within two weeks, they were singing ABC songs in the village, and within five months, they had hacked Android."[40]

This echoes the celebrated 1999 experiment when Ed Tech pioneer Sugata Mitra and colleagues placed a computer in a wall close by their IT office in New Delhi, near an extensive slum. In his own words: "What happened next astonished us. Children came running out of the nearest slum and glued themselves to the computer ... A few hours later ... the children were actively surfing the web".[41] Not all are

---

[40] Talbot, D. (n.d.). 'Given Tablets but No Teachers, Ethiopian Children Teach Themselves'. *MIT Technology Review*. Accessed February 2, 2018.
https://www.technologyreview.com/s/506466/given-tablets-but-no-teachers-ethiopian-children-teach-themselves/.
[41] Mitra, S. (2012). Edutopia, 03.02.

impressed, Donald Clark for one, who said it smacks of educational colonialism.[42]

These two episodes suggest however, how even 'untutored' children can achieve astonishing results, as long as they ae given sufficient guidance and motivating content. The 'KA-Pi' is an ambitious project to deliver Khan Academy's content from a Raspberry Pi. There would be no need even for an internet connection: local area networks can be set up and students can use wired or wireless access. Bridge International Academies, a US for-profit company, is one of the leading providers of Ed Tech currently in the developing world which has teachers delivering heavily-scripted lessons from electronic tablets. Teacher unions are not impressed with its standards and clashed with it.[43] Henry Warren is convinced these problems can be overcome.[44] This optimism lies behind the $15M Global Learning Xprize competition for those whose software "would enable children in developing countries to teach themselves basic reading, writing and arithmetic within 15 months".[45]

It is still premature to make bold claims about how education can be transformed through AI for the most deprived children. OLPC and similar initiatives require patience and a longer record of experience. It remains to be proved if dropping off tablets will spontaneously result in children teaching themselves to read. But the new technology, bolstered by AI machine learning, has the potential to, and we

[42] Clark, D. (2013) Plan B Blogspot, 02.06.
[43] *Times Educational Supplement*, 06.04.18.
[44] Interview with Henry Warren, 02.02.18.
[45] *Times Educational Supplement*, 06.04.18.

believe will, transform education for the world's children most unlikely to receive a conventional quality education. Imagine if we could, in the vein of the KA-Pi project, provide AI solar powered computers for all, stored in weather resistant casing, offering videos, text and lessons, with adaptive learning technology to serve as teacher and mentor. The technology can make learning plans, administer and grade assessments, provide feedback, all the while personalising the entire experience using data gathered from the students' tablet use. Such a system is theoretically possible today.

We cannot escape the question of cost. At present, the technologies that have the potential to make the most impact can be prohibitively expensive, as we have seen in the Silicon Valley experimental schools. So the concern is real that AI might deepen rather than mitigate existing educational divisions. Against this worrying possibility is the certainty that costs will fall dramatically. The anxiety is reduced too by appreciating the progressive role parents can play in the development. As Priya Lakhani and Rose Luckin put it, "The places most ripe for innovation are deprived areas in Africa, India and the Far East where parents are profoundly ambitious for their children's education: whereas in the Western world, the performance of students can be held back because parents do not always prioritise education to the same extent."[46] As we have seen also, it is not just in Africa that teachers are badly needed: they are in Britain and the US too.

---

[46] Interview with Priya Lakhani and Rose Luckin, 07.02.2018.

Will we need Teachers in the Future?

When the fourth education evolution arrives, what will be left for teachers to do? We do not believe that it is either possible or desirable for AI to eliminate teachers from education. The application of AI places more responsibility for learning certainly in the hands of the student, for how their time is spent and on what, even from a young age. Learners take time and encouragement to become more autonomous. The job of teacher will thus increasingly become to structure students' learning, help them with confusions and difficulties, run whole-class learning discussions, look after students pastorally, and guide them through their wider personal, social, cultural, sporting and character development.

So predictions by prophets of the future, in ways explicit and liminal, who suggest that the increased application of AI in schools will mean the disappearance of the teacher, are alarmist and will not come about. Teachers today are asked to perform a wide range of duties which takes them far away from teaching students. They are being prevented from giving their best energies to the task of developing the young by a mountain of administration and routine. "A recent survey sought the views of more than 3,000 teachers, with more than half saying they worked more than 55 hours a week, including nearly a quarter who said they worked more than 60 hours."[47] The factory model of education saw ever greater administrative demands on the teacher, not less.

---

[47] Adams, R. 2017. 'Demanding Workload Driving Young Teachers out of Profession'. *The Guardian*. Accessed 19.02.2018. https://www.theguardian.com/education/2017/apr/15/demanding-workload-driving-young-teachers-out-of-profession.

AI will change however the job of the teacher forever. There can be no going back. By *supporting* teaching in all their traditional five tasks, AI will usher in the biggest change the profession has ever seen. Imminent advances in virtual technologies will mean too that teachers no longer have to be physically present to offer their services. Students in remote Ethiopian villages will be able to receive supplementary mathematics instruction from a teacher in Brighton. Or Baltimore. Or Bangalore. The *Economist* concluded its 2017 survey of AI: "Education software is not making teaching obsolete. If anything it is making the craft of teaching more important".[48] There can be no complacency though: Jim Thompson gives a stark warning "Teachers will have a role if they work with the technology. If not, the technology will work round them".[49]

Teacher training will be revolutionised by the coming of AI. Teachers will be prepared for changed roles, while the technology will help them anticipate the challenges they will face, much as pilots learn on simulators. Chatbots will help them prepare for handling challenging students, and how to learn more about managing their own stress. Professional development of teachers will be revolutionised by AI and made much more stimulating the world over. Deadly PowerPoint presentations on the latest wheeze in teaching (confession: I've given a few myself) will be confined to the trash bin of history.

---

[48] *The Economist*, 22.07.17.
[49] Thompson, J. (2017). 23 December.

Will we need Physical Schools in the Future?

Will schools as physical entities be needed in the age of AI? What will be the point of students coming to school when the technology becomes the teacher? Home schooling has been on the increase in the developing world. In the UK, just over 15,000 children were classified as home taught in 2011: five years later, that figure had doubled to nearly 30,000.[50] The police and inspection regimes have become concerned by the increase because of risks of parental abuse or radicalisation. Psychologists worry about loss of opportunities for social and emotional learning, which are restricted where a child is taught at home – in a school effectively of one. This is the crux. Children in the future might be perfectly well served in their learning by spending their 'school day' at home in front of their AI technology, thereby saving travel time and inconvenience. But schools exist to educate human beings, and, for all the skills of the new technologies in enhancing emotional learning, education, and life, is and will always remain fundamentally *social* activity. So, we will need schools in 2030, 2050 and in all likelihood 2100. But they will look and feel different, as a contemporary open plan office looks different to 1970s offices.

Smart Schools

No one 'smart school', which highlights the human over the mechanical, exists in 2018. But elements of them are in evidence in schools worldwide. They will appear by 2030 and be common by 2050. Built of natural materials which are local

---

[50] Thomson, A. (2018). 'Take Home Schooling out of the Shadows', *The Times,* 28.02.

to the area in which the school is located (early twentieth century British architect Edwin Lutyens was a doyen of this approach), they will have green areas and plants inside and out. They will be powered and watered by local sustainable supplies (Ashley Primary School in Walton, UK, does this), and some of their food will be grown by the students. They will have animals which students will help look after.

Inside, there will be series of large open-plan spaces, with flexible seating, which students will use to work in alone or participate in discussions, projects and group work in designated zones. The school day will allow for some 30% of time in front of each child's AI software, which will give them individual learning plans. Human values will permeate every pore of the school's curriculum, values and structure. Dedicated space will be given to the arts and physical activity, both of which will figure prominently in the smart school. Areas will be set aside for quiet reflection. Well-being, flourishing, curiosity, creativity and the formation of individual character will lie at the heart of the education philosophy, which will develop all the children's aptitudes. Schools will be smaller in size than at present and be rooted in their local communities. Teachers will be present in similar numbers to today, but their roles will be different, as described above, and teaching assistants (both human and AI) will be ubiquitous.

We finish thus on a note of caution. AI and digital technology is neither a good nor an evil in itself: it has value only in as far as it allows us to enhance what it means to be human beings at our best. Joe Clement and Matt Miles published a useful warning in early 2018 about how AI and technology can make students less able, warning against the "assumptions perpetuated by the protechnology movement". We will all be better for heeding such warnings[51] while remembering that *nothing* will matter more in ensuring that AI is used for the best in the world ensuring that we have the right education system.

---

[51] Clement, J. and Miles, M. (2018). 'Screen Schooled: Two Veteran Teachers Expose How Technology Overuse is Making Our Kids Dumber'. *Times Educational Supplement*, 7.02.

Is this the university of the future?

Chapter Eight:

Universities of the future

Universities have been under considerable pressure worldwide in the last decade. This may be nothing though compared to the pressures they will face in the coming decade, from multiple quarters. In the age of quick-fix Uber, Amazon and Airbnb, what use for the long-form fixed-location university degree? Developments in AI and robotics will bring 'Olympian' levels of competition and pressure to universities globally said Vice-Chancellor of Sheffield University Keith Burnett, at the Asia Universities Summit in February 2018[1]. The following month, the University of London cut the price of its degrees by offering them on-line to attract a new market of part-time students. Daphne Koller, President of on-line company Coursera, pronounced that this was the tip of a new revolution. Online degrees are "more affordable and more accessible": hitherto they had been mostly for short courses from lesser providers, but within five years, she predicted: "leading universities will offer fully accredited undergraduate courses online".[2]

Whether universities offer students and governments value for money is one of the biggest questions of our age:

---

[1] *Times Higher Education*, 15.08.18.
[2] Sean Coughlan, BBC, 06.07.16.

Bryan Caplan[3] of George Mason University is one of those who emphatically thinks it doesn't. "Some of education's most heralded achievements are tiny at best", he writes. "We'd all like the education system to enrich our society and our soul. In practice, it's bad at both".[4] He's not just another wildman of academe. Laurence Brockliss, author of the official history of Oxford University, said that new technologies have the potential to make even universities like Oxford; "redundant" and it is "only a matter of time" before online transforms HE forever.[5] Is this the beginning of the end of the traditional residential university?

Why Universities?

The university came into being in the second education revolution era because of the call from religious, legal, governmental and commercial entities for people to acquire certain skills, which they absorbed from lectures and from books[6]. Before the advent of printing, when books had to be produced and reproduced manually, it was natural for education to spring up in close proximity to the great centres of learning and libraries, the temples of the university. As a consequence, expertise became concentrated in a small number of ancient locations, and students wishing to become

---

[3] *Times Higher Education*, 08.03.18.

[4] Bryan Caplan, C., (2018) *The Case Against Education: why the Education System is a Waste of Time and Money*, Princeton: Princeton University Press.

[5] Brockliss, L., (2016). *The University of Oxford: A History*. Oxford: Oxford University Press.

[6] Seldon, A., (2011). 'Why Schools? Why Universities?' Cass Foundation.

educated in them had physically to travel and set up lodgings where the experts and texts were located. This background helps explain why universities now face an existential threat.

A university degree was the guarantor that a student had become educated to an agreed and standardised level. Any two degrees of equal classification would theoretically indicate similar ability in students, regardless of the awarding institution or jurisdiction. The rapid spread of universities, not all of even quality, meant it became impossible to guarantee uniformity of standards. In the past, possession of a university degree was indication that the holder was themselves eligible to teach at any institution with no further examination. What a university degree may say now is that a student can be further shaped, not that they are the finished product.

In his 1963 BBC's Reith lectures, Albert Sloman, Vice Chancellor of the newly-opened Essex University, said universities had two primary functions, to teach and to engage in research (that is what "marks them out as universities", he said).[7] Sloman gave weight to the role universities had helping produce "the kind of man [sic] we believe that industry needs" but equally stressed their role in helping produce "rounded human beings", as when he spoke about the role of the university in the "fulfilment of lives".[8] This was encouraging.

The same year saw the publication of the Report of the Robbins Committee on Higher Education, which envisaged the doubling of university participation from 7% to 15% in

---

[7] Sloman, A. (1963). *A University in the Making*, Reith Lectures.
[8] Ibid. p. 63.

1980[9]. Nearly fifty years after Robbins, the higher education sector has expanded a further three times, and it is barely recognisable from the socially-elite, male-dominated institutions of 1963. Ivor Crewe, one of Sloman's successors as Vice Chancellor at Essex, described in 2009 the almost impossible demands on universities. 'Universities' are now expected to "create apparently useful knowledge and transfer it to businesses ... [be] proving the professional training for almost all the public services ... helping local schools to raise their standards and ambitions ... [and] to promote social mobility by widening participation".[10] Since then the burden of expectation on universities has intensified still more.

Will universities still exist in 2050 in anything like their current physical form? The continued need for them is far less obvious than the continuation of schools, once the AI revolution arrives. There is no unassailable case why residential universities, which arrived during the second revolution phase, flourished and spread rapidly during the third, will survive long into the fourth. In favour of their continuation though are many factors. They serve as networking centres: it is within them that many of the professional and personal relationships are forged that students will benefit from throughout their lives. Students are able to meet with, and be taught by, accomplished academics, engage in enriching intellectual and personal development,

---

[9] *Higher education report of the Committee appointed by the Prime Minister under the Chairmanship of Lord Robbins 1961-63*, Her Majesty's Stationery Office, 1963.

[10] Crewe, I., (2009). *The Role of Universities in the 21st Century*, HMC, 06.10.

and develop their thinking about future careers. Students learn how to negotiate the world much better if they entered it directly after school. But will AI change all this?

We begin by returning to the diagram that first appeared in Chapter 3.

'The university journey'

By 2030, to the extent that it has not already happened, the academic core of universities will have been transformed by digitalisation and AI. 'Lectures' in their present form are portrayed in the diagram in dark grey because they will have been mostly replaced, at least in monologue form with a lecturer standing at the front of a hall, by online lectures which students can listen to when and where and how they choose. Lectures will become more like interactive tutorials, with the old style banks of seats in lecture theatres replaced by clusters for perhaps 5-8 students, who can interact together under the stimulus and direction of the lecturer. Traditional lectures will still be given, but by those rare figures who manage to engage students for a full hour though the power of their voice and words. They will be among the stars of the universities of the future.

'Seminars' will continue to be held in physical locations, though MOOC technology will have become much more sophisticated to allow for much more meaningful and clear interaction between distance learners online. Physical seminars will provide a principal occasion when students meet together in the same physical space for academic study. Georgia Tech have already started employing Chatbots which have led to some reduction in teaching staff. Professor Ashok

Goel said in 2016 that some students were unaware Jill Watson, their first AI teaching assistant, was not a person.[11]

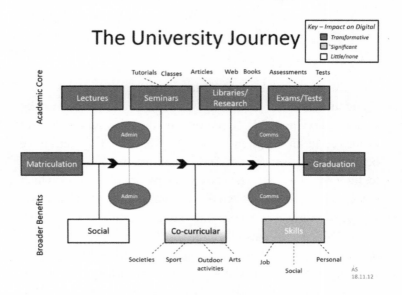

'Research' will have been transformed for students, with almost all materials that they want, and many experiments that they might need to conduct, available online, or through AR/VR. STEM research by academics will be more concentrated in expensive high-tech laboratories using AI technology. 'Libraries' will become study and learning centres: books will have been almost completely replaced by materials on-line: this will be particularly true of 'rare' books and archive records that will in future be accessed digitally without deterioration to the originals through handling them.

---

[11] Goel, A., (2016). TEDx San Francisco, 1.11.

'Exams' equally will have completely disappeared in their current form.

It is the broader benefits of university life, the social life, the co-curricular activity and the acquisition of skills which will still dictate a need for the students to meet together in one physical HE location. Many believe the main reason to go to university even after the digital revolution will be to grow up socially, and to learn how to become an adult. These benefits are profound, but are they sufficient to justify the continuation of physical buildings and universities as three dimensional entities, when the justification for doing so has tilted so far towards the 'non-academic' activities for requiring students to meet physically together?

Problems facing 21st century universities

The erosion of the case for students and teachers to be physically in one space together is one of many challenges facing universities.[12] A 2017 survey of university heads worldwide listed the impact of technology their top concern.[13] Others problems facing them include:

1. Affordability – costs are exploding, notably in the US, which is leading to increasing questions whether the economic model that has underpinned residential universities for the last 50 years will be sustainable for long into the future.

---

[12] Interview with Nick Hillman, 01.03.18.
[13] 'Rising to the Challenges of Tomorrow', Report, HEA, York, November 2017. Interview with Stephanie Marshall, 09.04.18.

2.   Maintaining quality – Africa, India and China will all see a vast increase in the provision of higher education over the next 25 years. The question is how well they can maintain a high quality and a personal education for all students in the face of the very considerable expansion in size.

3.   The challenge of autonomy – even in the United Kingdom, universities have found themselves increasingly regulated by the state, which demands accountability in return for the money it pumps into the sector. Maintaining quality and academic freedom to enquire, when autonomy is challenged and compromised by the state, is another problem likely to increase. China has negotiated this dilemma better than some, in that it manages to combine low autonomy with international quality at its top institutions.

4.   Maintaining internationalism – as the numbers of middle class parents expand across the world, they will demand a high quality education for their children. But a rise of nationalism, suspicion of overseas influences, and a rise in quality of home-grown universities, might see the high numbers of students who travel currently to university in the US and UK decline.

5.   Direct access into employment, and the decline of the ideals of liberal arts education – universities are seen increasingly by governments, and by some students, as institutions whose prime purpose is preparation for employment, rather than offering a rounded and pure

education with no specific career in mind. If universities are seen merely as passports to a job, the allure of going straight from school into work will become increasingly attractive. Many more large employers will offer in-service education directly to school leavers, obviating the need for university.

6. Mental health – despite increasing affluence worldwide, the indicators of mental illness and unhappiness among students are on the rise. Universities are blamed for not doing more, never more so than after an all too often student suicide: yet their scope is limited when students arrive at 18 having already presented difficulties. There are no easy solutions. Universities argue they are untrained to act as therapeutic institutions, many academics feel uncomfortable with a counsellor role, and the law in some countries prevents the universities communicating directly with homes. But this is a pet theme of mine, and let me say this. Universities must do more, not least by creating environments conducive to good mental health, based on the lifelong work of Professor Martin Seligman of University of Pennsylvania and mindfulness authority Jon Kabat-Zinn[14] at the University of Massachusetts Medical School. Monash University Melbourne is pioneering mindfulness in teaching its medical and other students.[15] Data analytics can be used far more imaginatively to help

---

[14] Seldon, A. and Martin, A., (2017) 'The Positive and the Mindful University', HEPI.
[15] Hassed, C., in Monash's Medical School, coordinates its programmes and has written extensively on the subject.

students by being on the front foot more. Non-engagement in the first week is a key indicator for example of future problems which analytics can diagnose early on.

7. Lifelong education – with the certainty that those in work will require new skills, and be likely to switch to altogether new occupations, as well as the spread of education into middle and old age, universities will be seen less as the preserve of the 18-22 year old, and more as institutions serving those of all ages.

8. Teaching quality and student demands – universities are under pressure to improve the quality of their teaching to satisfy ever rising student demands, while also performing at ever high levels on research. In the US, the Carnegie Foundation for the Advancement of Teaching, founded in 1905, helps support effective teaching,[16] as does the Higher Education Academy in the UK.[17]

The fourth industrial revolution: skills and the qualities demanded by future employers

The term the "fourth industrial revolution" was coined by Klaus Schwab, the German engineer and economist who founded the World Economic Forum that meets at Davos in

---

[16] Thanks to Ian Creagh, 09.04.18.
[17] Seldon, A., (2016). 'Solving the Conundrum, Teaching and Learning at British Universities', London: Social market Foundation.

Switzerland. In 2016, he published "The Fourth Industrial Revolution",[18] and "Mastering the fourth industrial revolution" was the theme of the 2016 annual meeting in Davos. The first industrial revolution Schwab says took place in the 18th and 19th centuries in Europe and America, the period when rural societies became industrial and urban, exploiting the technology of the steam engine. The second industrial revolution occurred between 1870 and 1914, utilising electricity, telephone, light bulb and the internal combustion engine. The third revolution did not begin until the 1980s, catalysed by the ICT revolution and the internet.

Schwab argues that the fourth industrial revolution, which is about AI, robotics, quantum computing, the internet of things and more, is fundamentally different to the earlier three that were all characterised by advances in technology. The fourth revolution will have a transformative impact on government, business and all other organisations, because of the inter-connectivity.

The fourth industrial revolution is of course equally the fourth education revolution. Yeon-Cheon Oh, formerly Head of Seoul National University, is one of many to believe that universities are "very, very static" in resisting the changes that need to be made to accommodate the fourth revolution[19]. A growing consensus is emerging that universities need to do much more to develop in students the employment skills that AI and robotics will never be able to replace. What might these twenty first century skills be?

---

[18] Schwab, K., (2016) *The Fourth Industrial Revolution,* New York: Crown Business.
[19] *Times Higher Education,* 23.03.17.

1. Creativity

Academics debate the extent to which machines will be able to think imaginatively and creatively. It is already clear that highly innovative thinking was evident in the successful defeats of human champions at both chess and 'Go', but human creativity is of a different order, and needs to be nurtured more in our universities (as in schools). As MIT academics Erik Brynjolfsson and Andrew McAfee have written in their book *The Second Machine Age*: "we have never seen a truly creative machine or an entrepreneurial one or an innovative one".[20] Creativity is a uniquely human but not an inevitably human quality: it needs to be drawn out of students, i.e. *educare*, at university. Whether graduates go on to work in large corporations or for themselves, they will all need an entrepreneurial, active-mindset outlook.

2. Social intelligence

Machines can certainly be trained to feign human empathy: but they can never *feel* emotions. Social intelligence is a quality that can be developed, and will need to be given a much higher priority in universities in the future. Carl Frey and Michael Osborne from Oxford University have said "while algorithms and robots can now produce some aspects of social interaction, the real-time recognition of natural human emotion remains a challenging problem, and the ability to respond intelligently to such inputs is even more difficult". Ian

---

[20] *Times Higher Education*, 28.07.16.

Goldin, former Director of the Oxford Martin School, is clear: machines "cannot give what is uniquely human, which is love, compassion and sympathetic reaction".[21] STEM, social science, humanities and other graduates all need to have their human qualities developed for more deliberately at university.

3. Ethics and moral choice

Moral behaviour and good character underpin good education, or should do, though the drive for exam success as the sole measure for the evaluation of the success of educational institutions has tended to negate or at least to downplay its value. Nevertheless, to make moral choices is the essence of what it means to be human, and only human beings should decide ethical questions about the future of other humans, animals, and the survival of the planet. Humanities may not give students the same sense of certainty that sciences, and even the social sciences, purport to give: but the sense of human value that they impart could become even more important, not least with humanities under threat in many universities in favour of more utilitarian courses. But again, *all* students need a thorough grounding and exposure to an ethical and moral education, and to have their characters development equally with their intellects.

4. Dexterity

Robots are becoming increasingly dexterous and life-like, but it is doubtful if they will ever be able to replicate the

---

[21] *Times Higher Education*, 28.07.16.

skill and deftness of the human being. Nor would we want them to. It is most unlikely we will want to go to a stadium to see robots taking part in sporting activities, or think it right that robots take critical decisions over life and death in war, or that we would want them to look after our elderly parents or children to the exclusion of ourselves. Universities need to rediscover the education of the physical body, which was often marginalised in the third education revolution. The body may or may not be a machine. But we need to teach our students better how it works, how to befriend it, how to connect it with the mind. Physical intelligence as we saw in Chapter Four, is lost when we allow ourselves to think that the human mind is all important. It isn't.

What will be the jobs for future graduates in the future?

We have argued throughout that education should develop *all* the aptitudes of the student, to help them prepare for living a meaningful life in society and at work. But what exactly is the work of the future for which universities will be preparing the young? Because at present, universities, like schools, are locked into set ways of delivering education and are not adjusting the curricula they have on offer sufficiently quickly. The literature on this subject is vast, but inconclusive. One of the best texts is by Richard and Daniel Susskind, *The Future of the Professions* (2015)[22]. This is their contention:

---

[22] Susskind, R. and Susskind, D. (2015) *The Future of the Professions. How technology will transform the work of human experts,* Oxford: Oxford University Press, 2015.

"Machines are becoming increasingly capable and are taking on more and more tasks that were once the exclusive province of human professionals. While new tasks will no doubt arise in years to come, machines are likely in time to take on many of these as well. In the medium term, during the 2020s, this will not mean unemployment but retraining and redeployment. In the longer run, however, we find it hard to avoid the conclusion that there will be a steady decline in the need for traditional flesh and blood professions."[23]

Expert opinion has given weight to their conclusion. A celebrated study from the Oxford Martin School in 2013 predicted that nearly half of US jobs would be at risk from digitalisation within the following twenty years[24]. Studies from McKinsey[25] and PriceWaterhouseCoopers[26] similarly suggested up to half of all jobs would disappear within the following twenty years.[27]

A report published by the Institute for Public Policy Research (IPPR) think-tank in 2017 was equally bleak, suggesting that digitalisation would wipe out a third of jobs in

---

[23] Paperback edition 2017, p. iX

[24] Frey, C.B. and Osborne, M. (2013). 'The Future of Employment: how Susceptible are jobs to Computerisation?' Oxford Martin School, September.

[25] McKinsey Global Institute, 'A Future that Works: Automation, Employment, and Productivity', January 2017

[26] PricewaterhouseCoopers, 'UK Economic Outlook', Section 4 'Will Robots Steal our Jobs? The Potential Impact of Automation on the UK and other Major Economies', March 2017.

[27] TAG, 04.11.17

the UK, specifying that some deprived areas would be even worse affected, including the north-east of England and north-eastern Ireland. Carys Roberts, one of the authors, said: "some people will get a pay rise, while others are trapped in low-pay, low-productivity centres. To avoid inequality rising, the government should look at ways to spread capital ownership and make sure everyone benefits from increased automation". The report singled out agriculture, transport, food processing and administration as areas at greatest risk, with women slightly more in danger of losing their jobs than men.[28] A mood of forlorn acceptance was taking hold. Sky's Economics Editor Ed Conway wrote in 2017: "it is increasingly apparent that Britain is rolling out the red carpet for the robots at the expense of its workers".[29] Foteini Agrafioti, head of the AI wing of the Royal Bank of Canada, says that robots are "still quite far away from replicating high-level [human] reasoning"; while it is clear human reasoning in the professions – accounting, banking, radiology, law, journalism – is being challenged by AI already.[30]

Not everyone is as pessimistic. The OECD produced a less alarming report in 2016, predicting that across the 21 OECD countries, only 9% of jobs would be automatable. It found digital machines were less likely to be able to replicate creativity, social interaction and the subtlety of human-to-human contact. But in April 2018, the OECD was gloomy again, warning some 66m workers in developing countries they faced unemployment. Economist Tommy Stubbing was

---

[28] *The Times,* 28.12.17.
[29] *The Times,* 31.03.17.
[30] *The Daily Telegraph,* 29.08.17.

provoked to write "the cumulative effect of all these studies is a growing conviction that the coming technological revolution will leave millions without work ... android hysteria is a thriving industry".[31]

In 2018, the Oxford Martin School teamed up with the education company Pearson and the innovation foundation Nesta to produce a report which concentrated on the jobs that digital and AI technology might *create,* rather than focussing on those that might be destroyed. It set itself up to challenge "the false alarmism that contributes to a culture of risk aversion and holds back technology adoption, innovation and growth". The report said that an optimistic approach is particularly important "to countries like the US and the UK, which already face structurally productivity problems".[32] It concluded by suggesting ten qualities which are most likely to correlate with future needs of employers: "judgement and decision making; fluency of ideas; active learning; systems evaluation; originality; learning strategies; deductive reasoning; complex problem solving; systems analysis and monitoring".

It is right to be optimistic about the future, but we must also be realistic. Our concern is not just with the quantity of jobs: it is also with their nature and meaningful *quality.* It is not going to satisfy graduates who have worked hard at school and university if they go on to careers where all the difficult intellectual work is undertaken by computers. We return to this question of quality of work in the final chapters. Nor do

[31] *The Sunday Times,* 08.04.18.

[32] Bakhshi, H., Downing, J.M., Osborne, M.A., Schneider, P.N., (2018). 'The Future of Skills: Employment in 2030', Oxford Martin School.

we believe that a world of leisure will satisfy humans, as some blithely believe, arguing for a universal basic income for all and a life in la-la land.

Perhaps the biggest lesson that universities should heed is the need to rethink the way they are preparing students for the world of work, given that such preparation will always be part of a university's purpose, even when offering pure academic degrees. Harvard's David Deming made this case in 2015,[33] when he found that nearly all job-growth since 1980 in the US had been in occupations that are social-skill intensive, and that social and human skills are thus what we should be teaching our students, alongside cognitive skills. Yet the traditional factory model trundles on, minimising human skills in favour of the very cognitive skills in which algorithms will always outperform humans. One way of addressing this would be to devise an 'AI-proof' or 'robot-proof' HE education.

A 'Robot-proof' University Education

Joseph E Aoun is President of Northeastern University in the US. He has thought more deeply than many university leaders about the adjustments that will be needed from universities in the age of AI. As he writes, "to ensure that graduates are "robot-proof" in the work place, institutions of higher learning will have to re-balance their curricula".[34] Aoun believes that this requires a new offer to students from

---

[33] Deming, D.J., (2015). 'The Growing Importance of Society Skills in the Labor Market', MBER Working Paper, August, revised 2017.
[34] Auon, J.E., (2017). *Robot-proof. Higher Education in the Age of Artificial Intelligence,* Boston. MA: Massachusetts Institute of Technology Press, p XVII.

universities, which he terms "humanics". Its goal is nurturing 'our species' unique traits of creativity and flexibility, building 'on our innate strengths' to allow students "to compete in a labor market in which brilliant machines work alongside human professionals".[35]

Humanics he explains has a "two-fold nature". The first consists of the "new literacies". Existing literacies in reading and writing, as well as numeracy, will no longer be sufficient alone. In future, universities need to add 'data literacy', to help students read, analyse and utilise the ever-growing volumes of information, 'technological literacy', which is necessary to give students a grounding in coding and engineering principles so they might understand how digital machines work, and finally, 'human literacy', to teach students about the humanities, design and communication, so they can understand and operate better in a human world.

The second aspect of humanics he says are the "cognitive capacities" or higher-order mental skills, mind-sets or ways of thinking about the world. These demand four separate skills. The first is "systems thinking, the ability to view an enterprise, machine or subject holistically and make connections between its functions in an integrated way". The second is "entrepreneurship", which is about applying the creative mind to the world of work and the economy. The third is "cultural agility", necessary for teaching students how to conduct themselves in complex, global environments, and understand different cultures and people. The fourth capacity, "critical thinking", which lies at the heart of the International

---

[35] Ibid, pXVIII.

229

Baccalaureate (IB), gives students the tools to engage in rational analysis and discernment.

Aoun is interested in developing lifelong learners for the new world they will face. By 2025, the planet will contain eight billion inhabitants who will have very different demands and expectations of life: nevertheless "we can predict that computers and robots and artificial intelligence will be even more intricately intertwined into the fabric of our personal and professional lives". Higher education he believes has a unique responsibility helping not just its students but all humanity adjust to this new world.

We do not know what universities will look like in 2030. But Aoun's humanics is a serious guide to the skills that are needed now at university (and indeed schools). There are others we suggest too.

What will drive change in higher education?

A celebrated survey in the *Times Higher Education* at the end of 2015 invited senior figures from universities to imagine how the sector might look in the year 2030. Only one of the seven asked mentioned artificial intelligence as a significant shaper of the future. There are several visionaries in the sector, like Helen Higson at Aston, Catherine O'Malley at Nottingham, and Wendy Hall at Southampton. But too often, leaders and academics are turning a blind eye to the AI revolution thumping down the track towards them: there are too many more immediate concerns that occupy their time. We sympathise. But standing still is not an option for higher education any more than it is for schools. Change is being driven by at least three factors:

1. Technology

MOOCs and online lectures are the tip of the iceberg. AI algorithms and adaptive learning is just beginning to personalise learning for HE students in the same way it is doing in schools. The technology is able to gain a penetrating insight into the mind, learning preferences and motivations of each individual student which allows them to benefit from personally tailored material and instruction. Virtual avatars and chatbots assess student learning in seminars either working directly with the student, or assisting the seminar leader by alerting them where a student is finding difficulty, and suggesting ways to help advance their learning. The New Media Consortia's horizon report in 2017 noted that these technologies will help teaching "in ways that more intuitively respond and engage with students", and equally will make a profound impact on research.[36] Wendy Hall, highlights the role that powerful increases in processing power and storage ability have made in allowing us the "capacity to build intelligent systems that can learn and begin to 'think' for themselves".[37]

2. Evolution and understanding of learning and the brain

Our understanding of how students learn, the way the brain works, and how to teach optimally, are progressing at a formidably quick rate. Finnish educator Pasi Sahlberg has argued the factor impeding the adoption of AI is not

---

[36] NMC. Horizon Report 2017 Higher Education edition.
[37] *Times Higher Education*, 26.12.17.

the technology but that "we don't know enough what good teaching is".[38] Dan Schwartz and Candace Thillie of Stanford University wrote that by 2030, "science will have made substantial progress in understanding how people learn to produce conditions that optimise learning".[39] The fields of neuroscience, neurology, psychiatry and psychology are all working together to help us understand how long and short term memory works, how the brain can best absorb information, and how to enhance the mind's effectiveness. The brain may or may not be a highly complex computer: but the evolution of this new learning will allow computers of the future to relate far more clearly to the minds of the future.

3   The impact of AI and automation on jobs

Michael Spence, Vice Chancellor of the University of Sydney, has been in the vanguard of calling for universities to help educate students to "tell machines what to do". He sets great store by teaching problem-solving and has been trying to re-design his university's programmes by establishing multi-disciplinary teams of students working together to tackle real life challenges. "The skills that the machines won't have particularly well – creativity, inter-personal skills, the ability to think laterally – [these are] the kinds of skills that you need". He does not minimise the difficulty of this transition, not the least from the parents, who want their children to take

---

[38] See Sahlberg P., (2011). 'Finnish Lessons: What can the World Learn from Educational Change in Finland?'
[39] *Times Higher Education*, 24.12.15

degrees in traditional subjects, which he describes as "table and chair" subjects with a view to "going on to the table and chair industry".[40] Mike Sharples of the Open University agrees that universities should be teaching these skills, along with global and technological awareness. They need to help students understand how they will have to work with AI systems in the future: "it's done piecemeal in some universities", he says, "but I don't think that any university does it in any systematic way".[41]

Types of Universities in the Future

Universities, for all their diversity across the world, will become still more so over the next 25 years, under the pressures of financial, social and above all technological change. The 'Carnegie Classification' of institutions of higher education, created in 1973, attempts to categorise the different types of universities and colleges in the United States. All accredited-degree granting universities and colleges across the US are described as follows: Doctorate-granting universities, with a high research focus; Masters' colleges, which focus on Masters' degrees while still undertaking research; Baccalaureate colleges, which see the focus on bachelors' degrees; Associate colleges, whose highest award is the associate degree; Special focus institutions, defined as offering degrees in a single field or set of related fields, and 'Tribal Colleges,' belonging to the American Indian HE consortium.

---

[40] *Times Higher Education,* 03.08.17.
[41] *Times Higher Education*, 03.08.17.

A more international and forward-looking model of university archetypes have been outlined by Glyn Davis, formerly Vice Chancellor of the University of Melbourne[42]. The 'influencer' university is international in perspective, strongly driven by research and tackling the major issues facing each individual country and the world. The 'agile' university is rich in AI and digital technology, and dedicated to applied research as well as giving students a competitive advantage. The 'consultant' university is focussed on the job market and its purpose is to serve organisational clients, who buy expert advice, education and research/innovation to boost their own performance. Finally, the 'community' university is less interested in national and international league tables, and has its *raison d'être* principally in serving local students and business, and championing them on national stages.

The Carnegie and Glyn Davis models are useful, especially the latter, but we need to go further to visualise how universities will adapt to the rise of AI and online learning, the fall in residential full-time students living away from home, a rise in part-time and all-age students, an increase is the number of accelerated degrees and those taking specific modules at university rather than completing a full degree at one university.

We see the market segmenting into six different kinds of institution.

---

[42] Davis, G., O'Brien, L. and McLean P., 'Growing in Esteem: Positioning the University of Melbourne in the Global Knowledge Economy.

234

1. Global

This will constitute a league of the top universities across the world, some 100 in number, including some ten from the UK, which compete internationally to attract world class academics and the very ablest researchers. They are heavily interlinked and research-focussed, addressing similar global problems. They will appeal to highly able undergraduate and postgraduates who relish independent study and being taught by cutting-edge academics. These will be truly the elite institutions, attracting a disproportionate amount of global research fundings and exerting considerable influence in their own countries and internationally. Their leavers will be employed internationally and paid commensurate high salaries. They will have little contact with their local or regional communities.

2. National universities

These will attract primarily national and regional students and staff, and will be engaged heavily in research, though the focus will be more upon undergraduate and postgraduate teaching than in the global institutions. They will nevertheless have significant numbers of doctoral students. National universities will scoop up the bulk of the research funding within each country, and work closely with their governments in solving problems of mutual interest. They will be predominantly residential.

3. Regional universities

These universities will play very significant roles in the economic, cultural and social life of their respective provinces, states and regions, working closely with those tiers of government and with businesses and other organisations of influence in the area. They will conduct research, to a more limited scale than for global and national universities, and the focus will be more heavily on teaching and learning. Many students will live at home.

4. Professional universities

These will make no attempt to offer anything other than training to achieve the qualifications required by the professions and services, among them law, finance, accounting, medicine, and architecture, the military and police. Many of them will be single subject institutions. They will offer programmes at undergraduate and post-graduate level, but will not undertake research unless paid for by clients. Large companies will also increasingly set up their own 'universities' within their own organisations to give bespoke professional training and qualifications to their staff. Corporate certifications are on the rise, such as Cisco Certified Network Associate, and Microsoft Certified Solutions Expert.[43]

British engineer and inventor James Dyson announced in 2016 he was setting up his own university to train engineers, he said because of their dearth. Apple were said to be thinking of starting a university. JLR has pondered it. KPMG is working with Birmingham, Exeter and Durham Universities in the UK.[44] Concerns have been raised whether quality might suffer if content and quality are decided not by universities but by employers.

---

[43] Interview with Martin Hamilton, 04.04.18.
[44] Interview with Rajay Naik, 1.02.2018.

Arun Sharma, deputy Vice Chancellor of Queensland University of Technology, is one to be vexed that India in particular is seeing an explosion of this form of higher education with employers "in effect replacing universities as the trusted guarantors of quality and credit".[45]

5. Digital

All six university types will invest heavily in digital and AI teaching, but specifically 'digital universities' will have no physical presence for students, and have headquarters purely or mostly for administrative purposes, much like The Open University in the UK. The number of digital universities will expand, though their growth will be contained by the conventional physical universities moving further online in a search for students.

6. Local universities

These universities will blend with further education (FE) colleges. They will not undertake research, and will offer only limited post-graduate activity. The focus will be on technical, vocational and applied undergraduate degrees, foundation programmes, apprenticeships, short courses and qualifications for those who require particular modules for their career progression, or for general interest and life-long learning. Every town of a size above 50-100,000 inhabitants, and many smaller, will have their own local university, which will work closely with schools, colleges, employers, social services and the third sector in the local area and will be heavily involved in

---

[45] *Times Higher Education*, 20.04.17.

teacher training, skills development and adult education. Almost all students will live at home.

The Dismembering of the Second and Third Revolution Era University

The European-Anglo-American residential university will be profoundly charged by the fourth education revolution. Medieval scholars would recognise the Sorbonne, Oxford and Harvard today. They may well not in 25 years. Libraries, research and examinations will all be changed beyond recognition by AI. The jury may still be out on web-based seminars and MOOCs, but they will grow, facilitated by the new technologies. But what of the mainstay of the traditional university, the lecture hall?

1. The end of the lecture hall at the University of Northampton

The new waterside campus at the University of Northampton in central England has been described by one insider as "the UK's most exciting higher education project".[46] At the heart of the new design is, "active blended learning", with students using digital learning technologies a variant of the 'flipped' classroom model, before attending seminars. Dean of Learning and Teaching, Alejandro Armellini, explains that the approach is designed to support "the development of subject knowledge and understanding, independent

---

[46] Nick Hillman, Director of HEPI, *Times Higher Education*, 21.06.17.

learning and digital fluency".[47] It allows students to play a more active role in their own learning, he says in the lab, seminar room, studio or workplace. The new campus has abandoned traditional large lecture theatres altogether, believing they are no longer appropriate for 21st century learning. Traditional office space on campus is equally regarded as wasteful. Staff will no longer have separate offices or even their own desks, having to adjust to hot desks and lockers to store their personal effects. Even Vice Chancellor Nick Petford will be in an open plan office: "a lot of [the staff] don't like it", he says "but this is how we will be running the university".[48]

John Hennessy, President of Stanford University and profound influence on the evolution of Silicon Valley, believes that the MOOC craze from 2012-15 was never going to fulfil the high expectations, but that the flipped classroom will have much more influence on the future of the universities under AI. He believes "we have some pretty good data ... that really demonstrates that [flipped classrooms] work".[49] He sees savings of some 15% in outlay from adopting this approach. It suggests that lecture halls, so central to universities in the past, should no longer be built, but instead converted into venues permitting small group discussion to presentations by speakers or film. Universities should still have one very large hall, for graduation which will remain a core rite of passage, and for 'star' lectures. The era of the lecture

---

[47] *Times Higher Education*, 11.01.18.
[48] *Times Higher Education*, 21.06.17.
[49] *Times Higher Education*, 21.07.16.

theatre as the dominant physical feature of the University is coming to a rapid end.

2. The 'C-Campus' or bilateral/trilateral degree

This is a virtual university collaboration, established in 2012 in between Beijing's Tsinghua University and the University of Melbourne, which from 2014 offered its first post-graduate programme on River Basin Management. The letter C is deliberately ambiguous, and could stand for Cloud Computing, Cyber Innovation, Cross-disciplinary or Collaboration. The partnership has been described as bringing "students and academics together across a broad range of topics, using the latest digital technologies without a physical campus".[50] Simon Evans, Pro-Vice Chancellor at Melbourne, says that digital technology "allows immediate and direct contact between two cohorts, facilitated by both universities having just a two hour time difference, which circumvents the universities being twelve hours flying time apart".

PluS Alliance is a three way collaboration engineered by three leading university leaders, Michael Crow of Arizona State at Phoenix (the 'P'), Ed Byrne at King's College, London (the 'L') and Ian Jacobs of the University of New South Wales in Sydney (the 'uS'). The universities work together on global issues including health, justice and sustainability. It is likely that in future many more universities will partner to form similar C-Campus or PluS Alliance relationships with ever cheaper

---

[50] MOOCs and Masters, *Times Higher Education*, September 2015.

and more effective technology meaning the communication between universities can become easier and more potent.

3. Virtual degrees or 'nanodegrees' from Udacity

Another possible future is pioneered by Udacity which is promoting a 'nanodegree' in self-driving car engineering. Students are offered an entire course online where they are mentored by teachers who are not university academics but engineers working in the car sector. Udacity has spotted the gap by going to the firms directly, deliberately by-passing traditional HE entirely. They talk to employers to discover the precise skills that they require and then tailor courses to meet that.[51] If companies like Udacity can guarantee undergraduates jobs, and a qualification to match that of an undergraduate degree, we will only see this variant of higher education growing.

4. The Blockchain, the University of One and Woolf University

Blockchain is the technology that underpins the bitcoin currency and has novel applications for HE, not least recording academic credits reliably and regulating contracts and payments. March 2018 saw the launch of the world's first 'blockchain university', described as 'Uber for students, Airbnb for academics'. Named 'Woolf University', it will have no physical presence but be based on an app that allows academics to sell their expertise to prospective students. It aims to organise itself

---

[51] *Times Higher Education,* 04.01.18

around several virtual colleges on the Oxbridge model, the first, Ambrose College, to have 30 academics, most with Oxford teaching backgrounds, It aims to have its degrees formally recognised within 10 years. It has yet to ignite the ire that AC Grayling generated when he launched his Oxbridge style private 'New College of the Humanities' in London in 2012, suggesting that tolerance for disruptive change in HE may have eased in Britain.[52]

Blockchain excels at garnering together the achievements of a student and giving future employers a verifiable record of what that individual might contribute – in a far more detailed and reliable way than the tired third revolution formula of written references. By allowing students to build up profiles in this way, it can open up the possibility of opting for 'a pick 'n mix' model of gaining credits on different courses from different universities across the world, which might constitute a more enterprising and intellectually challenging experience for a student than just attending a single university.

The Open University's 'Knowledge Media Institute' has pioneered this approach: its Director John Domingue enthuses about how the technology will allow students in the future to "move beyond the current structure of the universities". He calls this "the University of One", cutting out the middle man of the university: "if you are doing a course by Tim Berners-Lee on the internet, that"s going to [impress people]". In 2016, MIT released Blockcerts software that it plans will underpin the issuing

---

[52] *Times Higher Education*, 22.03.2018.

of academic certificates on the Blockchain in future.[53]
The 'pick 'n mix' model can also be seen in 'Studium
Irregulare', which students plan themselves, allowing
them to 'invent' new interdisciplinary education. Austria
is one country that allows this activity. It is early days for
this radical model, and students and their parents are very
conservative. But it poses a strong challenge to existing
university provision and asks searching questions of it.[54]

5. No universities at all

It is possible to envisage a future in which there will be
no universities at all, neither virtual nor physical.
Universities could go the same way that atheists see the
great cathedrals, temples and mosques going, sold off or
converted into shopping malls. Eric Cooke, formerly a
computer scientist at the University of Southampton, is
one who sees this happening: "in 15 years, we will have
no students to teach".[55] His argument is based on
computers being a thousand and more times more
effective in 15 years' time than they are today, as well as
the changing requirements of the job market. Robots he
says are already beginning to learn to express emotion in
human relationships, "simulating kindness and caring
better than most humans". He cites MITs establishment
of the "affective computing group", which is learning to
give robots an understanding of empathy. He sees IBMs
Watson as a clue to the future with its increasing ability

---

[53] *Times Higher Education*, 31.08.17.
[54] Interview with Gero Miesenboeck, 07.03.18.
[55] *Times Higher Education*, 24/31.12.15

to answer all kinds of questions put to it. This revolution he seems to be saying will happen all the more quickly if those in power don't "begin to work out what needs to be done before we all become road kill [sic] on the information highway".[56] He does not equivocate: "universities and academics will be assigned to history".

This will not happen in the fourth education revolution. It might in the fifth.

Smart universities

So, universities will not disappear. They will change fundamentally though, segmenting still more into the six types described above, but all with common 'smart' elements. These include: a heavy reliance on AI in teaching and learning; a focus on breadth of curriculum and twenty first century skills; medical, law, business, architecture and STEM students will all be taught humanities alongside science/social science; equally, humanities students will be taught science and mathematics; environments and culture will celebrate the human, the spiritual and the arts, with positive health and well-being of all at the core; student populations that embrace and celebrate learning by all from ages 18-120; institutions that nurture the mind, but also the body, curiosity, the imagination, the heart and soul; universities that encourage rather than deter 'irregular' and bite size studies, degrees and international collaborations; and a greater emphasis on inter-disciplinary work in research and understanding real human and global concerns.

---

[56] *Times Higher Education* 24/31.12.15

Universities, in the fourth education era, after their bumpy ride at the end of the third, will return to being the deeply vital and respected institutions they have been for much of their history.

Over one billion children across the developing world need a good education. But there are insufficient numbers of quality teachers to educate many of them. In the developed world too, there are severe teacher shortages in schools, while in universities, many academics would sooner research than teach. One of the many benefits of AI will be to help address these needs of students and offer them a high quality personalised and challenging education.

Chapter Nine:

The Benefits, Opportunities and Risks of AI in Education

The future fires the imagination. The past is gone, inert, impossible to reclaim. The future is there to be owned. People of action are interested in the future, how they can anticipate it better before it happens, how they can shape it before it happens, and bend it in their own or society's ends.

The advent of AI and the possibilities it creates can send creative minds into a frenzy. The stuff of science fiction - transhumanism and a cure for mortality - suddenly seem possible. Before we arrive there, if ever we do, if we ever want to, AI is making more prosaic and narrow leaps forward that are reshaping society and education.

AI will confer many benefits as long as it is used well but will also entail significant risks. What are these?

Gains from the Fourth Revolution

So let's take stock on how AI will address the five traditional limitations of the factory model of education.

1. Social mobility

Too much can be made of differences in ability at birth, which can engender a culture of low expectations. Differences grow from the very earliest weeks and months of life at home and are accelerated by differential school experience. The ratio of teachers per student, the quality and experience of the teachers, the motivation and behaviour in class, the pace of progress and the work expectation, capital spending per student and the information exchange between home and school, all differ very significantly between those who are at privileged schools compared to those who attend the least advantaged.

Two of the most important variants are the quality of teaching and class sizes. In proverbial terms, AI offers the prospect of "an Eton quality teacher for all". Class sizes for those children fortunate enough to attend a school will be reduced from 30 or more, where the individual student's needs are often lost, down to 1 on 1 instruction. Students will still be grouped into classes, which may well have 10, 20, 30 or more children in them, but each student will enjoy a personalised learning programme. They will spend part of the day in front of a screen or headsets, and in time a surface on to which a hologram will be projected. There will be little need for stand-alone robots for teaching itself. The 'face' on the screen or hologram will be that of an individualised teacher, which will know the mind of the student, and will deliver lessons individually to them, moving at the student's optimal pace, know how to motivate them, understand when they are tired or distracted and be adept at bringing them back onto task. The 'teacher' themselves will be as effective as the most gifted teacher in any class in any school in the world, with the added benefit of having a finely honed understanding of each student, their learning difficulties and psychologies whose accumulated knowledge will not evaporate at the end of the school year.

The teacher and teaching assistants (who may be a bot) will move around the class, ensuring that every child is learning, and will supervise 'whole class' learning experiences, where they ask questions, where students discuss and debate with each other, and engage in practical activities in and outside the classroom space. The rate of progress for each student will thus be optimised via the new AI technology. No longer will the 'best' teachers and the smallest class size be for the privileged few: they will now be for every child, from every background, from everywhere in the world.

2. Stage not Age

In the factory school, students move forward to a new year group each September. This is a poor format for helping students learn at their optimal pace. Student spend time bored at the slow progress of the class, or discouraged because they cannot keep up, and lack the confidence, motivation, or teacher time, to receive help. But with the fourth education revolution, each child will move forward at their own pace, and in each individual subject. The AI technology will take into account those days when students will want to move more quickly, and those when they are tired or unwell when the pace should be slower. It will know and understand how the student is reacting, and ensure the stimulus is optimal, and the material selected best challenges their understanding on each and every day throughout the academic year, and in their own time if they want to continue to study at home. The best teachers might recognise what each student needs day by day, but under the third era model, there was never be the time for them to give each the individual attention they need, and deserve.

3.   Teacher Time is Freed up

AI machines take away many of the routine burdens that stop teachers being able to give their best energy and attention to students and to teaching. AI will select the appropriate teaching materials tailored to each student. It will note when students are absent or distracted and put in place follow-up procedures. It will constantly monitor and assess each student's progress, enter scores and performance on central registers, ensure that parents remain well-informed about their children's progress, provide the data that the school managers and government need to be sure that learning is properly taking place, assess students' work so that teachers never have to mark another exercise book or worksheet, and send timely reminders to students when work has been left incomplete. The administrative burden which has handicapped teachers for hundreds of years will be taken off their shoulders, making their task far more rewarding. AI will make teaching a much more attractive, rewarding and stimulating profession, reduce early departures and boost the recruitment of promising new teachers.

4.   Breadth of Intelligence Developed

Under the factory model of education, schools and universities focussed on a narrow range of human intelligence and potential. Those institutions that did offer broader enrichment - emotional development, sporting achievement, wide exposure to the arts and moral leadership - were often those attended by the students from the better-off families, who had better learning opportunities open to them in their lives anyway. Accomplishment at these broader activities inculcate into children the behaviours and skills prized by top employers, perpetuating the privilege of elite groups into the future.

AI opens up an education offering a much broader enrichment for all. The technology will allow for more effective development of each child's cognitive capabilities. The greater speed with which linguistic and logical learning will take place in classrooms will free up time and energy for wider enrichment - time that at present is squeezed because of the treadmill of covering the curriculum in the limited time available, which in the third era model never seemed enough. Games, music, drama, dance, creative writing, painting, art history, reading, reflection time, project work, service learning and volunteering will all blossom in the schools and universities of the future.

AI technology itself has a major role to play in nurturing all students' 'multiple' intelligences. They will have time and more opportunities to extend their moral and spiritual sensibilities and interests. The technology will challenge them to think and respond in ways they might be reluctant to do so in class in front of other students. Their personal and social intelligences will be nurtured by AI machines, developing their self-confidence and ability to negotiate the world more ably. The sport and the art/creative intelligences will mostly be developed by working in physical interactions with other students: but the *theory* behind them, exercise, dance choreography, sporting techniques or chord harmonies can all be immeasurably enhanced by this new technology

5. Individualisation, not Homogenisation

Conventional education under the factory model had the unintended by-product of making students more like each other. Because there is a common body of knowledge to get through for all students, little space for individual reflection and responses, and often a 'right' or wrong answer that exam markers were looking out for, there was little scope for individualisation. Teachers in schools and lecturers in universities wanted for the time to give individual attention to all. Students in class learnt they got ahead by giving the 'right answer' rather than 'their answer'.

This personality straitjacket is changing under the fourth education revolution. In many subjects, mathematics, physics and social sciences there may still be a right answer, and a right way of getting to the answer that has to be learnt. But in the human sciences, in many aspects of the social sciences and above all the humanities, the individuated response by the student becomes more possible with AI technology. There is more time and opportunity at school and university for students to explore how they personally respond to material that is being presented to them, and for their thoughts to be heard and responded to. It is a world apart from the factory model, where students had their brains crammed full of knowledge without the opportunity to understand themselves or reflect. Reason and the intellect are important, but not all important. In this new era, we will have the promise, through greater opportunities for self-understanding, to learn more who we are, and to find more meaning and fulfilment in our lives.

***

There are a further five benefits AI will bring beyond merely addressing the five limitations of the third education revolution model.

1. Stimulus for Students

Why should academic study for students not be as enjoyable and challenging as playing computer games? Why do many students regard one as a chore and the other a delight?

As computer games have become more sophisticated over the last 25 years, they've increasingly engaged the intellects of students. Tech entrepreneur and game designer Jane McGonigal is a proselytiser who wants to see game use expanded: as early as 2010 she argued that the intense power of games over the minds of young people should be channelled for educational ends, rather than being seen primarily as a problem by educators and parents.[1] Game programmes can take students on interactive journeys of discovery that complement their curriculum subjects in science, history, geography, literature, psychology and more. Books and magazines have always been seen as supporting the task of teachers in educational objectives, whereas games have been overwhelmingly characterised as irrelevant or distracting. But they can give curriculum learning the same excitement as games to young females equally with males.

Games in future will increasingly tailor their output to individual students, deploying levels of sophistication far more complex than today, with enhanced potential to make their learning more rewarding and valuable. The new technology will help ensure that for each and every academic

---

[1] McGonigal, J. (2010) 'Gaming Can Make a Better World', TED.

subject games can be at the cutting edge of students' 'challenge zone'. The figurative Iron Curtain separating work and play could become consigned to history, as was the real Iron Curtain dividing East and West in the Cold War (we hope).

2. Increasing Stimulation for Teachers

Teachers commonly finish their careers and retire less enthusiastic about the profession than they were at the outset. Many have become tired and disenchanted. My challenge when I was a head to my teaching staff was to ask them if their final day in the profession could be as exciting as their first. This is difficult for many to achieve because of the repetitive nature of the teacher's work year on year, the workload and all pervasive lack of time, and the stress of coaxing students who are reluctant and poorly behaved into learning. Because AI technology will remove or reduce much that is humdrum and repetitive in the life of teachers, they can spend more time interacting and inspiring young people, and free them up to do what brought them into the profession. They will be able to read deeply and reflect on their subject, allowing them to be fellow learners alongside their students, dispelling the fiction that the teacher must be the font of all knowledge. AI will truly usher in a land of plenty for the teacher, and transform the profession forever into what it should always have been, inspiring students with learning and living better lives.

3. Continuity of Teachers

Under the industrial model, students typically have a new teacher in each subject at the start of each academic year. The model works well for students when a duff or unempathetic teacher disappears, but when a teacher who fired them up stops teaching them, not so good. Students can make considerable progress in an academic subject under a favourite teacher during one year, only to find their performance arrested when there is a change at the end of the year to a new teacher who the student finds unsympathetic, uninspiring or boring. We've all experienced this I'm sure.

In the fourth education model, each student will have a personalised 'teacher' for each subject, who will remain with them each September, indeed stay with them throughout their school journey. The same 'teacher' will be there to assist them in further or higher education and beyond, for as long as they retain an interest in learning. By adapting to the needs of each student for a preferred or optimal gender, age, ethnicity, character and dialect, never again will a student have to acclimatise to a new teacher. Because the 'teacher' equally will be available to them in the evenings, weekends and over the school and university holidays, the young will have far more control over their learning. The personalised face on the screen or hologram will even age along with the student themselves. Should boredom with the digital AI teacher become a problem, a new teacher can come into the student's life, tailored to their new needs. Incredible, and coming.

4. A Better Preparation for the World of Work

The job market we know will change very dramatically over the next 15 years. Generation Z (or Gen Z, iGen or post-millennials), were born from the mid-1990s, grew up with the internet and social media and have different demands and expectations of work than Generation Y, and certainly of their parents. Many expect to have several jobs requiring different skills, to work from home as well as abroad, to work hard but also to punctuate their careers with sabbaticals, to work for money but also to have work with a social purpose. AI learning and the fourth education revolution approach is much belter attuned to preparing the young for the work they will face.

5. The Encouragement of Lifelong Learning

The factory model, with its emphasis on formal learning in school and university, encouraged if unintentionally the notion that education finishes when a student leaves school, college or university. The stories, not always apocryphal, of students gleefully burning their exercise books and files on their last day in college to celebrate their freedom, captures a truth, especially with a model of education where they saw their education as something done to, not for, them. The new technology will open many more minds to the wonder of learning, and help the development of lifelong habits of mind including curiosity intelligence (CI). Learning is endless, and endlessly fascinating. It doesn't stop at 16, or 18, or 21, or 25. The truly enlightened human will be as eager to learn on his deathbed as he was as a mewling and puking infant.

Revisiting Future Work: Optimists vs Realists

This question of employment in the future is so central to the education that we must revisit it. A book published in 2017, *Teaching in the Fourth Industrial Revolution* written by internationally six prize-winning teachers, thoughtful though the text is, has virtually nothing to say about AI or the impact of digitalisation of jobs and life.[2] We can hardly say we had no warning of seismic change. It is 90 years since economist John Maynard Keynes discussed the approaching problem of 'how to occupy the leisure which science and compound interest' will make possible.[3] Had Keynes anticipated AI, he might have predicted change with even more confidence.

In the early 1960s, a seminal debate took place at MIT between one group, who we can term 'realists', led by John McCarthy and Marvin Minsky, who said AI computers would replace humans in the workplace, and those who said they would *complement* humans, spearheaded by two other major figures, Norbert Wiener and JCR Licklider.[4] The latter who we can term 'optimists' have had more supporters over the years. The IT company Cognizant produced a report in 2017 entitled *21 Jobs of the Future* which argued that jobs lost to AI will be replaced by ones that 'will create more employment, providing work for the many people in offices, stores and factory floors displaced or disrupted by technology[5]. Cognizant are optimists. So is the 2018 Pearson/Nesta/Oxford Martin report.[6] 'Far from being doomed by technology ... we find that many occupations

---

[2] Doucet, A. et al, (2018). *'Teaching in the Fourth Industrial Revolution. Standing at the Precipice'*, London: Routledge.
[3] Keynes, J.M. (1903) Economic Possibilities for our Grandchildren.
[4] Ridley, M. (2013). 'No need to fear the rise of the machines', *The Times*, 1 January.
[5] Cognizant, '21 Jobs of the Future', 27.11.2017.
[6] Bakhshi, H. et al (2018) *'The Future of Skills. Employment in 2030'*, Pearson, Nesta, Oxford Martin.

have bright or open-ended employment prospects'.[7] Scientist and public intellectual Matt Ridley is "unpersuaded" by talk of AI creating mass unemployment: "it will simply free people to do other things and fulfil other needs".[8] Optimists worry that predictions of job losses will depress creativity and damage economic prospects.

Do we need to reframe the discussion between optimists and realists? MIT professor Max Tegmark places himself firmly in the latter camp. The machines are no longer replacing "our muscles but our brains". Jobs requiring social intelligence, empathy and creativity will last longer, he says, but he sees these at risk too in the longer term.[9]

So which side is right? Optimists perhaps in the short term: pessimists/realists in the longer term? The quicker the fourth education revolution arrives, the better we will prepare our young for the world of work they will face, whichever world it will be. Generation Z will be better educated, be more creative, have more of their intelligence and strengths developed, and be able to enjoy Keynes' enhanced leisure time if it arrives, far more fully. We need to expect an optimistic future, but prepare for a realistic one. More on this later.

Potential Risks of AI

---

[7] Ibid, p.16.

[8] *The Times*, (2016). 21 November.

[9] Tegmark, M., (2017) 'AI is going to change working life forever', *The Times*, 2 December.

There are equally very real ten potential risks with the advent of AI in education, some the obverse of potential gains, others entirely new.

1. Social Immobility is Increased not Reduced

It is perfectly possible to envisage a world in which use of the latest technology is monopolised or colonised by existing elite groups with the most advanced (and best) forms of AI only available to those with the requisite cash. The likelihood is that this may happen in the early adoption phase. But rapidly falling prices of the technology as it evolves will ensure that it will become available on a widespread basis at a low cost, even if the latest iterations continue to be exploited unevenly by the well off. They will have better headsets, with more gadgets and designer labels. Elites throughout history have always found new ways of maintaining their competitive advantage. But once every child in the world has personalised adaptive learning software on laptops or devices, they have the prize. A pauper after all can watch the same latest television programmes as an oligarch, and benefit from them as much.

2. Education becomes Narrower and more Specialised at an Earlier Age

The new technology will allow astonishing rates of progress for gifted students, and will throw up a considerably greater number of gifted students than were ever cultivated in the factory age. It is entirely possible, likely even, that children as young as 11 will be studying mathematics at a university level. The factory model did not generally allow for this, though it could happen, as for Ruth Lawrence, who at the age of 12 in 1981 passed the Oxford University entrance exam in mathematics, coming first out of 530 candidates. Such child prodigies were exceptions in the old system, but when students start moving at their own pace, we will see many more Ruth Lawrence's.

There is a major downside however if students do so at the expense of progress in other subjects, and of their own emotional and social learning. In 2001, 5-year old girl Arran Fernandez successfully sat GCSE mathematics. Just because a child can do this doesn't mean to say that a child should do this. Tiger parents with restless eyes can be a menace and inflict great harm on their children. Lawyer and writer Amy Chua was lionised by many in the Anglo-American intelligentsia for her book advocating parents pushing their children very hard.[10] I think she has inflicted profound damage. The balanced development of each child is what matters. Careful watch will need to be made in the new education era to ensure that the child's interest, not those of a forceful and exploitative parent or school, prevails in this enormously exhilarating new world of learning.

3. Teachers Lose Control over their Students

Under the third educational model, teacher were both *an* authority and *in* authority. For a teacher to admit "I don't know" was widely if wrongly seen as a loss of credibility. The teacher needed to convince students of their mastery of the subject. Under AI, the knowledge of students will often outstrip that of their teachers educated under the old system.

---

[10] Chua, A., (2011). *Battle Hymn of the Tiger Mother*, Penguin, London. She was named as one of Time magazine's 100 most influential figures.

The student will become more authoritative than their teachers at any earlier age. This is desirable for research postgraduates, but potentially undermining for a teacher at school. The teacher will have to adapt to this loss of some of their traditional power. The brightest school students will acquire some of the prowess of the doctoral researcher. The teacher will have to learn to become their collaborators, fellow travellers at the borders of knowledge.

4. Deprofessionalisation of the Teacher

AI technology is so sophisticated and so adept at teaching students that teachers face compounding their loss of 'expert' subject status with loss of expertise at teaching. Some teachers may be tempted to ask why they should bother to keep abreast of knowledge in their specialist subject and latest pedagogical thinking? London taxi drivers no longer need the 'knowledge' of London streets in the age of the sat-nav. Why should teachers bother with knowledge in the age of AI? What many teachers most enjoy is helping their students learn a subject and develop as human beings. But if machines are performing both roles, then what is there left for the teacher? What satisfaction can teachers possibly derive in this new world? Professional changes to teacher training, and a completely new mindset and approach to the job of teaching, and to the task of school leadership, are urgently required. Teaching will be different: it should be no less, indeed more, satisfying.

5. Infantalisation of Students

Social media can make for superficial thought and relationships. Outgoing VC at the University of Adelaide, Walter Bebbington, said some students now graduate with "the attention span of a tweet, as competent surfers of the digital wave of bite-sized communicators, saturated in a sea of information but unable to navigate the wider ocean".[11]

Already our existing technology is rendering life simpler and more straightforward, allowing the young (and those of all ages) to cut corners. Who now can remember telephone numbers the way we did? Even our own? Let's return to Sat Nav. We no longer need to look at maps to discover how to get from 'A' to 'B' in cars. AI technology allows our route to be constantly recalibrated in the light of changing traffic. Neither do need to read maps to understand how to find our destination on foot. Many of us carry devices that tell us exactly what to do. It has many benefits including safety. But there are losses too. Understanding maps and working out how to use them is satisfying and enriching. It helps us to understand the relationship between spaces and how to appreciate an environment with its history, topography and sociology, rather than seeing space in a purely transactional way, i.e. how to reach a destination with the least effort and in the least time. Sat Nav, like out of town stores, sucks quality stealthily and subtly out of our lives under the guise of benefitting humankind. We are still only in the gentlest of foothills of AI technology and its impact. Vast swathes of human endeavour will be rendered pointless by these machines. Our lives may become easier and more convenient, but the depth, the adventure and struggle that have made life worthwhile risks becoming redundant. London taxi drivers could use the time freed up from thinking through the best routes to engage with passengers more and offer a better

---

[11] *Times Higher Education,* 20.04.17.

service. Many prefer instead to use it on origin to destination phone calls to their mates.

6. Education and the Risk of Boredom

Sophisticated voice recognition translation machines are calling into question the need for the teaching of languages. If the sole reason for learning a language is the transactional one of conversing with those of other nationalities, students could legitimately ask "why bother?" Computing Professor Stephen Heppell has said: "Simultaneous translation is coming, making language teachers redundant. Modern languages teaching in future may be more about navigating cultural differences".[12] Languages teaching must and will certainly continue, but AI will take away some of its justification. Translation machines though, however word perfect, will never fully comprehend cultural and psychological factors. Indeed, the need for language teaching could grow.

What might AI do to the teaching of some other subjects? If AI is going to commandeer or own large parts of human knowledge, students may feel there is little point in putting in the time and effort to learn, when the information no longer has to be committed to memory but is available at the click of a button, or a command of their voice. The fourth education age will need to reassert a non-utilitarian vision of education, including the importance of the liberal arts, as championed in earlier ages. Education is about much more than transactional objectives and making our lives simple.

---

[12] Interview with Stephen Heppell, 04.01.18.

7. Loss of Social Contact

Social media at best vastly extends the range of human contact. Mark Zuckerberg made this defence repeatedly when Facebook was under attack in April 2018. But the dangers are already evident. Video chats and holograms are a very different experience from being in the same physical space as someone we can sense, touch, smell and sense their unique presence as another human being. However sophisticated AI may make remote connection, it will never be the same as being present with another person. What then of machines which mimic empathy, understanding and even love for students, friends, patients and clients? It is 25 years since Robert D Putnam published his seminal essay *Bowling Alone: America's Declining Social Capital,* charting the decline of meaningful human relationships since 1950. Atomised modern society, he wrote, was militating against the very social interactions which made life enjoyable, worthwhile and happy.[13] The anonymising trend could be accelerated exponentially by AI. Not for the first time, we find ourselves on a pivot: AI could bring us untold social benefits, or untold damage. As Intel's Anshul Sonak has warned: "Technology-based education curriculums are lacking a focus on personal values, ethics and life skills … new generations are technically connected but socially disconnected. We should think about what kind of people we are generating."[14] Better connected does not necessarily entail more deeply connected.

---

[13] Putnam, R.D. (2000). 'Bowling Alone: The Collapse and Revival of American Community'.

[14] Sonak, A. (2017) Intel's regional Director for Education and Innovation, Asia. December.

8.   Unhealthy Lifestyles and Damage to Mental Health

The world of AI could prove so compelling to the young, and those of all ages, that the allure of remaining all day fixated in front of a screen, VR headset or hologram display could prove much more attractive than going outside, taking exercise, walking to work or taking part in social activities. Everything a human being could desire in terms of relaxation, stimulus, work and play will all be available for them as they sit or stand physically passive in front of the technology. The impact that this could have on obesity and general unhealthiness is imponderable. The human body evolved over millions of years to be physically active and not sedentary. Living too much in a world of cyberspace, including being vulnerable to online bullying, is one of the factors contributing to rising mental health worries among students. American psychologist Jean Twenge at San Diego State University has argued that smartphones were the most important cause of the rise of mental health problems among teens since 2012, and that 18 year olds are no less robust than they were.[15]

9.   Erosion of Values

At present, the young learn many of their values from interactions with their family and schools. The best teachers and schools will be working to develop ethical principles and values in each and every student. The system is far from perfect. Some teachers sexually exploit and abuse the young. Some have favourites and damage the self-esteem of the

---

[15] See Twenge, J. (2017). '*iGen: Why Today's Super-Connected Kids are Growing Up Less Rebellious ...*', Atria Books.

young. All teachers are affected to differing extents by cognitive bias which cloud their judgements. The Jubilee Centre for Character and Virtues set up in 2000 at the University of Birmingham has done much to provide a strong evidence base to justify schools devoting time and effort to strengthening character amongst students as well as staff and parents.

If students in the future are going to be primarily learning via AI, how can we ensure that they will absorb the right values? AI can be programmed to prioritise values which we consider important, such as honesty, kindness, perseverance and curiosity. But we may never be able to appreciate fully the nature of the relationship between the AI machine and the individual student, or whether the moral learning is being absorbed by each young person. Little is known about whether machines can be as effective at teaching moral values as humans. The AI itself will always lack any sense of morality. A way forward could be mandating a set amount of time at school when students work together with a teacher when virtues and ethics are stressed. The sheer amount of time that students spend in front of their screens in a largely private interaction with a soulless machine, which is able to bring the whole world of possibility tantalisingly to them, remains a worry. For some, the virtual will always trump any lessons that might be taught collectively at school.

10. Privacy and Ethical Concerns

We are rightly concerned about what the tech companies already store about us, how they use it, and the potential for this information to be misused by a third party. These concerns magnify many times over with the advent of AI. The machines interacting with students will know about the students' strengths and qualities, their intimate foibles and personality traits, their hidden weaknesses and vulnerabilities. They will know exactly what will be needed to persuade them to agree to do or say something they might not otherwise choose. This information is almost unimaginably powerful. It has already been used to manipulate students by the tech companies. What if it fell into the wrong hands?

The way is opened up for a nightmare future where manipulation rules and free will, already a fragile reality in some, is highly constrained. Can we trust the state if it stores such information about us? Can we trust the big technology companies, Alphabet, Amazon, Apple, Facebook, Google and Microsoft, to hold this most personal of information about students? AI opens up a Pandora's Box of ethical questions and we are a very long way from resolving them. We return to this topic later in the book.

Opportunities

The educational opportunities that AI will bring need us to transcend these risks. It is only by navigating these dangers successfully that we will make the most of the opportunities on offer. We close the chapter by rehearsing these.

1. A lifelong value

Education in the third revolution era was too often seen as a transaction. Graft at school was the price for good passes that were the path to enhancing economic opportunity in life. When the individual left formal education, the job of education was 'done'. AI will destroy forever the canard that education equalled just formal education till school or university finished which prevailed through the second and third eras. We will no longer need to sign up to formalised courses, but will be able to study our favourite subjects in in our own time and in our own way. AI will be liberating, reducing loneliness, boredom and isolation, and helping to make life as rewarding and enjoyable as it should be.

2. Depth of learning

The tyranny of distance meant that travel throughout much of history has been for the privileged few, not for the masses. Outward-looking teachers sought to take their students on trips abroad, to find schools abroad willing to set up pen-friends, to twin schools and in a host of ways to reach out to those of different nationalities and cultures. But teachers ran up against problems of time, money and language. In a tightly controlled school year, heads were often resistant to let students out during term-time, and parents, students as well as teachers were unwilling to go in holiday time. Overseas travel and accommodation was expensive, so it was disproportionately the better off student who travelled abroad on educational trips. The coming of AI, AR and VR will allow students to experience in a vivid way travel abroad and meeting those from very different cultures. Simultaneous translation will mean that language will no longer be a handicap, though cultural differences will remain. For the first time in history, students will be able to speak to those around the world in any language and to be able to understand each other. The world will become more interconnected, and, by and by, perhaps more peaceful.

3. Quality, not quantity of life

Even in a hundred years, there will be likely to remain significant economic disparities between the best and the worst off across the world. But there need not be inequalities in what matters much perhaps more, the sense of human fulfilment and happiness. The 21st century marked the beginning of a profound shift away from an obsession purely with quantitative data such as national income, corporate success, exam performance, and number of operations in the National Health Service. *Qualitative* measures became increasingly important as a complement to quantitative data (the NHS can double the number of operations, but if patients have a shoddy experience, the benefit is far less evident). AI technology will rapidly become more affordable and will spread its benefits in quality of life to each and every human, regardless of family, wealth or status.

4. Tackling the democratic deficit

Representative democracy has been handed down to us via the Roman Republic, the medieval parliament and the American and French Revolutions in the late eighteenth centuries, but always sat uneasily alongside plebiscitary democracy, which relies on referenda. Widespread use of affordable AI will have the benefit of spreading democracy to authoritarian countries, and making populations better informed than they have ever been in the past. AI can help revitalise democratic life, make schools more attuned to politics, and ensure that debate and discussion become far more part of school and university life.

We are at a turning point and taking the right actions will help ensure that the AI revolution maximises the gains and minimises the risks. But before we examine these in the Conclusion, we must look at some wider societal risks of AI.

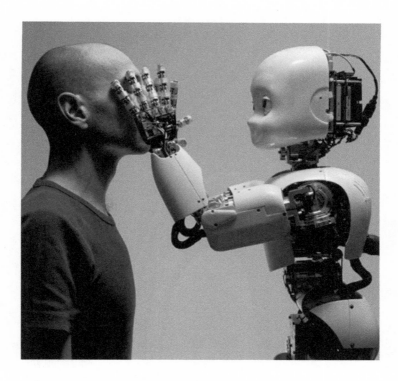

AI is infinitely seductive. It will know us better than our best friends, our parents, our partners. It probably already does. Under the guise of plausibility, is it opening our eyes, shielding our sight, or blinding us?

Chapter Ten

Will AI liberate or infantilise humanity?

Because education impacts all of life, and will become life-long in the fourth education era, in this final chapter, we move beyond the impact of AI on education to how it might affect life and society at large. There is no more important question for us to grapple with. Astronomer Royal Martin Rees has written "An explosion in artificial intelligence has sent us hurtling towards a post-human future".[1] Stephen Hawking said months before his death in March 2018: "AI will be 'either the best or the worst thing' for humanity ... Every aspect of our lives will be transformed. In short, success in creating AI could be the biggest event in the history of our civilisation".[2] But what constitutes that success and how might we master it? Inventor and entrepreneur Elon Musk[3] is another figure deeply concerned "Artificial intelligence is

---

[1] *Daily Telegraph* 23.05.15
[2] Hawking, S. (2016). Launch of the Leverhulme Centre for the Future of Intelligence, October.
[3] Musk, E. (2017) National Governors Association Summer Meeting, Rhode Island, 13-16 July.

the biggest risk we face as a civilisation and needs to be checked as soon as possible". This is no distant threat that need not concern us. Shahar Avin from Cambridge University's Centre for the Study of Existential Risk warned in early 2018 there could be major threats to humanity over the next few years from AI's exploitation by criminals, terrorist or rogue states.[4]

This chapter will examine whether AI could liberate humanity from the limitations of the third education revolution, or whether it could infantilise or even terminate human life forever, or at least life as it is recognisable today.

The core possibilities before the age of AI

AI can be seen as one of several severe challenges to face humanity in the 21st century,[5] which have been delineated clearly in Martin Rees's work, notably in his book: *A Scientist's Warning: How Terror, Error, and Environmental Disaster Threaten Humankind's Future in this Century – on Earth and Beyond*. Rees puts the chances of civilisation coming to an end in the 21st century as high (or low) as 50:50.[6] His concern is not so much destruction from events beyond human control, such as the impact of a massive asteroid, a gamma-ray burst, or a massive volcano eruption on a scale or bigger than Krakatoa in 1883. Rather his focus is on those eventualities over which human beings themselves do have control or agency. These include biotechnology and

---

[4] 'Malicious Use of Artificial Intelligence Report', Centre for the Study of Existential Risk, February 2018.
[5] Interview, Lord Rees of Ludlow, 26.03.2017.
[6] Morton, O. *The Guardian*, 14.06.03.

nanotechnology running out of control, biological terrorism, thermonuclear war or AI falling into the wrong hands. The defining feature of AI among this list of alarming prospects is that it can be as strong a force for the good as it can be for bad. If AI does indeed destroy humanity, we will only have ourselves to blame.

Logic suggests four possibilities for AI and the human race this century and beyond.

- Remove
  It is conceivable that AI-driven robots or some other form of higher intelligence evolved from AI will completely remove human beings off the face of the earth. This is the most radical scenario.
- Replace
  AI might enhance the bodies as well as the brains of human beings with ever more sophisticated implants and hence replace the race by a sophisticated blend of human beings and AI machine technology.
- Reform
  In this possibility human beings remain in charge on earth as life is understood today, but much reformed or enhanced by the benefits that AI will confer.
- Retain
  Equally possible is that AI will make very little difference to the daily experience of human life, which in the year 2100 will remain much the same as it was in the year 2000. This is the most conservative scenario, or optimistic/ pessimistic/realistic, depending on viewpoint.

Each of these four scenarios have powerful thinkers behind them. None are absurd. We have no way of knowing what the future will hold. Nor would it appear that any form of life in the future has ever mastered the ability to travel back in time and to tell us about it. Our thoughts therefore must be based upon conjecture and extrapolation.

Swedish-American cosmologist, now at MIT, Max Tegmark is one academic who has pushed conjecture far. In *Life 3.0: Being Human in the Age of Artificial Intelligence* (2017), he writes about the possibility of AI substituting itself for humans. He describes an epiphany moment: "it hit me like a brick that every time we understood how something in nature worked, some aspect of ourselves, we made it obsolete. Once we understood how muscles worked, we built much better muscles in the form of machines, and maybe, when we understand how our brains work, we'll build much better brains and become utterly obsolete"[7]. His epiphany begs questions. *Will* we ever understand how the brain works, including consciousness rather than just the mechanical parts? If we ever do, will we be able to build better brains in the same way we build better muscles?

Some thinkers on the extremes foresee the very nature of reality changing. Is reality they ask in fact immutable? This possibility caught the popular imagination when aired in the 1999 science fiction film *The Matrix*, in which the reality that humans experience is simulated in 'the matrix', created by advanced machines to pacify the human population. With virtual reality (VR) and augmented reality (AR) becoming

---

[7] Anthony, A. (2017). 'Max Tegmark: Machines Taking Control Doesn't Have to be a Bad Thing'. *The Guardian* 16.09.

steadily more sophisticated and seductively enticing, and with an arguably declining ability of some children and indeed adults to distinguish on-screen reality from the real thing, it is not mere fantasy to imagine that human beings could inhabit a created reality in the future: indeed, we might be living there now. The very notion of one objective reality is itself in contention.

Psychologists tell us that human beings construct their own subjective mental world of interpretation which they inhabit. For most, this works well, but if that subjective world deviates too far from a shared sense of reality, problems arise. Highly intelligent machines could quite easily convince us that the reality they wish to project is objective reality. Some already find it easier to live in a world of computer-generated reality and relationships, a possibility enhanced by AI software such as 'Replika', the chatbot which learns from human interactions.

Science writer Oliver Moody has written: "The strangest thing about the bot is the staggering candour with which people talk to it. A study showed that American army veterans with post-traumatic stress disorder found it significantly easier to open up to a computer-therapist than to a real one. Replika seems to benefit from a similar effect. In a lot of its uses, it appears to be more or less a person, only more patient and less judgemental"[8]. We are told that human empathy is unique. It may be. But if it is already being emulated convincingly today, where will we be with machines 10,000 times more powerful and convincing? What indeed is real? To

---

[8] Moody, O. (2017) 'As AI advances we risk losing our free will', *The Times* 14.10.

answer this question, we need to probe more what it means to be *human*. This is perhaps the most important question this book has posed.

Being Human: Four Facets

We will adopt the approach of segmenting what it means to be human into four quarters, represented below.

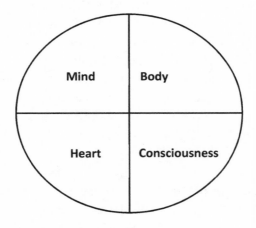

Let us take each of these one-by-one.

1. The *Mind*

The ability to think rationally is the essence of human uniqueness, according to Aristotle, Plato and Descartes. But human thinking is no match for computers, which will always be able to sift and organise data more quickly, reliably and objectively. But the mind is more than just a processing machine or engine room. It also consists of a control centre or, in shipping terms, a 'bridge' that takes the decisions, makes judgements based on values and experiences, can imagine futures and can pilot the self into it. Debate continues on whether it is capable of free will or not, as Kant and existentialists say it is, and neuroscience tends to deny. But as the essence of AI is personalisation, in education, health, work, in contrast to the conformity of the factory era, we may well see free will blossom. For the time being at least, perhaps always, machines have found it hard to replicate the human spark, whatever it may be. Perhaps AGI, if developed, will be able to do just this.

2. The *Heart*

Computers are thus able to replicate human emotions, and certain individuals feel they can communicate better with them than with human beings. Even if machines can only ever mimic human emotions rather than experience them themselves, we must accept that AI machines will be able to perform many aspects of human emotional interactions as well as or better than human beings. This has with profound implications for work including the caring professions, especially with an aging population. But AI will not be able to open the human heart. Many pass their lives with their heart centre closed, or only periodically opened at times of great emotional significance such as falling in love. Opening the heart is not an intellectual experience. Indeed, a life devoted to the mind and honing the intellect might even militate against such an opening, or believing it exists. It is experiential, utterly real, but only to those who know and experience it. Only when the heart is open do we become fully human. When it is, our

279

knowledge becomes very deep, and we are in touch with all others.

3. The *Body*

Whatever it is the human body evolved over many millions of years. Now scientists tell us more than half our body is not human (57% of us apparently is made up of microscopic colonists).[9] AI is already augmenting it, whether it is moving from fixing us to augmenting us and perhaps replacing us. Robots themselves will always find it hard to match the dexterity of the human body, however. But we must expect them increasingly to be able to replicate human movement and even human likeness. So it turns out we need our bodies to lead human lives, even if our bodies are not wholly our bodies, or indeed fully human.

4. Consciousness

We are least clear of all about consciousness, despite sixty years and more of intensive scientific research and many centuries of philosophical speculation. Computationalism is one theory spanning contemporary philosophy and neuroscience, which argues that consciousness is just another aspect of mechanical wiring yet to be comprehended by humans. It sees the brain as a computer and the mind is a result of that computer. It has strong supporters across academic disciplines. Philosopher Daniel Dennett proposed his "multiple drafts" variant in which consciousness is distributed over the brain in space

---

[9] BBC, 10.04.18.

and time[10]. Neuroscientist and psychiatrist Giulio Tononi has developed a scientific theory of consciousness, the "integrated information theory" which shows how it can be measured, correlates with brain states and factors in dreamless sleep. Fellow neuroscientist latterly at Caltech, Christof Koch, describes it as "the only really promising fundamental theory of consciousness".[11]

Others see consciousness as unique to animal life, and will never, not in another million years, be replicated by computers. This school of thought includes religiously-inspired figures, who believe that consciousness is the very seat of God in human beings. American Catholic theologian Richard Rohr has written: "There is a light in the soul that is uncreated and uncreatable, unconditioned, universal, deathless; in religious language, a core of personality which cannot be separated from God".[12] Thirteenth century German theologian Meister Eckhart believed the soul lies at the very centre of consciousness: that the soul is consciousness. In Indian mysticism, this divine core is called *Atman*, or 'the Self'. This is the same sense of consciousness as the 'I am' definition of God offered in the Jewish Torah and the Christian New Testament.

A third type of explanation is held by those who are neither atheistic nor expressly theistic. One holder is Italian physicist Federico Faggin, an inventor of the

---

[10] Dennett, D.D. (1991) *Consciousness Explained*, London: Little, Brown & Co.

[11] *New York Times*, 20.09. 2010.

[12] Rohr, R. (2018). 'Discovering Our Inner Divine Spark', Center for Action and Contemplation, 29.01.

commercial microprocessor. He describes this position thus: "I believe consciousness is a property of the 'stuff' of which all universes are made. This has little to do with atheism. I believe that animals are conscious, and so are living cells and molecules. Consciousness is about the capacity to have a sentient experience, not whether one believes in God. In my opinion, the concept of God of most religions is flawed, and I personally stay away from religious belief systems. The existence of 'spirituality' as a deep inner experience of connection with the universe, however, is real and is an indication that the nature of reality is holistic. That is also what quantum physics is telling us."[13]

The first school of thought believe that consciousness may eventually be replicable by AI machines: the latter two that it will never be, as long as the universe or universes exists.

Four dystopian possibilities

1. An Existential Threat to Humanity

Human beings have throughout history innovated beyond their capacity to control technology fully, and to prevent it falling into rogue hands. Chemical weapons were not first used in 1915 during the First World War as commonly believed, but during the Peloponnesian War between Athens and Sparta in the 5th century BC. Nuclear weapons, first used in Hiroshima and Nagasaki in August 1945, saw scientific inventions capable of wiping out

---

[13] From an e-mail from Professor Rosemary Sage, 31.01.18.

human life deployed in war with little thought to their future restraint. So too with the race to develop biological weapons, made up of bacteria, viruses and fungi, that replicate in their victims. Together, these Nuclear Biological Chemical (NBC) weapons, or weapons of mass destruction (WMDs), are poised to threaten our life, especially if they fall into the hands of the quartet of terrorists, criminals autocratic leaders unconcerned by international opinion or rogue states.

We must understand the risks of AI in precisely the same way. The Cambridge Existential Risk Centre is one of a burgeoning number of bodies to take the threat seriously not least because AI has the sophistication to corrode and trump human agency. Founder of the Future of Humanity Institute and philosopher, Nick Bostrom, can envisage a world in which superior intelligence might allow AI to hijack military, financial and political processes, resulting in human extinction. The Future of Life Institute (FLI) is a Boston Mass-based group of concerned scientists and technologists founded by Tegmark and Skype co-founder Jaan Tallinn. It includes Elon Musk, Stephen Hawking (R.I.P) and Martin Rees on its advisory board, who are actively campaigning to safeguard life in the light of WMD, with the use of 'Strong AI' a particular concern, including its use in warfare[14]. Drones will soon be able to be fitted with face recognition systems and explosive devices programmed to seek out and kill known individuals, capable of penetrating deep within buildings, and acting in

---

[14] Future of Life Institute, https://futureoflife.org/

association with each other – beyond the control of any human operator[15]. Nuclear technology has so far been harnessed to the benefit of humankind. There is no guarantee that AI will be subject to such control and oversight.

2. Manipulation

AI machines are already capable of knowing human beings intimately, not least their vulnerable points and what is required to prompt them to take a particular decision. The persuasive power of AI over our lives is already far greater than many realise, or want to acknowledge. In general, we don't like admitting we are not in control of our lives. We are still only in the earliest stages of sophistication of AI: its subtlety will develop more quickly than the capability of human beings to understand and mediate the influence of it over us. AI systems thus have the potential to change the way that we think about ourselves, the decisions we make, the way we relate to each, how we redefine our relationship with business and government; and all of this without us realising it.

A harbinger of the world to come came in 2017, when the Electronic Privacy Information Center (EPIC), a Washington research organisation, filed a complaint with the US Federal Trade Commission against a company, Universal Tennis: "The company, EPIC said, uses a "secret algorithm" to rank hundreds of thousands of amateur and aspiring tennis players, including children,

---

[15] *The Economist*, 14.12.17.

on a scale from 1 to 16. The system creates its ratings based on millions of match results. EPIC said the scores "define the status of young athletes in all tennis-related activity" and "impact opportunities for scholarship, education and employment". They may also, it argued, "in the future provide the basis for 'social scoring' and government rating of citizens".[16]

This still very basic system for ranking a field as perhaps unimportant as tennis suggests how systems in the future might rate wider human skills which could define career paths and success in life, becoming self-fulfilling prophecies. Governments, companies and any other parties who control the Alibabas will have extraordinary powers. Concern about technology companies, Amazon, Alphabet, Facebook, Microsoft and Uber etc. has raged through international discourse over the last few years. To some, they are the height of irresponsibility, making millions for the few, while destroying jobs and risking privacy for the many. To others, they are providing the lead where universities and government is not, driving innovation in education, medicine and elsewhere which will bring unheard of benefits to human beings. Whichever the view, the opaqueness of these companies is a major concern. Their eagerness to hide behind privacy is not always justified.

---

[16] Forston, D. (2017). 'Big data fuels the rise of the machines'. *The Times* 25.06.
https://www.thetimes.co.uk/article/big-data-fuels-the-rise-of-the-machines-lv65ndms2

3. The Frankenstein Syndrome

Mary Shelley's novel Frankenstein (1818) tells the story of a young scientist, Frankenstein, who creates a monster and is horrified that the creature develops a mind of its own. Regarded as the first science fiction story, the monster has often been called Frankenstein after the name of the creator. Algorithms are outstripping even now the ability of those who compose them to understand fully their reasoning. What was really noteworthy about AlphaGo, Google DeepMind's machine defeating Ke Jie, the world's no.1 player at the ancient Chinese game of Go in 2016, was some of the moves were beyond the ability of the best Google minds to comprehend. At present, the risks of a Frankenstein moment might be limited, as the AI machines are specifically focused on one particular task. But when and if AGI is developed, the concerns about monitoring and control of its operation will grow. Debate is likely to continue for many years over the 'singularity', when AI machines notionally will be able to improve themselves without human input and at a rate that will outstrip humans' ability to comprehend, will ever occur. In Shelley's Frankenstein, the monster outlives its creator, having killed his brother. But hers of course is a work of fiction.

4. Loss of work and the spread of social disorder

The Rise of the Robots (2015) by American futurist writer Martin Ford, envisages a world in which vast swathes of employment currently done by human beings are undertaken by machines. Hundreds of millions, billions indeed of people, could be driven out of work across the world, creating a crisis in societies, with people of all ages and education no longer in employment, finding their lives devoid of meaning. For the first time in human existence, we will not know how to fill our time with purposeful activity[17].

The debate on what will happen to employment in the future, and the ways schools and universities need to adapt to prepare students for it, has been a constant theme in the book. Our view is that work will always be available, especially in human-related activities, such as health, education, recreation, counselling, beauty and therapy, but the *quality* and the degree of *difficulty* of the work may become increasingly less satisfying. *The Economist* says this: "If research in automation does start yielding big pay-offs, the question is what will happen to the displaced workers? Recent trends suggest the economy can create unskilled jobs in sectors such as healthcare or food services where automation is relatively difficult. And if robots and algorithms become far cheaper than workers, their owners should become rich enough to consume much more of everything, creating more jobs for people. [But] the risk is that ... technology will relegate many more workers to the ranks of the low-skilled. To employ them all, pay or working conditions might have to deteriorate ... the eventual problem may not be the quantity of available work, but its quality."[18]

---

[17] Ford, M. (2015). *The Rise of the Robots* London: Bloomsbury, p. xvii.

[18] 'Economists grapple with the future of the labour market'. *The Economist*, 11.01.18.

We know that meaningful activity, in employment or at home, is one of the biggest contributors to personal *happiness*. Would we be content with no job, or no rewarding and challenging job, and no work at home bringing up children and homemaking? We are left with what? A life of pleasure? Isn't that what hedonists have told us is the ultimate aim of life? Ah, but their philosophy contains a fundamental misunderstanding between pleasure and *happiness*. The former depends on consumption of material and is always self-centred: the latter is deeper and based on harmony within oneself and with others.[19]

Techno-optimists utopias

Life for most people throughout most of history has been harsh, subject to violent and unpredictable events, prone to be cut short and diminished by illness, disease and old age, dominated by unsatisfying work, by mental illnesses and depression, and lacking the necessities let alone the luxuries that the elites alone enjoyed. Not for longer must the masses endure such a diminished existence, assert techno-optimists. The AI evangelists have an altogether different vision. For Max Tegmark in *Life 3.0,* AI will make life technological: post-humans "will be able to design their own hardware as well as their software". Life in this form (if we can still call it life), he says, will allow the human species to be "master of

---

[19] Seldon, A. (2015). Beyond Happiness. Hodder, London.

its own destiny finally fully free from its evolutionary shackles".[20]

Veteran American futurist Raymond Kurzweil has written about three stages of understanding human beings must go through in reaching an informed conclusion about the impact of AI on all our lives: "First is delight at the opportunity to overcome age-old afflictions: poverty, disease, and so on. Then alarm that these technologies can be destructive and cause even existential risks. And finally I think where we need to come out is an appreciation that we have a moral imperative to continue progress in these technologies because, despite the progress we've made ... there's still a lot of human suffering to be overcome. It's only continued progress particularly in AI that's going to enable us to continue overcoming poverty and disease and environmental degradation while we attend to the peril."[21] But how can we ensure that we see these benefits, and not the downsides? The question hangs.

Four distinct *utopian* visions emerge from our discussion.

1. Immortality

Death, the great certainty of our lives, may, it turns out, not be so certain after all, at least not in the minds of say Silicon Valley visionaries. Kurzweil is one of the strongest advocates for the controversial singularity (many of our interviewees like Tim O'Shea consider it a

---

[20] *The Guardian,* 16.09.17.
[21] Thompson, N. (2017). 'Ray Kurzweil on Turing Tests, brain extenders and AI ethics'. 13.11.
https://www.wired.com/story/ray-kurzweil-on-turing-tests-brain-extenders-and-ai-ethics/

chimera).[22] He has written: "2029 is the consistent date I have predicted for when an AI will pass a valid Turing test and therefore achieve human levels of intelligence. I have set the date 2045 for the 'Singularity' which is when we will multiply our effective intelligence a billion fold by merging with the intelligence we have created. That leads to computers having human intelligence, our putting them inside our brains, connecting them to the cloud, expanding who we are. Today, that's not just a future scenario. It's here, in part, and it's going to accelerate."

AI can theoretically allow human beings to achieve immortality by replacing biological elements of the body which age and degrade by mechanical parts, which can be renewed. Quadriplegics today can move arms and legs in response to brain impulses. Is it such an enormous leap of the imagination to conceive of our entire body being synthetic? If the brain can indeed be understood as a series of mechanical responses, then this too should be capable of replication in undegradable hardware. Kurz:eil has no such doubts, and is taking regular supplements to elongate his life in anticipation of his big day.

But do humans want immortality? The bounded nature of our lives is for many integral to our sense of meaning. Boundless life could spell a boundless mini-death of boredom. Yuval Noah Harari, the Israeli historian and author of, *Homo Sapiens* (2011) and the more tentative *Homo Deus* (2015) has no such doubts on this score. He denies that lack of meaning will pose a problem for humans if or once death is overcome.

---

[22] Interview, Tim O'Shea, 04.04.18.

"Over the past three centuries, almost all the new ideologies of the modern world don't care about death, or at least they don't see death as a source of meaning. Previous cultures, especially traditional religions, usually needed death in order to explain the meaning of life. Like in Christianity – without death, life has no meaning. The whole meaning of life comes from what happens to you after you die. There is no death, no heaven, no hell... there is no meaning to Christianity. But over the past three centuries we have seen the emergence of a lot of modern ideologies such as socialism, liberalism, feminism, communism that don't need death at all in order to provide life with meaning."[23]

Harari's understanding of religion is odd on several levels. For many of all faiths, purpose comes not from death in the future, but living a deeper, richer life *now*, in the present. It lies at the heart of the growing practice of mindfulness contemplation and meditation. It teaches one not to live or even think about the future, or death in the past, but how to live in the *present*. Some exponents of mindfulness are agnostic, but many others, like Oxford psychologist and best-selling co-author of Mindfulness (2011) Mark Wiliams, follow a religious faith: in his case, Christianity.[24]

---

[23] Andrew Anthony, A. (2017). "Yuval Noah Harari: 'Homo sapiens as we know them will disappear in a century or so'," 19.03.https://www.theguardian.com/culture/2017/mar/19/yuval-harari-sapiens-readers-questions-lucy-prebble-arianna-huffington-future-of-humanity

[24] Wiliams, M. and Penman, D. (2011). Mindfulness, a Practical guide to finding Peace in a Frantic World.

Immortality poses more immediately practical problems of space: if nobody dies, the population will rise relentlessly, which might be solved by more land reclamation from desert or sea, and eventually moving into space and colonising fresh planets. Problems too arise with consciousness: if religion is indeed true, and there is a God as the font of consciousness, it is unlikely this unique state will be possible for post-humans created by us or machines. If consciousness is not God-given, there are other questions about whether it can be implanted into machines.

2. Superabundance, no more war

AI machines and technology will be able to create more food, more drinking water more habitable areas, more goods, more cheaply than ever in history, while also tidying up our oceans of plastic and our land of centuries in debris. AR, MR and VR will enable experiences as close to reality as to be almost indistinguishable from it, yet far safer. Driving a Ferrari or a Formula One car, flying a private jet, or eating in the world's finest restaurant could be an everyday experience for all. In this era of superabundance, the theory goes, there will be no more need for war, because there will no longer be a struggle for resources. Steven Pinker argued in *The Better Angels of Our Nature* (2011) that the violence has decreased over time in human civilisation, and in his *Enlightenment Now* (2018) he supports his optimistic thesis by drawing on a variety of social science data. If he is right, and he is about levels of violence, then AI would be assisting in a direction that has already been long established.

The superabundance theory is flawed though. It assumes that human beings desire only the material benefits of pleasure and that when these are satisfied, they will be happy: evidence runs strongly against such a thesis. AI will undoubtedly lead to greater material possessions for all (and the illusion of experiencing them): the question is whether that will satisfy our deepest cravings, or make us any happier. We are lacking here a deeper context of meaning and purpose. We may have become less violent, but the change is due more to societal forces rather than an improvement for the better in human nature. It assumes too that violence and war are caused by want of material possessions, rather than by innate impulses within humans leading them into aggression.

3. Augmented humanity: some real and some fanciful applications

Mental ill health is spreading across the world despite, maybe even because of, growing prosperity. Unhappiness is often thought to be caused by lack of possessions, and it can be, so it is paradoxical that increasing affluence has seen an increase and not a fall in unhappiness and mental illness. The taking of antidepressants, sleeping pills and anti-anxiety medication is burgeoning across the developed world. The quality of human life everywhere is diminished because of suffering from mental afflictions. AI offers some real hope. It will systemically probe the chemistry of our bodies, and see exactly what medication might be required for that with chronic psychotic or neurotic illness to achieve optimum levels of balanced well-being. It will act as a personal therapist, offering advice and consolation to ensure we are able to operate at peak levels of well-being.

AI will equally assist with physical illness. Cancer may not be curable, but it and other life-limiting illnesses will be diagnosed much earlier, and treated far more effectively with AI. A revolution in health is arriving.

Techno-optimists go into overdrive on the subject of how the technology will enhance our brains. Kurzweil believes that a new age is not far away: AI "may not yet be inside our bodies, but, by the 2030s, we will connect our neocortex, the part of our brain where we do our thinking, to the cloud. ... we're going to be funnier, we're going to be better at music. We're going to be sexier".[25] British engineer and academic Kevin Warwick is one of those arguing that the age of the cyborg is not far away, with electronic implants inserted into the body. Warwick thinks: "we should upgrade humans and get them into the machines' decision-making loops ... AI would now be acting for us. You could plug your brain into a computer network so that you and the network become one. The brain is very plastic, it can adapt. Our brain cells would be lapping it up."[26] Even if brain-enhancement remains

[25] Galeon, D. and Reedy, C (2017) 'Kurzweil Claims That the Singularity Will Happen by 2045.' 05.10. https://futurism.com/kurzweil-claims-that-the-singularity-will-happen-by-2045/.
[26] Appleyard, B. (2017)'Robot wars: if we can't beat them, let's become them.' 06.08. https://www.thetimes.co.uk/article/robot-wars-if-we-cant-beat-them-lets-become-them-0887ldr8n

fanciful, some very serious thinkers believe it can happen. And the vision of more sexy computer boffins and AI technocrats is certainly one in which we can all rejoice.

4. Techno-realistic possibilities

We land, as we have throughout the book, on the side of realism, somewhere between the vision of those who say that AI will change little, and those who think it will change everything. It will certainly force us to reflect on what it is that makes us uniquely human, different to immaterial matter (easy), but also to animals (harder). It will force us to make choices about the kind of life that we want to have, and how to govern in a way which is fairer, more efficient and more principled than has been the case through much of human history. Professor of Philosophy Luciano Floridi[27] is one who advocates a middle way: "We can rest assured that new artificial agents will not confirm the scaremongers' warnings, or usher in a dystopian science-fiction scenario. ... All of these profound transformations oblige us to reflect seriously on who we are, could be, and would like to become. AI will challenge the exalted status we have conferred on our species. ... I suspect that AI will help us identify the irreproducible, strictly human elements of our existence".

Bostrom equally thinks that AI will be neither catastrophe nor utopia: but he urges intense thought to be given to the subject in the near future: "the problem may

---

[27] Luciano Floridi, "Charting our AI future," (02/01/17)
https://www.project-syndicate.org/commentary/human-implications-of-artificial-intelligence-by-luciano-floridi-2017-01

be difficult, but is not insoluble, provided we start early enough and apply enough mathematical talent". Together with colleagues at the Future of Humanity Institute, he believes that measured and profound thinking is needed now: "I don't think just ringing the bell and screaming is actually what the world needs", he says.[28] The talent that will be required to reach the right solutions will not be limited though just to left-brain thought. We return to the subject of what needs to be done in the concluding chapter.

Will AI Liberate or Infantilise Humanity?

The main ways in which AI could liberate humanity if wise voices prevail, are in summary as follows:

1. Enhanced fairness: AI will allow those who have less material means to enjoy better education and health, and more material possessions too virtually, if not in physical reality. The best that has been thought-created and conceived, by nature as well as by human beings, will be for everyone at last to enjoy.

2. Enhanced participation and decline of isolation: every human will be able to participate far more fully in communal and democratic life, and be able to communicate more meaningfully with friends and relatives through new technologies including holograms,

---

[28] John Thornhill, "Artificial intelligence: can we control it?" (14/06/16) https://www.ft.com/content/46d12e7c-4948-11e6-b387-64ab0a67014c

regardless of where they are in the world. We will see a decline of loneliness and isolation, one of the besetting problems of our age. AI will enable us all to enjoy our many talents and intelligence better, to bring meaning, fulfilment and joy in our lives.

3. Spiritual revival: because AI will help us to become aware of what is uniquely human, it will allow religion and spirituality to be taken far more seriously and help rescue it from the low credibility it widely has. One way it will do this is the highlighting of attention on the 'golden rule', present in all religions, to treat others as we ourselves would wish to be treated. It will focus attention on consciousness, said to be the presence of the divine in the material world. Individual religions, which have tended to particularise their own unique features, may find themselves challenged increasingly by those who wish to find the common *core* or the world's great religions while not denying their individual uniqueness.

4. Enhanced reflection on happiness not pleasure: AI will mean the likelihood of greater pleasure for all. This may well force us, as we have argued before, to search for the far more meaningful and utterly different human experience of *happiness*, which is grounded on harmony and not consumption[29].

But there is an equal risk that AI will infantilise and impoverish meaning in our lives. This dichotomy, the

---

[29] Seldon, A. (2015). Beyond Happiness.

leitmotif of the book, is going to the wire. We will attempt to answer it in the final chapter.

The ultimate body working to ensure that AI operates in the interests of all humanity must be a revivified United Nations. The UN has come under fresh attack in the last ten years from nationalistic leaders. The battle to ensure that it is the will of the UN that prevails, not that of individual countries, companies and malign individuals, will decide the future survival and flourishing of humanity in several domains, none more important than AI.

Recommendations

Five threats posed by AI

This concluding chapter brings together our thinking and recommendations. AI probably won't run out of control in a dystopian future with human beings snuffed out as an inferior race, treated as irrelevant ants trodden thoughtlessly underfoot by those of vastly superior intelligence. But there are real concerns and we would be foolish to ignore them. As Nigel Shadbolt said "there's a lot of scaremongering now. Everybody has become a self-appointed expert on AI. It's very complex. That said, there *are* risks".[1]

Change is happening far quicker than the ability of governments and others to keep pace. 'Amara's Law', named after the long-time head of the Institute for the Future in Palo Alto, argued that we overestimate the impact of new technologies in the short term and underestimate it in the long term. Well, we are entering the long term!

1. Infantilisation of humanity

Every new device, from calculating machines to early computers, aroused fears that the quality of human life would

---

[1] Shadbolt, 16.03.18.

be diminished as a result. AI is not just the latest technological innovation. It is qualitatively different to all earlier technological developments because it replicates not just our physical but mental and emotional activity. With generative AI growing, we may not even know what is human and what is machine. If AI, in the form of Sat Nav can guide us around our physical environment, what will happen when AI takes over our thinking in the rest of our lives? Niall Ferguson fears, for good reason: "the sum of human understanding may end up being reduced by AI."[2] Making our lives more convenient and comfortable has been a prime driver of change throughout history. Does it matter, some ask, if we are infantilised?

2. Loss of jobs and quality of life

The forces weighing in to say we need to wake up are growing. Governor of the Bank of England, Mark Carney, warned of mass job losses and the spread of Marxism due to AI and Robots.[3] Our concern in this book has been less about jobs disappearing than about the quality of the work that will remain. Will machines strip out the satisfying and challenging aspects of work, or will they merely take away the drudgery and allow us to focus on the most human and worthwhile aspects? The risk that we educate the young including those in poor countries but the economics don't keep pace is real. Out of town shopping malls in the last 25 years destroyed many local businesses and high streets, while rewarding the big retail companies. Now Amazon is taking even more local trade away. Does it matter if we lose our communities and

---

[2] *The Sunday Times*. 11.02.18
[3] *The Financial Times*. 15.04.18

local employment if our lives are more convenient? If people no longer work? Will it matter if parents talk less to their children because they are absorbed in cyber-space? AI nannies will after all be able to read bedtime stories and will respond sensitively to the child if growing sleepy.

3. Weapons

Considerable fears exist about the ethics of AI in drones and robots in armed conflict. The more quantum intelligence is wired into machines, the more difficult it will be to control them to ensure that they operate under human supervision. The detachment of the killer from the killed creates worrying ethical issues. What might a Geneva Convention for AI/robotic combat look like?[4] In April 2018 an international group of academics called for a boycott of the Korea Advanced Institute of Science and Technology over it collaborating with a defence contractor to build "killer robots".[5] Will killing become sanitised and clinical, and who will be controlling the decisions to kill?

4. Cyber security

AI will create ever subtler ways of compromising advanced systems. If the Pentagon can be hacked today by teenagers, the difficulty of maintaining security, with AI many thousands of times more high-powered than the human brain, becomes a major concern. Hacking into air traffic control, nuclear power stations or hospitals could create panic and massive disruption. Malicious actors who trick AI's into

---

[4] Commentary to authors, Martin Hamilton, 09.04.18.
[5] *The Financial Times*. 04.04.18

taking inappropriate action using adversarial input data is not the stuff of sci-fi: it could happen.

5. Ethical issues and privacy

To be fully effective, AI needs to know more about our individual bodies and minds than any human being has ever done. The benefits are considerable as long as this information is used ethically, but falling into the wrong hands could create great dangers. Users of Google Maps share a complete timeline of their movements with the company. Google's intentions can be trusted in the present. But who knows what use might be made of the vast quantities of data stored about us in the future? We find it hard to keep our children safe from predators: protecting our children is the greatest responsibility of any society: will AI help or hinder?

Five possible menaces

1. Individual hackers

As Martin Rees has memorably said, "the global village will have its village idiots, and they will have global range ... and with this power, just one could be too many".[6,7] Just one malicious person with a nuclear device could do existential harm. One exploiting AI with sinister intent could trigger widespread disaster.

---

[6] *The Guardian*, 28.05.2006.
[7] *Daily Telegraph*, 28.05.2015.

2. Rogue states

The term was coined by President Reagan in 1985 and has been controversial since because the US has used it to define any country of which it does not approve. But the phrase still has value. It can be applied to those countries which do not see themselves as part of the community of nations bonded together by a common framework of law and human rights. North Korea is one such risk. Russia under Vladimir Putin is another: it has almost certainly used AI and chemical weapons to further its own ends. We are less comfortable when we hear about the British or American governments misusing information. NSA whistleblower Edward Snowden famously revealed the existence of the Joint Threat Research Information Group whose task allegedly was to "deny, disrupt, degrade and deceive."[8]

3. Tech companies

Amazon, Facebook, Google and Microsoft spent $49M on lobbying in Washington in 2016, outspending Wall St by 2:1[9]. They have vast market power, hoovering up talent from smaller companies and universities to make themselves still more unassailable, in what the Economist describes as a "frenzy".[10] "It is hard to recall the misty, innocent days when we thought Steve Jobs was fun and Amazon was useful" wrote *The Times'* David Aaronovitch.[11] The fall from grace of the tech companies and their leaders has been described in

---

[8] Email, Martin Hamilton to authors, 09.04.18.
[9] *Observer*, 03.09.17.
[10] *The Economist*, 09.12.17.
[11] *The Times*, 13.01.18.

a battery of books, such as by *New York Times* writer Noam Cohen[12].

The companies are entities of prodigious power and influence, led by figures who have not been elected and who are accountable to no one government. Does being answerable to shareholders offer sufficient incentives to behave well and responsibly? We have repeatedly seen abuses of their power in the last ten years, most recently by Facebook and Cambridge Analytica in early 2018. Mark Zuckerberg responded by admitting his leadership had been "unforgivably lax" but said he was "still the man to run Facebook".[13]

By early 2018, a consensus had emerged: "It is no longer enough for technology companies to smirk behind algorithms and claim there is nothing they can do."[14] But not a consensus on the *action* to be taken.

4. Small companies

The risks from misuse of AI could come just as easily from the tens of thousands of start-ups which are appearing each year across the world, many of whom are poorly overseen, and all of which are striving for competitive advantage, some desperately. Cryptocurrencies like Bitcoin evaded regulation for a long time. We should not let our concern at the excesses of the big beasts blind us to the small.

---

[12] Cohen, N. (2018). *The Know-It-Alls: The Rise of Silicon Valley as a Political Powerhouse and Social Wrecking Ball*, The New Press.

[13] *New York Times*, 06.04.18.

[14] Leader. *The Times*. 13.04.18.

5. AI itself

We agree with veteran computer scientist Tim O'Shea who says: "I can't see how AI could get out of control. Computers and robots are not people. Rampant AI taking its own initiative is not a proposition that makes any sense to me".[15] Former AI chief scientist at Baidu Andrew Ng thinks similarly, saying he worries about superintelligence and AI killer robots in the same way he frets about overpopulation and pollution on Mars.[16] Nevertheless, there are many serious figures whose work we have discussed in this book who believe there is a risk, even if a small one, that AI could run out of control and pose an existential or serious threat. We would be wrong to discount that possibility.

Five possible courses of action

1. Do nothing

Let AI evolve independently, some say, and allow individuals to work it out autonomously, as they have done with the creation of Wikipedia, and they will ensure that truth and common sense prevail. Free marketers the world over believe AI is merely the latest technological wave and we should stand back and let it all happen: all will be well. Panic over. Economist and philosopher Friedrich Hayek warned explicitly about the dangers of governments trying to prescribe any particular future: any attempt to do so can lead

---

[15] Interview with Sir Tim O'Shea, 29.03.18.
[16] Williams, C. *HPC*, 19.03.15. Naughton, J. *The Guardian*, 25.02.18.

to totalitarianism.[17]The problem with doing nothing is that those who control AI have vastly greater resources than allowing individuals and *laissez-faire* to work it out alone. The internet has created global near-monopolies: there was no nineteenth of twentieth century equivalent of Amazon, Facebook and Google.

2. Let companies police themselves

Tech companies repeatedly claim they are moral and responsible agents and should not be tampered with by governments, who have their own agendas which may be far from benign. This is wrong. As security-expert, Edward Lucas has written: "The giant tech companies, cynical, powerful, wealthy, threaten our freedom … the real problem is we are soft on their anonymity".[18] They should certainly be forced to have maximum transparency, and to give far more back to the community than they do in their often paltry if showy charity activities currently. It would be naive to expect companies to have the integrity and public spirit to behave ethically unprompted, especially when they see others gaining a competitive advantage when not doing so.

3. Academic institutions and think tanks

There are a growing number of bodies we would be right to trust including the Oxford Martin School, the Future of Humanity Institute at Oxford, the Centre of the Study of Existential Risk at Cambridge and the Future of Life Institute

---

[17] Hayek, F.AS. (1944). *The Road to Serfdom*, Routledge, London.
[18] *The Times*, 09.02.18.

in Boston.[19] Some individuals including Demis Hassabis and Mustafa Suleyman at DeepMind and Jaan Tallinn, co-founder of Skype and Kazaa, and founder of the Existential Risk Centre, have far-seeing contributions to make. We are more likely to find wisdom for the future from them than from the big tech companies and governments. They are the custodians of our future. We depend on them.

4. National governments and legislatures

They certainly have a role to play. The House of Lords set up an enquiry into AI and UK economy in September 2017, which reported in April 2018, that the UK has a unique role to play in the ethics of AI.[20] The US Congress is displaying similar interest. In March 2018, the British Cabinet Minister overseeing digital, Matthew Hancock, said the government "would put rules in place so that tech can be harnessed for the good of people". He said "the wild west for tech companies is over". The British Government's 'Digital Charter' lays out rules and norms on internet safety and ethics of AI and intellectual property on-line[21]. Governments need to take strong leads certainly, especially in modernising their education systems and fostering research. UCL's Rose Luckin argues for governments to set up interdisciplinary centres of expertise in AI education to provide long-term funding and stability for in-depth research.[22] She is right. But

---

[19] The Future of Humanity Institute's 'Malicious use of AI Report' (2018) February is an example of excellent work.

[20] The Financial Times. 16.04.18.

[21] *Evening Standard*, 22.03.18.

[22] Luckin, R. and Holmes, W. (2018). *'Intelligence Unleased, An Argument for AI in Education'*. Open Ideas at Pearson.

these are international problems and the scope for national governments responding unilaterally when the internet and the tech companies operate globally is heavily restricted.

5. The United Nations

The UN is by far the most important forum for producing and policing a framework for the governance of AI which all should follow and it needs to play a major role in ensuring that AI operates in the interests of all humanity, and the underprivileged in all nations, and not just the rich and powerful.

Five levels of response

"We will have just one shot to get it right" said Stephen Cave, Director of the Centre for the Future of Intelligence in Cambridge.[23] We should employ a variety of strategies.

1. All companies should be required to be totally transparent in their use of AI, and responsible for their content. Why should we know so little about the companies that know so much about us? Transparency must be a red line. Sandra Wachter of the Oxford Internet Institute says we "need to hold algorithms to the same standard as humans".[24] "We have got to have transparency. If a company is collecting data on individuals and groups we have to see what they are doing", says Tim O'Shea.[25] But what happens when the companies resist/deceive?

---

[23] Cave, S., *The Times* 24.01.18.
[24] *The Daily Telegraph.* 03.08.17.
[25] Interview Tim O'Shea, 29.03.18.

2. Codes of good practice should be insisted upon universally. We should control the operation and impact of AI, as Oren Etzioni and Carissa Schoenick argue when proposing 'three rules' for any AI system. It must respect the same laws that apply to its creators and operators; it must always disclose it is not human; and it must never share confidential information without approval from the source.[26] Matthew Gould, the official who oversees the British Government's digital policy, is clear that an effective digital framework is the *sine qua non*.[27] What sanctions are there in place though when AI systems and companies ignore them?

3. National laws should demand compliance. The companies should be forced to pay taxes in the jurisdictions in which their profits are earned.[28] But the companies operate internationally, so how much influence can any national government have?

4. Fines and sanctions should be imposed on all companies and governments which break the rules, and the large tech companies could be broken up by anti-trust legislation, as the US government and European Union have often debated. But no action has been successful so far. How one might break up companies like Amazon and Facebook raises great problems. But that should not

---

[26] Etzioni, O. and Schoenick, C. '*AI: What Educators Need to Know*', Alla Institute for AI, 10.01.18.

[27] Interview with Matthew Gould, 02.03.18.

[28] Keen, A. (2018). '*How to Fix the Future: Staying Human in the Digital Age*'. Atlantic Books.

discourage them being broken up. If break-ups slow down the pace of introduction of AI, that might be a boon.

5. International laws should be written and updated to ensure that they keep abreast of the AI threat. This is the locus where ultimate decision-making and enforcement must lie. Supranational bodies have a key role to play: the European Commission has imposed large fines on tech companies over failures to pay tax. But ultimately only the United Nations can ensure order. 75 years after the UN's formation, the time has arrived for major reform to give it the teeth and the tools to do the job.

Five actions specifically for educational institutions

Nothing but nothing is more important than education in ensuring that AI works in the interests of all humanity. We need to reimagine our schools from the ground up to teach our young to be more fully human and not be content any longer with giving them just 'factory era' skills.

1. End early specialisation at schools (Britain is particularly bad at this) and have a third common core element at university, as the Harvard report above recommended in 1945. All students should study the arts (and perform in them), history of art, philosophy, maths, science and language. The evidence is strong that depth need not be sacrificed to breadth on academic quality. As Venki Ramakrishnan, President of the Royal Society in Britain has said: "Our narrow educations system, which

encourages early specialisation, is no longer fit for purpose in an increasingly interdisciplinary world."[29]

2. Emphasise the human across *all* education. Much greater weight should be given to the encouragement of individual responses from students, rather than the 'right' answer, to project work, to character development, problem solving, critical thinking, empathy, entrepreneurship, leadership and well-being. Curiosity needs to be developed ('CQ') in preparation for life-long learning. Medical Schools need to emphasise the human element much more in their education, to balance the learning of purely scientific and technical knowledge. Law Schools, Business Schools, indeed every single university department needs, to prioritise the human.

3. Staff preparation. Invest in staff who understand learning and analytics, and machine learning and AI, and invest in technology optimally to deliver AI to all students. As Margaret Boden said: "We're going to have to start teaching children from primary years and all the way up about AI because the pace of change is absolutely drastic".[30]

4. Personalised learning preparation. Students need to prepare for individualised learning programmes. Schools and universities have to catch up with their students

---

[29] Ramakrishnan, V. Royal Society, October 2017. The Royal Society maintains that breadth as well as depth in education should be prized.
[30] Interview, Margaret Boden, 27.02.18.

quickly. Equally, they must prepare for life-long learning, which will spread rapidly.[31] Credit transfer will become the norm rather than the exception. Students should all be taught computer, digital and AI literacy, and how to understand the difference between the human and the machine. The Welsh government is ahead of other UK nations on this.

5. Challenge preparation. Students should be stretched and challenged: it needs to be engineered into schools and universities. AI will always promise to make our lives easier. But life is fulfilling when we are challenged. We need to educate the young to celebrate and seek challenge, not avoid it. To Stephen Heppell, the gains are considerable. "I would say for about 50% of children in education today, the system is not working for them".[32]

Five Educational Benefits

If we can shape AI to our advantage, we can reduce or remove the five inherent problems the earlier education phases never solved i.e.:

1. Stagnant or declining social mobility.

2. Students moving by age not their stage of ability and understanding.

---

[31] Watson, D., former VC of Brighton University, wrote that we should end the idea 'that one's first attempt at a degree is one's only attempt'. THE.

[32] Interview with Stephen Heppell. 30.12.17.

3. Teachers weighed down by administration being prevented from teaching.

4. A narrow range of abilities and intelligences only educated.

5. A system that homogenised, not individuated, students.

Five Leading Nations/Blocs

Most countries are waking up to AI. Many do not know how to respond to it. Some want to lead. The United States currently does, but will it still be in ten year's time? The blossoming in Silicon Valley and elsewhere in the US has been phenomenally quick. Google started in a garage in 1998 and has 4.2 billion search requests a day by 2018. YouTube started in a room above a Pizzeria in 2005 and today people watch 8.8 billion of its videos.[33]

Miles Brundage of the Future of Humanity Institute is one who believe momentum is being lost in the US.[34] China is eager to fill the gap, working to establish itself as the world's primary 'AI innovation centre' by 2030.[35] We've seen above how Alibaba, Baidu and Tencent are powering ahead, and how it's publishing twice the number of papers on AI than the US.[36] We should be looking less at Silicon Valley and turning our attention more to start-ups in Shenzhen and Shanghai, and to companies like Wan Xing and Hero Entertainment. David Rowan, Founding Editor of Wired UK, said in 2018: "Two

---

[33] *Sunday Times*, 01.10.17.
[34] Interview, Miles Brundage, 27.02.18.
[35] *The Times*, 12.03.18.
[36] *THE*, 25.05.17.

years ago I wrote ... It's time to copy China. Today, I'd upgrade that: it's time to fear China".[37] China benefits greatly from "tonnes of data, oodles of computing power and boffins aplenty", according to *The Economist*.[38] India is stealing up quietly not far behind, and the EU has ambitions to become a major presence in AI on the world stage post Brexit.

Which takes us to Britain. It has been coming from behind in some quarters: it has 33 robots per 10,000 workers, compared to 93 in the US and 213 in Japan.[39] But it has been catching up fast, with AI leading the Prime Minister's Industrial Strategy, announced in November 2017. London now raises twice the amount to fund digital companies of any other European capital. The number of start-ups in East London rose from 16 in 2008 to an estimated 6000 by 2018.[40] Tech City, founded in 2010 by David Cameron and adviser Rohan Silva, has helped power progress in the 'Silicon Roundabout' area of London. Much of the coordinated drive has come from former schoolteacher now the country's first national technology adviser, Liam Maxwell. Journalist Harry De Quetteville argues that Britain has become "by almost any metric – the most powerful technology hub in the world".[41]

Patriotic exaggeration aside, there is no doubting Britain's determination to be a global player on AI, especially ethics. International competition has its role in driving innovation

---

[37] Rowan, D. 'Fear the great tech armoury of China', *The Times*, 12.03.18.

[38] *The Economist*, 09.12.17.

[39] Elliott, L. 'Robots will take our jobs. Plan now before it's too late'. *The Guardian*, 01.02.18.

[40] *Daily Telegraph*, 19.03.18.

[41] *Daily Telegraph*, 19-21.03.18.

and diversity, and choice to consumers. At some point, however, more international cooperation on AI must take over from flag-waving. Because the benefits, and risks of AI cannot be nationalised. They are global.

Five final reflections

1. Pleasure vs happiness

The first to third education revolutions were much concerned to maximise pleasure and minimise pain. The fourth education revolution opens the door for the development of fulfilled, challenged and happy students who take responsibility for their own well-being. Happiness, is utterly different to pleasure.[42] No-one who read *50 Shades of Grey* became happier as a result: it may have given them pleasure. Or so we are told.

2. Closed vs open

The first three revolutions did not do enough to challenge closed thinking, the discovery of 'right' answers, excellence as determined exclusively by peer review and learned academies, individual rather than collective achievement. The fourth revolution will usher in much greater openness to those of other nationalities, faiths and backgrounds. The collective will become as important as the individual. The internet has already paved the way and made a significant impact on academic collaboration, famously the Higgs Boson paper

---

[42] Seldon, A. (2009). Trust: How We Lost it and How to Get it back'. Biteback, London.

with 5,000 authors.[43] To say that thinking is not all important should no longer be considered irrational.

3. Brain vs holistic

The mind was the sovereign of the first three education evolutions. Yet the mind could never satisfactorily answer the question 'why', because it can never solve ultimate questions or reach the deepest levels of understanding. Only an individual using far wider capacities and intelligences, including body intelligence and an opening of the heart centre, can discover profound truth. As American theologian Richard Rohr has written, "Deep knowing and presence do not happen with our thinking minds. To truly know something, our whole being must be open, awake and present".[44]

4. Atheistic Certainty vs humility and unknowing

The poet WB Yeats wrote in the *Second Coming*, one hundred years ago exactly, "the best lack all conviction, while the worst, Are full of passionate intensity". Atheist thinkers dominated the late third revolution era with their dismissal of those who did not accept their materialistic, mind-dominated interpretation of truth. These thinkers tend to conflate religion and spirituality, and highlight the excesses of religious fanatics while denigrating the human and artistic achievements of those inspired by faith. Their appalling black and white approach to truth is typical third education revolution thinking. Its leading atheistic thinkers, may never have encountered the spiritual in their own lives, but were

---

[43] Thanks again to Martin Hamilton, interview 04.04.18. *Nature News and Comment*, 15.05.15.
[44] Rohr, R. 'Bodily Knowing', Daily Meditation, 04.04.18.

single-minded in their determination to use the power of their intellects and academic and literary authority to disparage the quest for the spiritual in others.

In the fourth era, there will be much greater tolerance and respect for ambiguity and uncertainty, and awareness that there are limits to what the mind alone can know. In the quantum age, we may well know even less about how machines let alone minds are thinking. We must move beyond passionate and intolerant intensity, because it is only in informed acceptance that we understand more about what it means to be human. This becomes crucial when AI machines will be able to replicate so many human attributes. In so doing, we move beyond mere cognitive intelligence, through understanding, to wisdom.

5.   Fear of the future to belief in the present

We must not be afraid of the future, whatever it holds. The third education revolution did little to discourage or question the mind ranging unconsciously over the past and the future. In the fourth education revolution, aided by the technology, including apps like Headspace, we will learn to live in the present. Doing so gives us an utterly different window on life. The philosopher and novelist Iris Murdoch, argued for a mindful, present, moment approach to life in her late work, including *The Sovereignty of Good* (1970). Drawing on the work of French mystical philosopher Simone Weil, she invites us to focus our attention on what is 'good' and present moment by moment, because doing so alone will connect us to the "true nature of things". She says that attending to the present is "the ultimate condition to be aimed at". Doing so will make us "humble": such a person "sees himself as nothing" and can "see other things as they are".[45] When we are fully conscious, and fully present, we know life at a much deeper level, including the spiritual, but we can only experience this ourselves wholly, not by thinking alone. Only by living in the present moment, being fully aware of passing thoughts and feelings, do we become entirely awake ('falling awake') and fully human, a state AI will never replicate.

Conclusion: Three Big Thinkers, One Synthesis

What of the future? Steven Pinker is optimistic and we are right to be. In *Enlightenment Now: A Manifesto for Reason, Science, Humanism and Progress* (2018), he draws inspiration from the Enlightenment's belief in our ability to apply knowledge systematically to problems to make our lives longer, happier and more meaningful. But he cautions us against complacency. The Enlightenment taught us that human agency is all-important. Progress, nor disaster, are guaranteed.[46] For Ian Goldin, latterly of the Oxford Martin School, the Renaissance is his inspiration, arguing that our era is "the second renaissance" because it is marked by "the same blend of wild intellectual innovation, trade, migration and social friction seen five centuries ago".[47] He too stresses the need for individuals and governments to take smart and wise decisions, by being outward-looking, taking care of the dispossessed and celebrating human virtues and the arts. Get it right, and we can "co-create a blossoming that the world

---

[45] Seldon, A. *Beyond Happiness,* 2015.

[46] *THE*, 22.02.18.

[47] Goldin, I. and Kutarna, C. (2016). 'Age of Discovery'. *Financial Times*, 10.07.16.

will still talk bout in 2500".[48] Historian Niall Ferguson similarly looks back 500 years but to yet another landmark event: "the global impact of the internet has few analogues in history better than the impact of printing on 16th century Europe".[49]

Our journey concludes where the third education revolution began, with the printing press. That revolution failed often to realise its hopes for progress, fairness and rigour. It fell short in part because of the Enlightenment's insistence upon reason and a narrow Cartesian understanding of what it means to be human. The fourth education revolution will be and needs to be, very different.

So what is the answer finally to the question, will AI infantilise or liberate humanity? The answer is we do not know for certain. Either eventuality is possible. Ensuring the right education system that develops our full humanity is more important than anything else we might do. What will decide whether we make the right choices? Our actions will decide. We are the deciders. We alone.

---

[48] *Observer*, 15.05.16.
[49] *Sunday Times*, 01.10.17.

Acknowledgements

It always takes a village, and here is ours.

First, we would like to thank Tim Bunting for suggesting the book to Anthony back in 2015, and for constant support and encouragement throughout, and to Adam Seldon, a teacher, for researching and writing down, in 2016, the broad ideas that would eventually become this text.

We are fortunate at Buckingham University to have had the support of Purnima Anhal, who took care of real world logistical details; the bones that hold up everything else. We must also thank Sarah Rush, Jenny Carter and Sarah Bouderballah who were also an integral part of that effort in the Vice-Chancellor's Office. Vice-Chancellors should research, write and contribute to the public debate on today's world. The task of doing that and running a busy university, even a smaller one, is eased greatly if one has a superb team, as Anthony has across the University.

We are grateful to Sebastien Ash for his research support in early drafts and organising the material resulting from numerous interviews, as well as to Raymond Newell. Integral to the entire process has been the work of Julie Cakebread who typed every single word, kept track of and made the corrections to the multiple iterations of this book with huge intelligence.

We would like especially to thank our two guiding stars and inspirations, Rose Luckin of UCL, for her explanations of AIEd, and Priya Lakhani of Century Tech, for her analysis of the AIEd industry, and for their enthusiastic support throughout of our efforts.

There are many members of industry and academia without whom this book would not be possible. We are grateful to them for taking the time to speak to us, sharing their insights and pointing us in fruitful new directions. Three figures stand out. We would like to thank Donald Clark, Martin Hamilton of JISC and Peter Read in particular for helping us understand AI in the most abstract and specific of terms.

We are grateful to Simon Balderson, Martin Hamilton, Peter Read, Alan Smithers, Patrick Watson, Henry Warren and Ian Yorston for reading early versions of the book. John Adamson read the first chapter.

We are immensely fortunate to have *The Fourth Education Revolution* published by the University of Buckingham Press and we would like to extend our thanks to our publisher, Christopher Woodhead, for his patience and professionalism, and to his wife Chloe. Thanks too to Midas Public Relations.

We would like to thank Ralph Allwood, Jake Ayres-Thomson, Simon Balderson, Margaret Boden , Kristopher Boulton, Rod Bristow, Jamie Bristow, Miles Brundage, Donald Clark, Sarah Ellis, Matthew Gould, Demis Hassaabis, Stephen Heppell, Nick Hillman, Mads Holmen, Nick Kind, Jim Knight, Priya Lakhani, David Levin, Rose Luckin,

Stephanie Marshall, Riccarda Matteucci, Liam Maxwell, John McDermott, Gero Miesenböck, Charlie Muirhead, Rajay Naik, Simon Nelson, Sir Tim O'Shea, Peter Read, Lord Martin Rees of Ludlow, Lisa Marie Rowland, Sir Nigel Shadbolt, Russell Shilling, Matthew Smalley, Mark Stevenson, Jim Thompson, Lyle Ungar, Brad Vanstone, Henry Warren, Charles Wyles and Duncan Wilson for agreeing to be interviewed for the book.

Oladimeji would like to thank Anthony. His simultaneous efforts as teacher, cheerleader and collaborator is the major reason this book exists. I am grateful to Harin Sellahewa for connecting me to Anthony. I am grateful to Stratten Waldt for being my sounding board and willing debate partner. Finally, I am grateful to Megan Pearson, Paris Howell and my parents Layi and Derin Abidoye for their support while writing this book.

Anthony would like to thank his three children, Jessica, Susannah, Adam and late wife Joanna for their encouragement for this book and patience in teaching him about the digital world. Joanna was the best teacher and educator he has ever known. Colin and Fiona Prior proved particularly stimulating discussants one weekend in France. Rohan Silva opened his eyes to the possibilities of AI and invited him to give the seminar at Number 10 discussed in the book. He is grateful to all those colleagues in schools and universities who have tried to coax him into the use of digital technology, including Ian Burgess and Tim Pratt at St Dunstan's, Mary Anne Brightwell, Angie Moore and Debra Lewis at Brighton College, and Angela Reed, Roger Auger and John Rawlinson at Wellington College.

The best writing and thinking for this book was done at Joanna's favourite home at St Jean de Cole in France, where Anthony would like to thank Anne, Herman and Cate at Agence Immobilier, and when he was leading trips to the trenches.

He would like to thank the organisers of many literary festivals including Cuckfield in Sussex and Shute in Devon, and to the Science Festival in Brighton and to the IAPS (Oxford Group) for letting him air early versions of this book. He would like to thank his colleagues in the Schools G20 and the Universities G20, who provided wonderful stimulus and insights. At HMC, he would like to thank Vivian Anthony, Geoff Lucas, Ian Power and William Richardson. Among often lifelong friends in schools from whom he has learnt much he would like to thank Mike Buchanan, John Claughton, Joe Davies, Jonty Driver, Robin Dyer, David Fletcher, Andrew Grant, Brian Griffiths, Andrew Halls, Chris King, Barnaby Lenon, Tony Little, Neil and Jane Lunnon, David James, John James, Lucy Pearson, Jonathan Smith, Simon Smith, John Spencer, Paul Taylor and David Walsh.

He'd like to thank all the contributors to Wikipedia, on which he drew extensively when writing the book. When footnotes do not appear it is because Wiki was again and again the source. It is then appropriate that the royalties from the book are going to charity, specifically to the Jo Cox Foundation. Two other vital sources were the incomparable THE and TES.

He would like to thank the governors and colleagues at the University of Buckingham especially, Chairman of Council Rory Tapner and his deputy John McIntosh and colleagues John Clapham, John Drew, Susan Edwards,

Anthony Glees, Paul Jennings, Geraint Jones, Alan Martin, Harin Sellahewa, James Seymour, Karol Sikora, Alan Smithers, Martyn Smith and Jane Tapsell. Four others who have been helping us at Buckingham have given him great insights: Ian Creagh, Mary Curnock Cook, Nick Hillman and Stephanie Marshall. He would like to thank Oladimeji Abidoye, finally, for teaching him so much about digital technology and about writing. The best passages in this book were all penned by him. He has a remarkable insight and talent.

Sir Anthony Seldon: Biography

Sir Anthony Seldon, Vice-Chancellor of The University of Buckingham since 2015, is one of Britain's leading contemporary historians, educationalists, commentators and political authors.

He was a transformative head for 20 years, first of Brighton College and then Wellington College. He is author or editor  of over 35 books on contemporary history, including the inside books on the last four Prime Ministers, was the co-founder and first director of the Institute for Contemporary British History, is co-founder of Action for Happiness, honorary historian to 10 Downing Street, UK Special Representative for Saudi Education, a member of the Government's First World War Culture Committee, was chair of the Comment Awards, is a director of the Royal Shakespeare Company, the President of IPEN, (International Positive Education Network), is patron or on the board of several charities, founder of the Via Sacra Western Front Walk, and was executive producer of the film *Journey's End*. He appeared on the Desert Island Discs in 2016. For the last fifteen years he has given all his profits from writing and lecturing to charity.

He has three children; his wife of 34 years, Joanna, died of cancer in December 2016.

Oladimeji Abidoye

Oladimeji Abidoye is studying Computer Science at the University of Buckingham.

Bibliography

Books

Al-Khalili, J. *What is Next? Even Scientists Can't Predict the Future – or Can They?* London: Profile Books (2017)

Auon, J. Robot-proof. Higher Education in the Age of Artificial Intelligence, Massachusetts Institute of Technology Press, (2017)

Barbier, F. *Gutenberg's Europe, New Jersey*: John Wiley (2016)

Benei, V. *'Introduction: manufacturing citizenship: confronting public spheres and education in contemporary worlds'. Manufacturing Citizenship: Education and nationalism in Europe, South Asia and China.* New York: Routledge, (2005)

Christodoulou, D. *Seven Myths about Education.* London: Routledge (2014)

Climer, N., in *'What's next'*, Al-Khalili, J. (2017)

Culliford, L. *'The Psychology of Spirituality'* London: Jessica Kingsley (2011)

Dennett, D.D. *Consciousness Explained*, London: Little, Brown & Co. (1991)

Doucet, A. *'Teaching in the Fourth Industrial Revolution. Standing at the Precipice'*, London: Routledge. (2018)

Eisenstein, E.L. The Printing Revolution in Early Modern Europe, Cambridge: Cambridge University Press (1993)

Ford, M. *The Rise of the Robots London*: Bloomsbury (2015)

Gardner, H. *Frames of Mind: The Theory of Multiple Intelligences.* New York, NY: Basic Books. (2011) [Online]. Available at: http://ebookcentral.proquest.com/lib/duke/detail.action?docID =665795

Good, H.G. & Teller, J.D. *A History of Western Education.* London: Macmillan (1969)

Bibliography

Keynes, J.M. *Economic Possibilities for our Grandchildren* (1903)
King A. *'From Sage on the Stage to Guide on the Side'* Taylor & Francis Ltd. (1993)
Kulke, H. & Rothermund, D. *A History of India*. London: Routledge (1990)
Maag, K. 'Education and Literacy'. The Reformation World. London (2000)
McCorduck, P. *Machines Who Think: A Personal Inquiry into the History and Prospects of Artificial Intelligence. 25th anniversary update*. Natick, MA: A.K. Peters. (2004)
Molloy, C., Shakespeare, S., and Blake, C. Beyond Human: From Animality to Transhumanism. London. UK: Bloomsbury Publishing PLC. (2011) http://ebookcentral.proquest.com/lib/duke/detail.action?docID=894596
Mulgan, G. Big Mind: How Collective Intelligence Can Change Our World. Princeton, NJ: Princeton University Press. eBook Collection EBSCOhost (2018)
Musgrove, F. *Youth and the Social Order*. London: Routledge and Kegan Paul (1964)
Napier, J. *Mirifici Logarithmorum Canonis Descriptio* (1614)
Putnam, R.D. *'Bowling Alone: The Collapse and Revival of American Community'* (2000)
Robinson, M. *Preparing young people for the future with lessons from the past*. London: Independent Thinking Press (2013)
Rosch, E., Thompson, E. & Varela, F.J. *The Embodied Mind: Cognitive Science and Human Experience*. Boston MA: MIT Press (1993)
Seldon, A. *Beyond Happiness: How to Find Lasting Meaning and Joy in All that You Have* (2015)
Seldon, A. *Trust: How We Lost it and How to Get it Back* (2009)
Seligman, M. *The Hope Circuit: A Psychologists Journey from Helplessness to Optimism* (2018)
Sharkey, N. *"Robotics" section from "What's next"* Al-Khalili, J.
Strauss, G. *'A sixteenth century encyclopaedia: Sebastian Muenster Cosmography and its edition'*. From the Renaissance to the Counter Reformation. New York, NY: Random House, (1965)

Susskind, R. and Susskind, D The Future of the Professions: how technology will transform the work of human beings, OUP Oxford (2015).

Turing, A. M. *'Computing Machinery and Intelligence'*. Mind (1950)

Tversky, A Kahneman,D. 'Judgement under uncertain ties; Heuristics and Biases', Science, Vol 185, No 4157 (1974).

Twenge, J. *Why Today's Super-Connected Kids are Growing Up Less Rebellious'*, Atria Books. (2017)

Walker, M. *"Transhumanism"* in *"What's next?"* Al-Khalili, J. (ed.) (2017)

Walsh T. *Android Dreams: the Past, Present and Future of Artificial Intelligence*, C Hurst & Co. (2017).

Williams, M. and Penman, D. *Mindfulness, a Practical guide to finding Peace in a Frantic World* (2011)

Academic Papers

Bakhshi, H. (2018)'*The Future of Skills. Employment in 2030'*, Pearson, Nesta, Oxford Martin (2018)

Bakhshi, H. Jonathan Downing, M. Michael A Osborne, Philippe N Schneider, *'The Future of Skills: Employment in 2030'*, Oxford Martin School, (2018)

Benedikt Frey, C. and Osborne, M. *'The Future of Employment: how Susceptible are jobs to Computerisation?'* Oxford Martin School, September (2013)

Black, P. and Wiliam, D. *'Assessment and Classroom Learning'*, Assessment in Education: Principles, Policy and Practice, Vol. 5, Issue 1. (1998)

Boydston, Jo Ann. *'The Middle Works of John Dewey, 1899-1924'*, Vol 1. Southern Illinois University Press (2008)

Bransford, J. D., Brown, A.L. & Cocking, R.R. *How People Learn: Brain, Mind, Experience and School.* Washington DC: National Academy Press (2000)

Brockliss, L. *The University of Oxford*: A History. Oxford, (2016)

Caplan, B. *'The Case Against Education: why the Education System is a Waste of Time and Money',* Princeton University Press, (2018)

Cf. Waterhouse, L. (2006a). *'Inadequate Evidence for Multiple Intelligences, Mozart Effect, and Emotional Intelligence Theories'*. Educational Psychologist, 41(4), pp.247–255. doi: 10.1207/s15326985ep4104_5 / Waterhouse, L. (2006b). 'Multiple Intelligences, the Mozart Effect, and Emotional Intelligence: A Critical Review'. Educational Psychologist, 41(4), pp.207-225. doi: 10.1207/s15326985ep4104_1 / Klein, P. D. (1997). 'Multiplying the Problems of Intelligence by Eight: A Critique of Gardner's

Chamorro-Premuzic, C. *'Curiosity is as Important as Intelligence'*. Harvard Business Review, 27 August 2014. [Online]. Available at: https://hbr.org/2014/08/curiosity-is-as-important-as-intelligence

Chingos, M.M. & Whitehurst, G.J. *'Class Size: What Research Says and What it Means for State Policy'*. Brookings Institute.(2011) [Online]. Available at: https://www.brookings.edu/research/class-size-what-research-says-and-what-it-means-for-state-policy/

Claxton, G. *'Expanding the Capacity to Learn: A new end for education*?' (2006)[Online]. Available at: https://docs.wixstatic.com/ugd/84a7e9_7c2c7b0cb542445cb3 e972c2f7180709.pdf

Cobban, A.B. *The Medieval Universities*. London: Methuen (1975)

Conant, B. *General Education in a Free Society*. Cambridge, MA: Harvard University Press (1950)

Darlington, R. 'Factor Analysis'. [Online]. Available at: http://node101.psych.cornell.edu/Darlington/factor.htm

Davis, G. and O'Brien, L. and McLean, P. *'Growing in Esteem: Positioning the University of Melbourne in the Global Knowledge Economy.*

Dr Sloman, A. *University in the Making*, Reith Lectures, (1963)

Dustdar, S. "Cloud Computing" (2016) https://doi.org/10.1109/MC.2016.46

Gardner, H. *'Multiple Intelligences: Prelude, Theory and Aftermath'*, In Sternberg, R. J., Fisker S. T. & Foss D. J. (eds.), *Scientists Making a Difference*. Cambridge: Cambridge University Press (2016)

Gesche, P. 'Schulunterricht in Babylonien im ersten Jahrtausend v. Chr. Alter Orient und AltesTestament'. The Oxford Handbook of Cuneiform Culture (2000)

Gillard, D. 'Education in England: a brief history'. (2011) [Online]. Available at: http://www.educationengland.org.uk/history/chapter02.html

Goldthorpe, J.H. 'The Role of Education in Intergenerational Social Mobility: Problems from Empirical Research in Sociology and some Theoretical Pointers from Economics'. (2013) [Online]. Available at: https://www.spi.ox.ac.uk/sites/default/files/Barnett_Paper_13-02.pdf

Greenstone, M. '*Thirteen Economic Facts about Social Mobility and the Role of Education*'. (2013) [Online]. Available at:, https://www.brookings.edu/wp-content/uploads/2016/06/THP_13EconFacts_FINAL.pdf

Hendrick, C. and Macpherson, R. '*What does this look like in the classroom? Bridging the gap between research and practice*', Woodbridge UK: John Catt Educational (2017)

Kramer, S.N. '*Schooldays: A Sumerian Composition Relating to the Education of a Scribe*'. Journal of the American Oriental Society (1949)

Luckin, R., Holmes, W., Griffiths, M. & Forcier, L. B. *Intelligence Unleashed: An argument for AI in Education.* London: Pearson Education. (2016) https://www.pearson.com/content/dam/corporate/global/pearson-dot-com/files/innovation/Intelligence-Unleashed-Publication.pdf

Omar,L. '*Schools as agents of cultural transmission and social control*'. Revue Sciences Humaines (1991)

Phillips, D.C. & Siegel, S. '*Philosophy of Education*'. Stanford Encyclopaedia of Philosophy. (2013) [Online]. Available at: https://plato.stanford.edu/entries/education-philosophy/

Pressey, S.L. '*A third and fourth contribution towards the coming 'industrial revolution' in education*'. School and Society (1932)

Rose, D. and Dalton, B. Learning to Read in the Digital Age. Mind, Brain, and Education,(2009)

Sage, R. and Matteucci, R. *'The Robots are Here'*, University of Buckingham (2018)

Seldon, A. *'Why Schools? Why Universities*? Cass Foundation, (2011)

Silver, D., Hubert, T., Schrittwieser, J., Antonoglou, I., Lai, M., Guez, A., Lanctot, M. 'Mastering Chess and Shogi by Self-Play with a General Reinforcement Learning Algorithm'. ArXiv:1712.01815 [Cs], December. (2017) [Online]. Available at: http://arxiv.org/abs/1712.01815.

Sloman, A. 'The Training of Minds'. BBC Reith Lectures.(1963) [Online]. Available at: http://downloads.bbc.co.uk/rmhttp/radio4/transcripts/1963_rei th3.pdf

Sonak, A. *Intel's regional Director for Education and Innovation*, Asia. December (2017)

Susskind, R and Sussking D. *The Future of the Professions. How technology will transform the work of human experts,* Oxford University Press, (2015)

Theodore de Bary, W.M. *Sources of Chinese Tradition*. New York, NY: Columbia University Press (1960)

Theory'. Canadian Journal of Education,

Walton, L. *'Educational Institutions'*. In The Cambridge World History, vol. 5 (2015)

Willetts, D. *A University Education. Oxford*: Oxford University Press (2017)

Yorke, H. 'Number of children home taught doubles in six years amid increased competition for school places' The Daily Telegraph 7 July 2017. [Online]. Available at: http://www.telegraph.co.uk/education/2017/07/07/number-children-home-taught-doubles-six-years-amid-increased/

Zhou, K. *'Education for people and planet: Creating sustainable futures for all'*. Paper commissioned for the Global Education Monitoring Report (2016)

Web Content

"*Student-Centered Learning - Education Writers Association*". (2016) Ewa.Org. Accessed 21 February 2018. https://www.ewa.org/student-centered-learning.

"*Tear Down This Wall! A New Architecture For Blended Learning Success - Edsurge News*". (2015) Edsurge. Accessed 19 February 2018. https://www.edsurge.com/news/2015-06-29-tear-down-this-wall-a-new-architecture-for-blended-learning-success.

"*IEICE Paper on MR.*" Accessed 11 February 2018. http://etclab.mie.utoronto.ca/people/paul_dir/IEICE94/ieice.html

Bledsoe, W. '*Facial Recognition System*', Wikipedia (1966)

Future of Life Institute, https://futureoflife.org/

Galeon, D. and Reedy, C. '*Kurzweil Claims That the Singularity Will Happen by 2045.*' (2017) https://futurism.com/kurzweil-claims-that-the-singularity-will-happen-by-2045/

Graves, A., Wayne, G., Reynolds, M., Harley, T., Danihelka, I., Grabska-Barwińska, A., Gómez Colmenarejo, S., et al. '*Hybrid Computing Using a Neural Network with Dynamic External Memory.*' (2016) https://doi.org/10.1038/nature20101.

Glatter, H. and Wong, A. 2016. "*The Classroom Of The Future*". The Atlantic. Accessed 19 February 2018. https://www.theatlantic.com/education/archive/2016/09/reimagining-the-modern-classroom/498224/.

http://www.tandfonline.com/doi/pdf/10.1080/14681366.2016.1256908?needAccess=true

https://kurani.us/riverbend/

https://www.edsurge.com/news/2017-05-12-pearson-an-investor-in-knewton-is-phasing-out-partnership-on-adaptive-products

https://www.edsurge.com/news/2017-11-30-hitting-reset-knewton-tries-new-strategy-competing-with-textbook-publishers

https://www.scientificamerican.com/article/how-big-data-taking-teachers-out-lecturing-business/

Independent Teacher Workload Review Group, 'Eliminating unnecessary workload around planning and teaching resources: Report of the Independent Teacher Workload Review Group' (2016) [Online]. Available at: https://www.gov.uk/government/uploads/system/uploads/attachment_data/file/511257/Eliminating-unnecessary-workload-around-planning-and-teaching-resources.pdf

Floridi, L. *"Charting our AI future,"* 2 January 2017
https://www.project-syndicate.org/commentary/human-implications-of-artificial-intelligence-by-luciano-floridi-2017-01

Office for Fair Access (OFFA) *'Outcomes of access agreement monitoring for 2015-16'*. (2017) [Online]. Available at:
https://www.offa.org.uk/wp-content/uploads/2017/06/OFFA-Monitoring-Outcomes-Report-2015-16-Final.pdf

Rose Luckin *'Towards artificial intelligence-based assessment systems'*, Nature Human Behaviour, (2017)
https://www.scientificamerican.com/article/how-big-data-taking-teachers-out-lecturing-business/

Seldon, A. "On Positive Psychology and the Positive University" [Online]. Available at:
https://emotionsblog.history.qmul.ac.uk/2017/06/on-positive-psychology-and-the-positive-university/

Social Mobility Commission. *'Time for Change,* [Online]. Available at:
https://assets.publishing.service.gov.uk/government/uploads/system/uploads/attachment_data/file/622214/Time_for_Change_report_An_assessement_of_government_policies_on_social_mobility_1997-2017.pdf

Talbot, David. n.d. *"Given Tablets but No Teachers, Ethiopian Children Teach Themselves."* MIT Technology Review. Accessed 2 February 2018.
https://www.technologyreview.com/s/506466/given-tablets-but-no-teachers-ethiopian-children-teach-themselves/.

Taylor, B. *'Factors deterring schools from mixed attainment teaching practice'*. Pedagogy, Culture & Society, [Online]. Available at:
https://www.tandfonline.com/doi/pdf/10.1080/14681366.2016.1256908

Thompson, N. *'Ray Kurzweil on Turing Tests, brain extenders and AI ethics'*. (2017) https://www.wired.com/story/ray-kurzweil-on-turing-tests-brain-extenders-and-ai-ethics/

Tucker, M. *'What Does It Mean to Be an Educated Person Today?'* Education Week. (2015) [Online]. Available at:
http://blogs.edweek.org/edweek/top_performers/2015/10/what_does_it_mean_to_be_an_educated_person_today.html

Van der Berg, S. *'Social mobility and education'*. [Online].
Available at:
http://blogs.worldbank.org/futuredevelopment/social-mobility-
and-education

Wei, F. and Bifet, A. *"Mining Big Data: Current Status and
Forecast to the Future"*, (2013) SIGKDD Explor News 14(2):
1-5. https://doi.org/10.1145/2481244.2481246.

Wikipedia. *'Sure Start'*. [Online]. Available at:
https://en.wikipedia.org/wiki/Sure_Start

Wikipedia. 'Theory of multiple intelligences', [Online]. Available
at:
https://en.wikipedia.org/wiki/Theory_of_multiple_intelligence
s (accessed on: 16 January 2018).

Zunger, Y. *'Asking The Right Questions about AI'*. Medium.
(2017) [Online]. Available at:
https://medium.com/@yonatanzunger/asking-the-right-
questions-about-ai-7ed2d9820c48

Newspaper articles

Adams, Richard. 2017. *"Demanding Workload Driving Young
Teachers Out Of Profession"*. The Guardian. Accessed 19
February 2018.
https://www.theguardian.com/education/2017/apr/15/demandi
ng-workload-driving-young-teachers-out-of-profession

Anthony, A. "Yuval Noah Harari: *'Homo sapiens as we know
them will disappear in a century or so' (*2017)
https://www.theguardian.com/culture/2017/mar/19/yuval-
harari-sapiens-readers-questions-lucy-prebble-arianna-
huffington-future-of-humanity

Appleyard, B. *'Robot wars: if we can't beat them, let's become
them.'* (2017) https://www.thetimes.co.uk/article/robot-wars-
if-we-cant-beat-them-lets-become-them-0887ldr8n

Barnes. J. 'Nicomachean Ethics', Book X, 1172a.17 / *The
Complete Works of Aristotle*: The Revised Oxford Translation.
NJ: Princeton Univ. Press. (1984)

Forston, D. (2017). 'Big data fuels the rise of the machines'. The
Times 25 June 2017 https://www.thetimes.co.uk/article/big-
data-fuels-the-rise-of-the-machines-lv65ndms2

Ingmire, J. 'Learning by doing helps students perform better in science'. Uchicago News, 29 April 2015. [Online]. Available at: https://news.uchicago.edu/article/2015/04/29/learning-doing-helps-students-perform-better-science/ http://journals.sagepub.com/doi/pdf/10.1177/0956797615569355

Joe Clement and Matt Miles, '*Screen Schooled: Two Veteran teachers Expose How Technology Overuse is Making Our Kids Dumber.* TES, (2018)

Josh Worth, 'What Next for EdTech', TES Guide to Ed Tech, (2018)

Markoff, John. 2017. "*New Test For Computers: Grading Essays At College Level". Nytimes.Com. Accessed 20 February 2018.* http://www.nytimes.com/2013/04/05/science/new-test-for-computers-grading-essays-at-college-level.html

Morrison, N. '*Will AI be the next big thing in the classroom*', Forbes, (2017)

Murray, C. '*The Bell Curve' and its Critics'.* Commentary Magazine (blog). [Online]. Available at: https://www.commentarymagazine.com/articles/the-bell-curve-and-its-critics/

Richmond, E. "*When Students Take Over The Classroom*". The Atlantic. Accessed 21 February 2018. https://www.theatlantic.com/education/archive/2014/10/what-happens-when-students-control-their-own-education/381828/

Seldon, A. "Sir Anthony Seldon publishes plan to tackle teaching quality at British universities". [Online]. Available at: http://www.smf.co.uk/press-release-sir-anthony-seldon-publishes-plan-to-tackle-teaching-quality-at-british-universities/

Thornhill, J. "*Artificial intelligence: can we control it?*" 14 June 2016 https://www.ft.com/content/46d12e7c-4948-11e6-b387-64ab0a67014c

Worth, J. '*What next for Ed Tech'*, TES Guide to Ed Tech, (2018)

Yee, V. 'Grouping Students by Ability Regains Favor in Classroom'. New York Times. [Online]. Available at: http://www.nytimes.com/2013/06/10/education/grouping-students-by-ability-regains-favor-with-educators.html

Index

Sloman, Albert, 56, 57, 243, 379, 381
smart schools, 156
Social Mobility Commission, 69, 70, 85, 383
Socrates, 41
Sonak, Anshul, 302, 381
Song Dynasty, 93
Southampton University, 263
Sparta, 14, 321
Spearman, Charles, 95
special education needs and disabilities (SEND), 181, 227
specialisation, education and, 38, 355, 356
Spence, Michael, 196, 265
SPI Incubator, 209
Spielman, Amanda, 36
spiritual intelligence, 103
Spiritual revival, 338
Sproull, Bob, 138
Standard Attainment Tests, 72
Stanford University, 174, 265, 273
state intelligence, 3, 106
Steed, Mark, 219
STEM subjects, 55, 185, 225, 246, 254, 279
Stephenson, Neal, 177, 178
Stimulation, 290

Stoke Mandeville Hospital, 143
strong AI, 120
Stucomm, 157
Student Agents, 185
Sumerians, 12
Summit Public Schools, 207, 220
Sung Dynasty, 17
Sure Start, 66, 384
Susskind, Richard and Daniel, 199, 256, 377, 381
Sutherland, Ivan, 138
Tahoe Expedition Academy, 205
Talbot, David, 229, 230, 383
Tallinn, Jaan, 322
Tavenner, Diane, 204
Teacher Advisor, 181
teacher training, 272, 299
tech companies, 16, 1, 145, 161, 305, 347, 350, 351, 354, 355
Tegmark, Max, 295, 313, 314, 322, 328
Tencent, 160, 359
Terman, Lewis, 94
textbooks, 25, 46, 167, 191
Thattai, Madhav, 152
Thatti, Madhav, 152
think tanks, 351
third education revolution, 3, 4, 24, 25, 32, 58, 59,

61, 62, 63, 71, 89, 157,
161, 197, 255, 289, 311,
363, 364, 366
Thomaz, Andrea, 147
Thompson, Jim, 191
Thrun, Sebastian, 174
Times Higher Education,
175, 240, 241, 253, 254,
263, 264, 265, 266, 271,
273, 274, 275, 276, 277,
278, 279
Tononi, Giulio, 319
transhumanism, 4, 144,
282
transparency, 350, 353
Treaty of Westphalia, 104
trivium, 18, 58
Tsinghua University, 274
Turing, Alan, 98, 117,
122, 124, 126, 132, 133,
329, 377, 384
Tversky, Amos, 186, 377
Twenge, Jean, 303, 377
Twitter, 155
Udacity, 174, 183, 275
United Nations, 100, 341,
352, 355
University College
London (UCL), 71, 188,
220, 226, 352
university journey, 164,
169, 245
University of Essex, 56,
125, 243
University of Manitoba,
174

University of Melbourne,
250, 267, 274, 275, 379
University of Nalanda, 16
University of One, 276,
277
University of Oxford, 9,
14, 15, 16, 18, 21, 22,
23, 24, 33, 36, 45, 53,
86, 172, 199, 241, 254,
256, 257, 259, 272, 276,
294, 297, 331, 351, 365,
370, 377, 378, 379, 381,
385
University of Paris, 16
University of
Pennsylvania, 175, 250
University of Sheffield,
146, 240
University of Sydney,
196, 265, 275
University of Texas, 101,
147, 152
US Congress, 351
utopias, 328
VeinViewer, 140
Ventilla, Max, 202
Virtual degree, 275
virtual reality (VR), 4, 7,
314
Virtual Retinal Displays,
139
Viv, 149
VKontakte, 150
vocational qualifications,
73